□ *Essentials of Classroom Teaching Series* □

Essentials of
Elementary Mathematics

Second Edition

C. Alan Riedesel
State University of New York at Buffalo

James E. Schwartz
Houghton College

Allyn and Bacon

Boston   London   Toronto   Sydney   Tokyo   Singapore

To Ardeth and Elaine:
Your love and companionship are vital in helping us
to keep growing and learning. Thank you!

Vice President, Editor in Chief, Education: Sean W. Wakely
Series Editor: Frances Helland
Editorial Assistant: Bridget Keane
Marketing Managers: Ellen Dolberg and Brad Parkins
Editorial Production Service: Chestnut Hill Enterprises, Inc.
Manufacturing Buyer: Suzanne Lareau
Cover Administrator: Jennifer Hart

Copyright © 1999 by Allyn and Bacon.
Essentials of Classroom Teaching: Elementary Mathematics © 1994 by Allyn & Bacon.
A Viacom Company
160 Gould Street
Needham Heights, MA 02194

Internet: www.abacon.com
American Online: keyword: College Online

Between the time Website information is gathered and published, it is not unusual
for some sites to have closed. Also, the transcription of URLs can result in typographical
errors. The publisher would appreciate notification where these occur so that they may be
corrected. Thank you.

Library of Congress Cataloging-in-Publication Data
Riedesel, C. Alan.
    Essentials of elementary mathematics / C. Alan Riedesel, James E.
Schwartz. — 2nd ed.
        p.   cm.
    Rev. ed. of: Essentials of classroom teaching / James E. Schwartz,
C. Alan Riedesel. c1994.
    Includes bibliographical references and index.
    ISBN 0-205-28750-6 (pbk.)
    1. Mathematics—Study and teaching (Elementary)   I. Schwartz,
James E.   II. Schwartz, James E.   Essentials of classroom teaching.
    III. Title.
QA135.5.S327   1998
372. 7'2044—dc21   98-17350
                                                                          CIP

Printed in the United States of America

10 9 8 7 6 5 4 3 2   RRD-VA   03 02 01 00 99

Contents

Preface

The world of elementary mathematics teaching is undergoing dramatic changes. Initiatives for reform have come from professional organizations as well as from political voices and the general public. Teachers and teacher educators have shown a willingness to find better ways to teach elementary mathematics, but learning new ways is sometimes difficult. If we could observe the kind of teaching that groups such as the National Council of Teachers of Mathematics (NCTM) recommend in *Curriculum and Evaluation Standards for School Mathematics,* perhaps we would be more successful in making such teaching more common.

In *Essentials of Elementary Mathematics,* Second Edition, we invite you into many classrooms to observe the interactions between and among children and teachers. Following each visit we offer an analysis of some of the key features of each lesson or interaction. Our use of classroom situations (vignettes), and our analysis of these vignettes, provide a powerful teaching tool. We recognize that, just as children must construct their own understanding of mathematics, the pre-service teacher must also construct his or her own understanding of mathematics pedagogy. By focusing on vignettes, we project a realistic alternative to the "show-and-tell" method of *learning to teach* elementary mathematics.

One of our goals was to show the reader the integration of the NCTM *Standards* throughout the text. We have used four different icons to point out instances where each of the four most general standards is illustrated. These four standards: Mathematics as Problem Solving, Mathematics as Reasoning, Mathematics as Communication, and Mathematical Connections, form a recurring theme throughout the text. The following four icons are used for this purpose.

 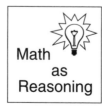  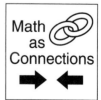

A fifth icon is sometimes used to draw attention to instances where the teacher is dealing directly with symbolic representations. There is a time in the development of children's mathematical thinking when the use of symbolic abstractions is desirable and appropriate. This time occurs *after* the child has constructed a conceptual understanding of the material under study. Whenever the icon for Increasing Abstraction is used, the reader should note that much concrete conceptual work has preceded the use of abstract symbols.

Leaders of professional organizations have become increasingly aware of the need to integrate technology instruction in all courses dealing with teaching methods. In this second edition we have added a sixth icon to highlight the many places in the text where we discuss technology. This technology icon is shown on the left.

Perhaps the most notable physical feature of *Essentials of Elementary Mathematics* is its much shorter length than the usual comprehensive text for an elementary mathematics methods course. This smaller size is an intentional design feature. Calls for reform have included recommendations that pre-service teachers spend more time in field experiences. As courses have been restructured to permit more field experience, there has been a corresponding decrease in the amount of time spent in the college classroom. Also, instructors often want to make use of current journals or their own materials. This has led to a tendency to underutilize the comprehensive methods texts that were designed for college-classroom-based courses. We have had to make many difficult decisions in writing this text; there is so much to say about teaching elementary school mathematics. However, we believe that this text will meet the needs of today's field-based courses more precisely than would a more comprehensive text. We do not pretend that a 240-page book provides *all* of the material that is necessary. We urge the instructor to supplement *Essentials of Elementary Mathematics* with readings from current research and with activities from some of the many excellent activity books that are available. In this second edition we have provided a number of activity cards that can be used as the basis for thinking about lessons.

Finally, we want to acknowledge the contributions of the following reviewers: William E. Lamon, University of Oregon; and Paula Lee White, Marshall University.

1 Today's Classroom

LOOKING AHEAD

Each generation of children and teachers has seen changes in the content of school courses and in the approach used to teach these courses. The present generation is not different; in fact, changes occur more rapidly now, owing to the speed of communication. During the 1950s and 1960s, there were significant changes in the content of the elementary school mathematics program; new content was added, and standard content was taught at an earlier grade level. During the 1970s, there was a slowdown in content change, and a good deal of attention was given to "system of delivery" of content.

In the late 1970s and early 1980s, the "back-to-basics" movement gave a heavy emphasis to drill and practice in mathematics. In the late 1980s, National Assessments Scores reflected this movement, indicating a need to increase emphasis upon teaching concepts and problem solving.

To improve mathematics programs, the National Council of Teachers of Mathematics issued their *Curriculum and Evaluation Standards for School Mathematics* (1989). (This document is explained in detail in later sections.)

The 1990s were an exciting time for mathematics in the elementary school,with the increased use of computers and calculators and the increased emphasis on estimation, problem solving, and in-depth thinking. The improvement of education was a major issue in the 1992 election and continues to be a major issue throughout the United States. International studies comparing countries in their mathematics achievement conducted during the middle 1990s indicated the United States still has a distance to go. With the current emphasis and improved teaching the goal of excellence in mathematics education can be reached early in the 21st Century.

No matter what the emphasis, the single most important variable in the mathematics instructional program is the *teacher*. The way he or she guides the child in thinking and feeling is the crucial ingredient. Thus, it is of major importance for the teacher to be able to approach teaching mathematics with excitement and enthusiasm. Toward this end, the approach to teaching needs to focus on involving both children and teacher intellectually and emotionally. The procedures that follow in this book are designed to foster that type of involvement. Up to the present time, no single best method has been found for teaching and organizing for teaching. There have been a number of specific theories and movements that have affected mathematics instruction in the elementary school, and each has made important contributions. But, it is the presupposition of this book that no single set of materials, no single sequence of instruction, no single motivational technique, or no single model is appropriate for all the children in the United States. The teacher must be familiar with a variety of ideas so that he or she may use them when appropriate.

CAN YOU?[1]

- Describe several strategies for teaching elementary school mathematics?
- Give suggestions for procedures useful for any teaching strategy?

---

[1] In each chapter, the "Can You?" section provides a preview of the chapter in question form. After studying the chapter, you should be able to answer the questions.

- List and diagram three needs for curriculum construction in elementary school mathematics?
- Sketch the history of mathematics teaching in the elementary school?
- Describe the emphases of the National Council of Teachers of Mathematics (NCTM) *Standards*?

TEACHER LABORATORY

1. Think back to your elementary school years. How was mathematics taught? Outline a typical lesson. What was the role of the teacher? of the child?

2. How do current elementary school mathematics textbooks compare with those of a few years ago?

3. Obtain three elementary school mathematics textbooks: one published before 1960, one between 1965 and 1970, and the most recent one you can find, hopefully after 1998. How do they compare in approach and content?

4. What do you believe to be the most current set of questions concerning elementary school mathematics teaching? Look through the index of this book. Where are these questions discussed?

5. Become familiar with this book. Look over the chapter features, such as "A Look Ahead," "Can You?," "Self-Test," "Think About," and "Selected References."

6. If possible, obtain copies of *Teaching Children Mathematics* (NCTM) and *Mathematics Teaching in the Middle Grades*. What seems to be the major focus of the articles?

7. Recall your elementary school years. What types of mathematics lessons can you recall?

VISITING CONTEMPORARY CLASSROOMS

A picture of the role of the teacher of elementary school mathematics can be developed by looking into several classrooms of today. Three of the strategies seen in these classrooms—Socratic questioning, group thinking, and pattern searching with laboratory work—are developmental in nature. The other, the explanatory method, is didactic in nature and involves the teacher's telling and showing. In such a classroom the emphasis is usually on computation with little problem solving.

Explanatory Method

For many years one of the authors has begun the teaching of a class dealing with elementary school mathematics instruction by using question 1 of the "Teacher Laboratory" in the previous section. Well over ninety percent of the responses received have outlined what we would call the explanatory method. See if you have ever been taught this way:

The lesson begins by the correction of the previous day's assignment. When the work is corrected, the children are told to open their books to a particular page. On the top of the page is an explanation of the steps necessary to do some mathematics. The teacher then makes another illustration of the material and again explains the steps to the children. Several examples are worked by the class together and a homework assignment is given.

Developmental Patterns

In contrast to the explanatory approach, developmental patterns involve active involvement of the children and pupil discovery. Here is an examination of several developmental strategies.

KIDS IN ACTION

Math as Problem Solving

GROUP THINKING AND LABORATORY (The teacher presents a problem that causes the children to use previous experience, and manipulatives are often used to help children construct or discover a new mathematical idea. The children exchange their ideas to synthesize and develop new ideas.)

A teacher using this developmental pattern describes a lesson she taught in the following manner: "I started the lesson with this problem: 'You are wrapping presents for a party and you only have a limited amount of wrapping paper. You must use just the right amount of paper on each package to cover it and have about 1 inch extra on each side for overlapping and taping. What are you going to do?' We discussed the question, without talking about suggestions for solutions, just to make sure that everyone understood what was being asked. Then, I handed out the boxes and wrapping paper. Students worked in groups of two to solve the problems.

"I moved about the room making sure that everyone was on task and had ideas for getting started. I gave the children free reign over any materials in the room that they thought would be useful. I challenged them to try to find as many ways as they could to solve the problem. Students used rulers, square-inch blocks, various types of paper, scissors, and tape as some of their materials. I allowed them to use any method that they wanted and encouraged different and creative solutions.

"There was a wide range of methods that students used to arrive at solutions. Some used wrapping paper and boxes. Others measured every face of the box and marked out the wrapping paper very precisely. Some children used manipulatives such as square-inch blocks or squared paper.

"After all students had at least one solution, we shared our findings. Pairs volunteered to explain their methods with the class.

"To tie everything together and apply mathematical terms, we discussed what type of problem we were solving and what we might need to know to work with similar problems. It was suggested that part of this type of problem might be finding the areas of surfaces, which could be done in several ways.

"After further discussion I gave each child a sheet containing several practice problems involving surface area. While the children worked I helped any that were having trouble with the concept and any calculations. Many children made use of a calculator as they worked. In the days that followed, generalizations concerning area were developed by the children."

We call this strategy *group thinking*. Further analysis of this procedure will follow in later chapters.

KIDS IN ACTION

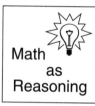

Math
as
Reasoning

PATTERN SEARCHING   (Children work as individuals or in a small group to discover a "rule" for a pattern.)

The teacher began by saying, "The other day my father said to me, 'You do things differently than when I was a boy. However, I bet that you can't figure out the practical, everyday use of the kind of mathematics I'm going to show you.' He then told me several addition combinations. I'll show you on the board. See if you find the sums that I've omitted and also see if you can figure out how you might use this type of addition."

$$8 + 5 = 1 \qquad 4 + 4 = 8 \qquad 6 + 8 = ?$$
$$3 + 11 = 2 \qquad 9 + 5 = 2 \qquad 10 + 6 = ?$$
$$3 + 10 = 1 \qquad 12 + 4 = ? \qquad 9 + 7 = ?$$

As the individual children worked on the pattern, the teacher moved about the room asking the children who were experiencing difficulty leading questions (Socratic questions) to aid in their discovery of the pattern. When she noticed that a child had found the pattern, she suggested that he or she make up several word problems in which the pattern could be used.

Here are two of the problems the children developed:

KIDS IN ACTION

USING CLOCK MATHEMATICS   (Draw a clock to help, if you wish.)

- A 10-hour countdown is planned for a space shuttle launch. If the countdown begins at 5 in the morning and there are no delays, at what time will the shuttle be launched? (5 + 10 = 3)

- The Martin family is planning a Labor Day weekend trip to Washington, D.C. They plan to leave at 9 in the evening to avoid the holiday traffic. At what time will they arrive in Washington if the trip takes 5 hours? (9 + 5 = 2)

PATTERN SEARCHING (another example)

The teacher said, "I want to add 58 + 37 using my calculator, but the 5 button and the 7 button are broken. How can I use my calculator to do this? How many different patterns can you find for the use of a calculator with broken 5 and 7 buttons? After you've worked for a while, check your work with your partner."

KIDS IN ACTION

SOCRATIC QUESTIONING   (The teacher directs children's discovery, in large or small groups, through a series of leading questions.)

I wanted the children to find out several ways of figuring out a forgotten addition fact. I used this dialogue:

Teacher: I used to have trouble remembering 8 + 9. How much is it?

Pupil: 17

Teacher: Good. Are there any easier addition combinations that add to almost 17?

Pupil: 8 + 8 = 16

Pupil: 9 + 9 = 18

Teacher: Keep those facts in mind. What ideas could you use to find 6 + 7 if you forgot?

Pupil A: 6 + 6 = 12. 6 + 7 is one more: 13.

Pupil B: 7 + 7 = 14. 6 + 7 is one less. It's 13.

Teacher: Great. Could you give me a statement of what we've been doing?

(Pause.)

Pupil: Well, if we are adding to numbers that are "next to each other", that is, one number is one larger than the other, we know all of the numbers added to themselves, so we can add one to the smaller double or subtract one from the larger double.

Teacher: Fine. Give me an example.

Pupil: $8 + 9$ is one more than $8 + 8$, or 17. Or, it's one less than $9 + 9$; also 17.

DIFFERENCES IN APPROACH

It is obvious that no teacher makes exclusive use of explanatory procedures while another uses only developmental procedures. By the very nature of teaching, some aspects of each approach are used. However, many teachers tend to emphasize one of the two approaches. Also, not all superior teaching procedures are related to the issue of "teacher telling" as opposed to "pupil developmental thought." The comments that follow attempt to accomplish two things: (1) to point out differences between the "explanatory" and "developmental" procedures used in the preceding lessons and/or other lessons to follow and (2) to make several suggestions for teaching mathematics that are considered effective but not tied to either method.

1. The developmental patterns emphasize active learning. Rather than waiting for the teacher to tell them "what" or "how," the students attempt to develop a solution by themselves. If a pupil is not able to solve a problem, the teacher helps with a question or a comment designed to provide insight. Actively involved in the learning process, the student is more likely to be attentive. In the explanatory approach, the pupil's role requires listening rather than acting. Often, the pupil is not sure whether or not to listen to what the teacher is saying and thus may give the teacher's explanation halfhearted attention.

2. The developmental approach stresses building new knowledge on the foundations of experience, so it is of value to students in social situations as well as in academic endeavors. It also closely resembles the approach taken by mathematicians and scientists. Pupils taught by the explanatory method have a tendency to see if they can find a teacher or a book that will answer any questions they have. Thus, they are much more intellectually dependent in problem-solving situations.

3. Because developmental methods stress pupil thinking, the classroom is pupil-centered. The teacher must ask the right question or provide the right activity at the right time; to do this, it is necessary to understand the pupils. The explanatory approach fosters a classroom climate in

which the teacher is the fount of all wisdom. Pupils wait to find out what the teacher thinks before they think or form opinions.

4. The developmental approach stresses a search for relationships and patterns and leads to an understanding of mathematical structure. Such insight is valuable at all levels of mathematics. In contrast, when patterns are pointed out by the teacher they tend to be sensed by the children rather than understood.

Now that we have listed the major differences between explanatory teaching and developmental procedures, let us focus on differences in the various developmental teaching strategies or approaches, as illustrated in Figure 1-1, Table 1-1, and Figure 1-2. It should be noted that these strategies are used most often in introductory lessons and that the line between them is a thin one. The various strategies should not be considered as pure or scientific but as methods of varying discovery-type teaching to meet the needs of specific mathematical topics, children, and teachers.

Figure 1-1 shows a general progression from pure telling to pure discovery teaching. The chart should not be considered at all absolute. Thus, it is quite possible for a "pattern-searching" strategy to be more developmentally oriented than a "group-thinking" or "laboratory" strategy. The degree of developmental orientation will depend upon the type of subject matter studied and the approach of the teacher.

Table 1-1 provides some general characteristics of the types of developmental teaching strategies described earlier in the chapter. Figure 1-2 reveals the overlap of the teaching strategies.

As you can see, there is a great deal of overlap between the group thinking and laboratory approaches.

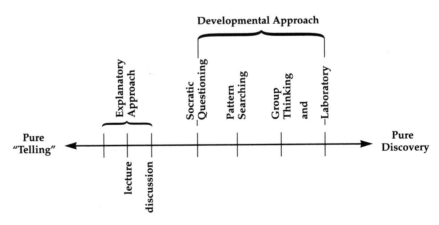

Figure 1-1   The Relationship of Developmental Teaching Strategies to Discovery

Table 1-1   An Analysis of Specific Teaching Strategies

SOCRATIC QUESTIONING	PATTERN SEARCHING
1. Teacher directs children's discovery through a series of leading questions.	1. Several worked examples of the pattern to be discovered are presented.
2. This is a large- or small-group activity under direct teacher guidance.	2. Children work as individuals or in small groups.
	3. Children discover a "rule" for the pattern and then test it.

GROUP THINKING AND LABORATORY

1. The teacher presents a problem that causes the children to use experience to discover the new mathematical idea. It may require exploration and activity.

2. Children exchange their ideas to synthesize and develop new ideas.

3. A variety of procedures are developed.

4. Manipulative materials are often used.

5. Often individual work is done first, then group work.

6. Children often work in small groups.

7. Often "science experiment"-type procedures are used.

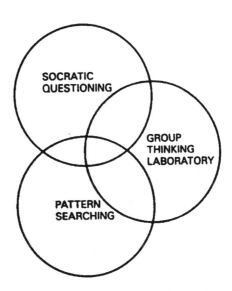

Figure 1-2   The Relationships Among Teaching Strategies

The single examples of the various teaching strategies and the charts are designed to introduce the reader to thinking about strategies of teaching elementary school mathematics. In the chapters that follow, many other classroom illustrations are given by using the various strategies. Thus, this brief introduction should be considered as explanatory; many examples will often be needed to clarify the strategies.

Two other important points need to be considered:

1. The best strategy to use often varies with the mathematical topic, the children to be taught, and the teaching style of the teacher.

2. The teaching strategies considered are not "pure." The components of each strategy can be combined in several different ways.

SOME GENERAL PROCEDURES

There are a number of procedures that lend themselves to good teaching with any strategy. Some of the best follow:

1. *Verbal problems.* Such problem situations are effective for introducing new topics, for they provide the student with a physical-world model from which to abstract mathematical ideas. They also identify a use of the material; when students see a need or use for the phase of mathematics being taught, their motivation to learn is heightened.

2. *Multiple methods of solution.* The use of several methods of solving a problem or an exercise is helpful in several ways. (1) It allows for individual differences in approach and level of abstract thinking; one child can count to find the answer to an addition problem, while a more advanced pupil can think the answer. (2) It develops self-confidence; pupils are better able to attack new materials when they have developed several methods of approaching mathematical situations. (3) It leads to several solutions, encouraging the kind of pupil discussion and debate valuable for developing mathematical thinking.

3. *Materials.* A wide variety of manipulative, experimental, and/or environmental materials can be used effectively to make mathematics interesting, understandable, and relevant to children.

4. *Orally presented problems, computations, and challenges.* Teachers and researchers have found that spending 10 to 15 minutes daily on non-pencil-and-paper tasks (sometimes called *mental arithmetic*) greatly improves the problem-solving, computational, and mathematical thinking achievement of the children.

5. *Readiness.* Providing children with readiness for mathematical abstractions and readiness for new material should be built into the program 1 to 2 years before the topic is considered in a paper-and-pencil form. For ex-

ample, simple orally presented word problems such as, "There are four of you at the table. If you each get two soda straws, how many do we need for the table?", can be used as kindergarten readiness for multiplication.

6. *Calculators and computers.* All children should have access to calculators, and there should be one computer per classroom.

7. *Enrichment.* Challenging problems, puzzles, historical materials, and computational algorithms should be provided for all children.

8. *Reintroduction.* Reintroduce topics from a different perspective than they were first introduced. This provides a challenge and also a variety of procedures to aid the children.

9. *Review.* Provide challenging reviews periodically. To keep sharp, the children need to review.

CURRENT ISSUES AND CONCERNS

As we end the 1990s, there is a clear-cut interest in a number of areas concerned with elementary school mathematics instruction. The Commission on Standards for School Mathematics of the National Council of Teachers of Mathematics (1989) has identified these five areas of need in student development: (1) becoming a mathematical problem solver, (2) learning to communicate mathematically, (3) learning to reason mathematically, (4) valuing mathematics, and (5) becoming confident in one's ability to do mathematics.

Becoming a Mathematical Problem Solver

Math as Problem Solving

Development of each child's mathematical problem-solving ability is essential if he or she is to be a productive citizen. Developing these abilities requires the child's discovery and development of problem-solving strategies; this involves working problems that take seconds, problems that take minutes, problems that take hours, problems that take days, and even long-term problems. (Emphasis on this phase is given throughout this book, with particular emphasis in chapter 4.)

Learning to Communicate Mathematically

Math as Communication

Presently, mathematics is used to represent complex problems in business, economics, physics, and so on. The almost universal use of the computer illustrates the tremendous importance of the communication of ideas by all kinds of language: spoken, written, and mathematical. It is, in fact, almost impossible to differentiate between "language" and "mathematics" in computer use. Students must be helped to see that communication is a vital part of mathematical thinking.

Learning to Reason Mathematically

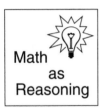

Children learn to make conjectures, gather evidence, build arguments supported by mathematical reasoning, and find correct answers. Development of these attributes requires doing a lot of mathematics. The discussions and suggestions in each of this book's chapters place emphasis upon mathematical reasoning. In today's world, one cannot be considered to be mathematically literate without an ability to reason mathematically. Remember: It is almost impossible to spend too much time working on this.

Valuing Mathematics

Mathematics should play an important role in children's lives, whether in school or out of school. Teachers of history or science can aid in the student's valuing of mathematics by developing lessons about Pascal or Newton, or the mathematical contributions of the Mayans, Greeks, Babylonians, Egyptians, and Romans, for instance.

Teaching mathematics by introducing each new topic with a meaningful problem to which the children can relate also contributes to their understanding of the value of mathematics. Some teachers have invited parents and other adults whose occupations use mathematics to discuss their use of mathematics with the class.

Becoming Confident in One's Ability to Do Mathematics

"Nothing succeeds like success." This is certainly true in the area of confidence concerning one's ability to do mathematics. The attitude toward mathematics and the enthusiasm for teaching mathematics that the teacher brings to the class greatly affect children's confidence. Numerous studies have shown that if teachers and parents believe that a child can do mathematics, the child can. In over 30 years of teaching mathematics, one of the authors has found that children always improve when they have two attitudes: first, they must *want* to do mathematics, and second, they must believe they *can* do mathematics. When these two attitudes occur, children learn mathematics and also enjoy mathematics, problem solving, and mathematical discovery. A key person to establishing these attitudes is the teacher. Children must feel comfortable with problem solving and the computation used in problem solving.

Careful study of the suggestions made by NCTM concerning changes in curriculum and teaching will reveal that these changes are reflected in the approach taken in this book.

Summary of Changes in Content and Emphasis in K–4 Mathematics

TOPICS TO RECEIVE INCREASED EMPHASIS	TOPICS TO RECEIVE REDUCED EMPHASIS
Number	
Number sense	Early attention to reading, writing, and ordering
Place-value concepts	numbers symbolically
Meaning of fractions and decimals	
Estimation of quantities	
Operations and Computation	
Meaning of operations	Complex paper-and-pencil computations
Operation sense	Isolated treatment of paper-and-pencil
Mental computation	computations
Estimation and reasonableness of answers	Addition/Subtraction without renaming
Selection of an appropriate computational method	Isolated treatment of division facts
Use of calculators for complex computation	Long division
Thinking strategies for basic facts	Long division without
	remainders
	Paper-and-pencil fraction computation
	Use of rounding to estimate
Geometry and Measurement	
Properties of geometric figures	Primary focus on naming geometric figures
Geometric relationships	Memorization of equivalencies between units
Spatial sense	of measurement
Process of measuring	
Concepts related to units of measurement	
Actual measuring	
Estimation of measurements	
Use of measurement and geometry ideas throughout the curriculum	
Probability and Statistics	
Collection and organization of data	
Exploration of chance	
Patterns and Relationships	
Pattern recognition and description	
Use of variables to express relationships	
Problem Solving	
Word problems with a variety of structures	Use of clue words to determine which operation
Use of everyday problems	to use
Applications	
Study of patterns and relationships	
Problem-solving strategies	

Summary of Changes in Content and Emphasis in K–4 Mathematics (continued)

TOPICS TO RECEIVE INCREASED EMPHASIS	TOPICS TO RECEIVE REDUCED EMPHASIS
Instructional Practices	
Use of manipulative materials	Rote practice
Cooperative work	Rote memorization of rules
Discussion of mathematics	One answer and one method
Questioning	Use of worksheets
Justification of thinking	Written practice
Writing about mathematics	Teaching by telling
Problem-solving approach to instruction	
Content integration	
Use of calculators and computers	

Summary of Changes in Content and Emphasis in 5–8 Mathematics

TOPICS TO RECEIVE INCREASED EMPHASIS	TOPICS TO RECEIVE REDUCED EMPHASIS
Problem Solving	
Pursuing open-ended problems and extended problem-solving projects	Practicing routine, one-step problems
Investigating and formulating questions from problem situations	Practicing problems categorized by types (e.g., coin problems, age problems)
Representing situations verbally, numerically, graphically, geometrically, or symbolically	
Communication	
Discussing, writing, reading, and listening to mathematical ideas	Doing fill-in-the-blank worksheets
	Answering questions that require only yes, no, or a number as responses
Reasoning	
Reasoning in spatial contexts	Relying on outside authority (teacher, answer key)
Reasoning with proportions	
Reasoning from graphs	
Reasoning inductively and deductively	
Connections	
Connecting mathematics to other subjects and to the world outside the classroom	Learning isolated topics
Connecting topics within mathematics	Developing skills out of context
Applying mathematics	
Number/Operations/Computation	
Developing number sense	Memorizing rules and algorithms
Developing operation sense	Practicing tedious paper-and-pencil computations

Summary of Changes in Content and Emphasis in 5–8 Mathematics (continued)

TOPICS TO RECEIVE INCREASED EMPHASIS	TOPICS TO RECEIVE REDUCED EMPHASIS

Number/Operations/Computation (continued)

Creating algorithms and procedures	Finding exact forms of answers
Using estimation both in solving problems and in checking the reasonableness of results	Memorizing procedures, such as cross-multiplication, without understanding
Exploring relationships among representations of, and operations on, whole numbers, fractions, decimals, integers, and rational numbers	Practicing rounding numbers out of context
Developing an understanding of ratio, proportion and percent	

Patterns and Functions

Identifying and using functional relationships	Topics seldom in the curriculum
Developing and using tables, graphs, and rules to describe situations	
Interpreting among different mathematical representations	

Algebra

Developing an understanding of variables, expressions, and equations	Manipulating symbols
Using a variety of methods to solve linear equations and informally investigate inequalities and nonlinear equations	Memorizing procedures and drilling on equation solving

Statistics

Using statistical methods to describe, analyze, evaluate, and make decisions	Memorizing formulas

Probability

Creating experimental and theoretical models of situations involving probabilities	Memorizing formulas

Geometry

Developing an understanding of geometric objects and relationships	Memorizing geometric vocabulary
Using geometry in solving problems	Memorizing facts and relationships

Measurement

Estimating and using measurement to solve problems	Memorizing and manipulating formulas
	Converting within and between measurement systems

Instructional Practices

Actively involving students individually and in groups in exploring, conjecturing, analyzing, and applying mathematics in both a mathematical and a real-world context	Teaching computations out of context
	Drilling on paper-and-pencil algorithms
	Teaching topics in isolation
	Stressing memorization
	Being the dispenser of knowledge

Summary of Changes in Content and Emphasis in 5–8 Mathematics (continued)

TOPICS TO RECEIVE INCREASED EMPHASIS	TOPICS TO RECEIVE REDUCED EMPHASIS
Instructional Practices (continued)	
Using appropriate technology for computation and exploration	Testing for the sole purpose of assigning grades
Using concrete materials	
Being a facilitator of learning	
Assessing learning as an integral part of instruction	

From: National Council of Teachers of Mathematics (1989) *Curriculum and evaluation standards for school mathematics.* Reston, VA: National Council of Teachers of Mathematics.

ESTABLISHING A BALANCE

A number of factors interact to create curriculum change. Glennon and Callahan (1975) suggest that decisions on selection of content for inclusion in the elementary school mathematics program may be attained with help from three sources: (1) social theory (needs of society, sociological theory, or social-utility theory); (2) the needs of the subject theory (logical organization theory and meaning theory); and (3) psychological theory (needs of the individual, felt-needs theory, or expressed-needs theory). They further suggest that any time these three theories are not well balanced, the curriculum suffers. The extreme child-centered approach, which results in mathematical instruction only when the child expresses a need for it, may weaken the program. This is the approach sometimes referred to as the "Summerhill" approach (Neill, 1960). Some educators have noted that an extreme application of the social-utility theory may have weakened the mathematics program for the 30 years prior to 1950. In the 1960s, the movement in the direction of the needs-of-the-subject approach may have been inappropriate because it failed to take into account the developmental needs of children. It is hoped that the present trend is toward a balanced approach.

It may be helpful to consider the three extreme positions as the vertices of a triangle. A balance among the three theories could be considered to be a ring held in place by three springs (see the following figure). Thus, applying extra pressure to any one of the springs would move the curriculum out of balance. This diagram is helpful when considering individual differences in children or groups of children. For example, children with extreme psychological problems might need to have the program moved toward psychological theory; children from a disadvantaged area might benefit from a program moved toward social theory; and children with strong academic goals might benefit most from a program moved toward the needs of the subject.

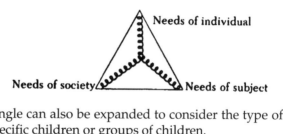

The triangle can also be expanded to consider the type of motivation to give to specific children or groups of children.

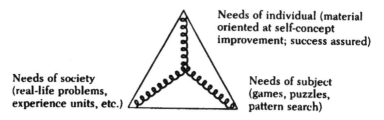

As can be noted, children with an academic orientation are often motivated by mathematics itself in the form of games, pattern searching, and puzzles. Children who see mathematics as of practical importance in the everyday world benefit from situations based on real-world problems. Children who are in need of an improved self-image are probably motivated best through material that ensures success and provides a feeling of achievement. It is true that most children benefit from a mixture of all three types of motivation, but specific groups of children should probably have a greater concentration of one type.

A PHILOSOPHY OF TEACHING ELEMENTARY SCHOOL MATHEMATICS

The material that follows was written by Nancy Redanz at the end of a course in teaching elementary school mathematics. We believe that it summarizes the type of teaching that this book is designed to help you learn.

GOAL: To teach children to learn for themselves . . . Mathematics plays an important role in everyday life. Unfortunately, many of us have learned to fear or dislike mathematics as a subject. This needs to be changed by instilling an enthusiasm in students for solving problems and exploring numbers. As a teacher, I fully agree with and strive to attain the goals put forth by the National Council of Teachers of Mathematics. Specifically, students will learn to value mathematics, become confident in their mathematical ability, become mathematical problem solvers, communicate mathematically, and reason mathematically. The focus of mathematics should be on expanded thinking through the discovery of different strategies to approach a problem. This skill would be most useful and applicable to children's everyday, non-academic life.

Listed below are the main elements of my philosophy of Mathematics:

The teacher's main role should be that of a motivator and facilitator.

Whenever possible, lessons should begin with a problem which makes that topic relevant to the children so they do not have to ask, "Why are we learning this?"

Discussion/Introductions to new topics should start with concrete examples (perhaps suggested by the students) and then work up to discussion of the more abstract ideas pertaining to that topic. In other words, readiness should first be built at a concrete level. Proper readiness would eliminate the term "remedial." Spending more time on the development of an idea at the beginning pays off later.

A combination of teaching methods should be implemented in the classroom. The various Developmental Approaches should overlap (Socratic Questioning, Group Thinking, Pattern Searching, Cooperative Learning, and Laboratory Techniques). These approaches help children to develop mathematics concepts.

Paper and pencil mathematics should be reduced. Emphasis should be placed on orally presented problems, computations, and challenges. "Hands-on," interactive displays should be an integral part of the classroom as well as proper use of manipulatives such as Unifix™ cubes, Cuisenaire rods, geoboards, etc. Computers and calculators play an important role in today's society and should therefore be available and used in the classroom where appropriate.

The child's ability to solve problems is a prerequisite for computation and this fact should be reflected in the teaching format. In other words, straight drill and practice/rote memorization of formulas, without a clear understanding of the concepts, is absolutely unacceptable. Vocabulary/terminology (e.g., perimeter) should follow problem solving. Emphasis should be placed upon various techniques/ways of solving things so the student does not get discouraged if s/he cannot solve the problem or computation in a particular way. It is helpful if the student knows that there is more than one correct way to arrive at an answer because then, rather than hastily "giving up," the child will persevere.

When reintroducing a topic, an approach other than the original one should be taken. Enrichment should be a program available for ALL students, not just the "gifted." Enrichment activities are equally appropriate for the slower students as well as the "bright."

SELF-TEST—HOW WOULD YOU RESPOND TO EACH OF THESE STATEMENTS?

- • ____ In the explanatory method, the pupils can try out their own methods and explain them to the class.

- • ____ Of the many variables affecting the mathematics program, the teacher is the most important.

- • ____ The explanatory method is essentially didactic rather than developmental.

- • ____ Under a developmental pattern of instruction, children are encouraged to experiment with different solutions.

- • ____ Pupil discussion and analysis of solution strategies is an important aspect of the explanatory method.

- • ____ The explanatory method usually encourages pupils to seek answers from an authority rather than to create their own solutions.

- • ____ Pattern searching and finding relationships are characteristic of developmental teaching.

- • ____ In developing a mathematics curriculum, the only relevant concerns are the subject-matter needs and society's needs.

- • ____ When the majority of class time is spent on developmental activities, students seem to perform better on achievement tests in problem solving, computation, and concepts than when the time is spent on drill and practice.

- • ____ Reading periodicals such as *Teaching Children Mathematics* has little value for elementary teachers.

- • ____ Proper mathematics terminology is essential to understanding the concepts; thus, vocabulary should be developed prior to any conceptual work.

- • ____ The theory of social utility dictates that the only math to be taught should be that which is most used in the daily life of adults.

THINK ABOUT

1. Develop an introductory geometry lesson on the classification of shapes for your first-grade class, using the techniques of Socratic questioning.

2. Explain the three contributory needs in determining a math curriculum as described by Glennon and Callahan.

3. Discuss the advantages and disadvantages of the explanatory method and the developmental method of instruction.

4. Prepare a lesson on addition of whole numbers for a fourth-grade class. What method(s) did you use? Why?

5. List your goals in teaching mathematics. Get together with two or three friends to determine the goals each of you considers most important. Defend your views.

6. Look at the NCTM *Standards* material. How is this different from your childhood mathematics?

7. Think through your feelings about the use of calculators in school mathematics. How important are calculators in everyday life?

8. In your imagination, teach a lesson by using each of the lesson types described in this chapter.

9. Obtain elementary school mathematics textbooks; compare the grade placement of topics with those shown at the end of the chapter.

10. The American philosopher George Santayana said, "Those who do not study history are doomed to repeat it." What implications does this have for elementary mathematics teaching?

SELECTED REFERENCES

Glennon, V. J. & Callahan, L. C. (1975). *Elementary School Mathematics: A Guide to Current Research*. Washington, D.C.: Association for Supervision and Curriculum Development.

National Council of Teachers of Mathematics. (1989). *Curriculum and evaluation standards for school mathematics*. Reston, VA: National Council of Teachers of Mathematics.

National Council of Teachers of Mathematics. (1980). *Research in mathematics education*. Reston, VA: National Council of Teachers of Mathematics.

National Council of Teachers of Mathematics. (1983). *The agenda in action, 1983 Yearbook*. Reston, VA: National Council of Teachers of Mathematics.

National Council of Teachers of Mathematics. (1986). *Estimation and mental computation, 1986 yearbook*. Reston, VA: National Council of Teachers of Mathematics.

National Council of Teachers of Mathematics. (1995). *Assessment standards for school mathematics*. Reston, VA: National Council of Teachers of Mathematics.

National Council of Teachers of Mathematics. (1986). *Estimation and mental computation, 1986 yearbook*. Reston, VA: National Council of Teachers of Mathematics.

National Council of Teachers of Mathematics. (1989). "Let's count," in *Curriculum and evaluation standards for school mathematics*. Reston, VA: National Council of Teachers of Mathematics.

National Academy Press. (1989). *Everybody counts*. Washington, DC: National Academy Press.

Neill, A. S. (1960). *Summerhill*. New York: Hart.

Post, T. R. (1988). *Teaching mathematics in grades K-8: Research based methods*. Boston: Allyn and Bacon.

PERIODICALS

The following journals are devoted almost exclusively to mathematics teaching.

Teaching Children Mathematics, National Council of Teachers of Mathematics, 1906 Association Drive, Reston, VA 22901.

Journal of Research in Mathematics Teaching, 1906 Association Drive, Reston, VA 22901.

Learning, Education Today Company, Inc., 530 University Avenue, Palo Alto, CA 94301.

Mathematics Student Journal, National Council of Teachers of Mathematics, 1906 Association Drive, Reston, VA 22091.

The Mathematics Teacher, National Council of Teachers of Mathematics, 1906 Association Drive, Reston, VA 22091.

Mathematics Teaching, Association of Teachers of Mathematics, Market Street Chambers, Nelson, Lancashire, BB9 7LN, England.

School Science and Mathematics, Central Association of Science and Mathematics Teachers, Inc., 535 Kendall Avenue, Kalamazoo, Ml 49007.

The following journals and newsletters have published articles of interest to mathematics educators in recent years. They range from highly practice-oriented publications to research-oriented publications.

Action in Teacher Education

American Educational Research Journal

American Journal of Education

British Journal of Psychology

Cognition and Instruction

Cognitive Science

Cognitive Science and Mathematics Education

Curriculum Inquiry

Curriculum Review

Developmental Psychology

Education

Educational Leadership

Educational Research Quarterly

Educational Researcher

Educational Studies in Mathematics

Elementary School Journal

For the Learning of Mathematics

Journal of Education

Journal of Educational Psychology

Journal of Experimental Child Psychology

Journal of Experimental Psychology: General and Cognition

Journal of Learning Disabilities

Journal of Negro Education

Journal of Research and Development in Education

Journal of Research in Science Teaching

Mathematics in Schools

Mathematics Teaching

Memory and Cognition

Peabody Journal of Education

Science

Teaching and Teacher Education

Theory into Practice

LOOKING AHEAD

A Variety of Children: Culturally Relevant Mathematics

In today's elementary classroom we have a wide variety of individual differences. Since World War II the mix of children in our classroom has greatly increased. We need to consider that children differ in physical attributes, cultural background, gender, intellectual ability, and emotional stability.

This chapter takes an approach somewhat different from the other chapters inasmuch as in this chapter, answers are provided to some questions about children and their learning of mathematics that students of the teaching of elementary school mathematics need to consider in the entire framework of mathematics teaching. Many of the topics are illustrated in later chapters; however, it is worthwhile to take an overview at this time.

Children in Our Multicultural Society

Multicultural education reflects the premise that the United States is not as much a "melting pot" of cultures as it is a salad bowl with many cultures existing within the whole. It is a country where many cultures maintain their identities but contribute to the whole. Such a concept requires a respect for diversity.

Children have a variety of needs. All children have the need to be and feel safe, to be well fed and healthy, to belong and have friends, to be able to work and play effectively in their environment, and to feel some satisfaction from their school work. Certainly there are many other needs, but those needs already mentioned can start us thinking about ways of helping children develop to their fullest.

Children come to us with general needs. However, because of mental, physical, emotional, and social differences, some children will have special needs.

Here are a few questions to help you consider a "fair" treatment of every group. Often the answers will present philosophical dilemmas.

1. Should we refer to groups by culturally descriptive names or just identify children as "persons"?

2. Should we use the same norms for all groups? (Note that this is difficult. It is hard to get culturally diverse groups into some enrichment programs. However, using different norms implies that some groups are not able to achieve as well as others.)

3. What do we do about opportunities that cost extra money?

4. Should we use any homogeneous grouping (also called *ability grouping*)? Why yes? Why not?

5. Should we expect that same standard of classroom behavior of all groups?

6. How do we develop a curriculum that is inclusive of and fair to all groups?

7. What do we do in situations where children from an animal rights activist family and children from a culture that eats canines are in the same classroom? This happens.

8. What is the role of English in our culture? Is there standard English? When should it be advocated?

IN THE CLASSROOM

Ms. Jefferson was teaching a very diverse group of students for the first time. Her former classes had been composed entirely of mainstream, white, middle-class children. Today she was meeting a fourth-grade class that was composed of children of African-American, white, Asian, and Hispanic backgrounds. In addition there was a great deal of difference within each of the ethnic groups as to the income and educational background of their parents.

To get started in mathematics Ms. Jefferson said, "I met a student in the hall who said, 'I think math is a waste of time.' What do you think?"

There was some agreement and some disagreement.

Ms. Jefferson: Let's see if we can find out if math is a waste of time. Look at the sheet I'm handing out. What is it?

Student: A daily record with space for writing after every half-hour.

Ms. Jefferson: We're going to try a math scavenger hunt. Keep track of anything that occurs involving any type of math during the day and at home tonight, and we'll break up in teams tomorrow and see how much mathematics affects our lives.

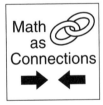

Math as Connections

The following day the children worked in small groups and developed lists of ways that mathematics occurred in their day. Most were surprised that math use was so widespread. Later in the day, as a part of social studies, the children were asked to list the things that they most like to do. Ms. Jefferson resolved to make use of these activities in developing mathematical problem-solving lessons and units. Some of the activities that the children mentioned were as follows:

playing basketball; watching basketball

listening to top 40 on the radio

playing football; watching football

playing video games (Games were listed.)

talking with friends

skating

eating

playing games (Games were listed.)

TEACHER LABORATORY

1. Read the chapter. What questions would you add to the list of questions that are addressed? Record your questions. Keep them on a sheet of paper in the back of the book. If they are not answered in the chapters that follow, perform the proper research to answer them.

2. Providing for individual differences is one of the greatest problems facing the elementary school mathematics teacher. Before reading this chapter, think about or write tentative answers to each of the following questions. Discuss your answers with others. Ask several children to comment on your suggestion.
   a. How can I interest children who are having difficulty with mathematics?
   b. What are the advantages and disadvantages of a completely individualized program?
   c. How many groups could I handle in a class of 30 children?
   d. What are different worthwhile activities that could be occurring simultaneously in an elementary school mathematics classroom?

3. Work out a lesson designed to help a child to be his or her own teacher.

CAN YOU?

- Suggest several generalizations concerning individual differences?

- Indicate specific mathematical learning disabilities that a child might have?

- Give suggestions for making mathematics culturally relevant to a variety of children? don't discriminate   don't insult   relate to all cultures   cultures

- Tell how to recognize varying abilities?

- Explain the use of learning stations?

- Comment on the need of all children for enrichment?

- Suggest how the constructivist view can be used with children of all cultures and abilities?   have gifted + slower students   work stations   interests of children

Think about teaching elementary school mathematics, children's thinking, individual differences, and materials. What do you need to know?

HOW DO CHILDREN LEARN MATHEMATICS?

Why Teach Mathematics to Children?

In the second half of the twentieth century the need for mathematical knowledge and problem-solving skill has expanded at a tremendous rate. In 1960 a distinguished professor of economics reported that "in his day" you could earn a Ph.D. in economics with little or no college-level mathematics. Today much of economics involves mathematical modeling. As a biology major, one of the authors took 20 hours of college mathematics; however, none was required. Today biology is very mathematical. There is reason to believe that with continued development of technology, mathematics will continue to grow in importance and that children with poor mathematical backgrounds will be handicapped in their ability to make choices concerning the directions of their future careers.

It is very important that we help children to develop an understanding of, appreciation for, and facility with mathematics. To do this we must be sure that children truly see a need for mathematics and that they learn to apply mathematical ideas to solve problems of importance to them.

What Type of Behavior Do We Want from Children?

In earlier times the major role of the child was to "sit and get." In reality most children developed their thinking skills outside the classroom setting. This mode of teaching was particularly harmful to children from disadvantaged homes, for often they had little opportunity to develop thinking skills.

The NCTM *Professional Standards for Teaching Mathematics* (1991) suggests that children should behave in the classroom in the following manner:

- Listen to, respond to, and question the teacher and others.
- Use a variety of tools to reason, make connections, solve problems, and communicate.
- Initiate problems and questions.
- Make conjectures and present solutions.
- Explore examples and counterexamples to investigate a conjecture.
- Try to convince themselves and one another of the validity of particular representations, solutions, conjectures, and answers.
- Rely on mathematical evidence and argument to determine validity.

How Do We Produce That Behavior?

As was previously mentioned, the major goal in education is to help each child to become his or her own teacher. Therefore, we need to help the children assume responsibility for their behavior and help them learn independently. Here are some things we know about the prerequisites for successful problem solving by children:

- knowing the goal
- having related previous experience
- possessing an attitude that says, "what in my past experience will help me with what I'm trying to figure out?"
- a "problem-solving" attitude
- confidence

Some children experience the following difficulties:

- insufficient motivation or attention
- inability to disregard irrelevant information
- inability to understand the problem
- lack of any planned approaches
- inability to organize
- difficulty in retaining information
- inability to shift attention to relevant problem details
- frustration leading to inattention and inefficient use of strategies (adapted from: Ashman & Conway [1989], p. 91)

What Is Metacognition? What Is the Role of Metacognition in Elementary School Mathematics?

Metacognition deals with the knowledge and control that a person has over one's thinking. In other words, do you have techniques that help you to learn, solve problems, and think? A great deal of interest in learning to learn and becoming your own teacher fits into the framework of metacognition.

Help in Teaching Elementary School Mathematics

Teachers can give important aid to the children they teach by helping each child to be aware of the way in which he or she studies and learns mathematics. For example, some metacognitive reflections that can be learned are as follows:

- I make computational errors when I hurry.

- Pulling out the numbers without knowing what a word problem is about works some of the time, but not enough to rely on.

- If one way does not work, there is usually another method that I can use to find an answer.

Math as Communication

Teachers can help students develop awareness of their best learning techniques by asking questions, conducting discussions, and rewarding children's thinking about thinking. The following are some questions that might be used on occasion: "What do you do when you see an unfamiliar problem? Why? Is it important to take one's time in working on a problem? When? What can you do when you're stuck with a computation and can't seem to get an answer? How often does it work? How can you keep track of what you're doing? What kind of errors do you usually make? Why? When is it useful to check your work? Why? What kind of problems are you best at? What kind of problems are you worst at? Do all problems take the same length of time? Why or why not? How many ways can problems be solved? When? Do you think you are good at mathematics? Why? How could you be better? What are things you could do to help yourself?"

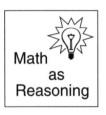

Math as Reasoning

In addition to helping children think through and improve their thinking strategies, the teacher can model good thinking behavior. Modeling requires that you let the children in on your thought processes. Too often we give children polished solutions rather than showing how we think and plan. A teacher who makes the classroom a place where both teacher and children are learning provides a setting for improving the metacognitive process of both. (See Garafalo, May, 1987, April 1986, Schoenfield, 1988.)

How Can "Meaning" Be Maintained?

Often, teachers introduce new topics through exploratory procedures that lead to understanding of the mathematical idea and then proceed to teach efficient computational processing without constant stress on "meaning." It is suggested that each time a topic is reintroduced later in a school year or in a different school year, the teacher review the ideas behind the processing. The teacher should also periodically ask questions such as, "I noted that you all renamed in this subtraction situation without writing any changes in the numerals. Can you tell me what the basic principles of this process are?", or "You've been inverting and multiplying when you divide fractions. Why does this work? What mathematical principles are involved?", or "You multiplied the measure of the length by the measure of the width to find the area of this rectangle. Why?" Mathematical meanings, as well as computational procedures, need to be reviewed and reinforced.

Written Communication
Superior teachers of elementary school mathematics have used short reports or themes as an aid in improving the mathematical understanding of the children.

What Procedures Help Children Remember the Mathematics Taught to Them?

Researchers have found a number of techniques that help children to remember mathematical material. Several rather easily used techniques are these:

1. Teach mathematical content in a meaningful manner, helping children to understand mathematical principles and computation.

2. Adjust the learning tasks to the appropriate achievement and intellectual level of the child.

3. Make use of intensive review procedures. (When several concepts have been taught, develop a day's work that involves probing review questions.)

4. Periodically retest. (Several weeks after you have given a quiz or test on material, repeat the quiz or test.)

5. Give children opportunities to diagnose their own errors. (Children can correct their own papers and then try to determine the reasons for mistakes they have made.)

6. Use guided-discovery teaching approaches.

How Can We Improve Children's Attitudes toward Mathematics?

In addition to the proper development of mathematical ideas, it is of prime importance that the feelings and "attitudes" of the child become a part of the planning for instruction. Figure 2-1 calls attention to the various forces that affect a child's attitude toward mathematics. The teacher should consider each of the areas for each child in the class.

It should be noted that none of the levels or the factors contributing to a child's achievement in the cognitive domain or to his or her attitude in the affective domain is absolute. They are provided to draw attention to some of the levels and ideas that should be considered in learning more about a child and his or her relationship to elementary school mathematics.

Another idea to consider in dealing with a child's feelings toward mathematics and in thinking about the teaching of mathematics to children is the "need orientation" of the child. Looking at the "needs" box in Figure 2-1, we can see five types of needs that are listed in developmental order. That is, a child who is cold and hungry will not be interested in a mathematics activity designed to develop self-esteem. The wise teacher motivates children at their need level.

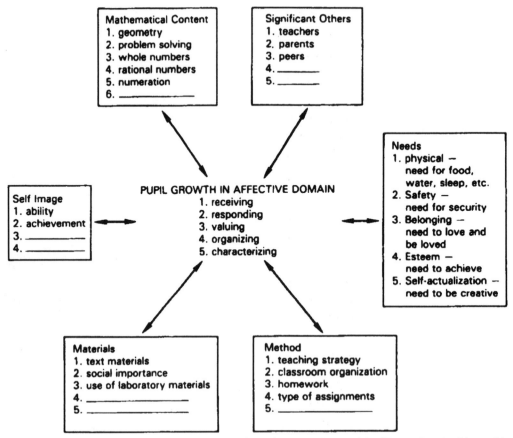

Note: The blank spaces are used to indicate that these lists are not complete The reader should consider the addition of other categories

Figure 2-1   Factors Affecting Pupils' Attitudes toward Mathematics

WHAT CAN BE DONE TO HELP CHILDREN WITH SPECIAL NEEDS?

There are several categories of special needs of children. Think about it for a minute. What are some categories of special needs? It is possible to develop quite a number of categories; however, the following can be considered to be broad umbrellas to cover all of them: difficulty in learning; giftedness; cultural differences; and socioeconomic disadvantages.

Special Learning Needs

What About Slow Learners?
The following characteristics are often observable in slow learners in mathematics:

1. Possessing little motivation or drive. They are willing to just sit.

2. Enjoying "drill-type" work.

3. Possessing short attention spans. They are easily distracted.

4. Possessing a less-than-average memory. They may forget material from day to day.

5. Low ability in verbal comprehension. They have difficulty in interpreting written material.

6. Inability to be original in their thinking.

7. Being physically weaker, socially less secure, and emotionally less stable than the average.

These traits vary from pupil to pupil, but awareness of them should serve the teacher as a guideline in observation. In addition, the power of motivation should not be overlooked. It is possible for the slower pupils to do very fine work on a topic in which they are greatly interested or that they believe they have a chance of mastering.

The suggestions that follow are designed to improve the interest of the slow learner, although many of them apply equally well to the average and the above-average student.

1. Show interest yourself. Interest inventories reveal that arithmetic rates at or near the top as a favorite subject of children, but teachers do not rate it as high. Below-average pupils often reflect the enthusiasm or lack of enthusiasm of the teacher.

2. Often, the bright pupils are provided with attractive supplemental materials. Provide appropriate supplemental materials of equal attractiveness for the below-average pupils.

3. During a class discussion, use the "levels-of-depth" approach to discussion, in which the teacher allows the pupils who have used a very simple means of arriving at an answer to express their views first. Then the teacher builds on the children's explanations by getting suggestions next from the average pupils, and last, from the bright students. By such an approach, all ability levels are able to make a contribution to the class consideration of a topic in mathematics.

4. Slow learners have few opportunities to present unique contributions to the class. During the course of the year, work out a "special" presentation with one of the slower pupils. "Knowing something first" is often a good incentive for continued work.

5. Provide situations that "make sense" to the slow learner. Bright mathematics pupils are often interested in the abstract-puzzle aspects of mathematics. Although some slow learners are also interested in these aspects, in general it is important for them to see a use for the mathematics they study.

6. Know the interests of the pupils, and capitalize on them in the mathematics class. Many boys who are below average in arithmetic understand baseball percentages very well, for example.

7. Be impartial. Show that you like each pupil and that you are interested in the work of each, even if you feel the person may never be a good mathematician. Be positive rather than negative. Almost all slow learners react much better to "You're coming along better; let's see if we can do well on the next lesson" than to "If you don't improve, you're going to fail mathematics."

8. Point out the value of praise to the parents. Encourage them to take pride in some of the good work a slow learner accomplishes.

9. Be patient. When a pupil is trying very hard and working as fast as possible, it is very discouraging to hear, "Hurry up; quit loafing!"

10. Last and probably *most important*, give the slow learner a feeling of being important to you and of being liked as a person.

What About the Gifted?
Giftedness is very difficult to define. The trait may be the result of various combinations of high intelligence, creativity, interest, motivation or drive, and curiosity. Further, the child may be gifted in many areas or traits or may have a gift or talent for particular subject matter.

The following characteristics often are observable in gifted students in mathematics:

1. More persistence in pursuing a task than is seen in other students.

2. Ability to quickly perceive mathematical patterns, structures, and relationships.

3. Possession of a greater amount of intellectual curiosity and imagination than is seen in other students.

4. Being physically stronger, socially more secure, and emotionally more stable than average.

5. Possession of a superior vocabulary.

6. Ability to transfer mathematical learning to new or novel situations that have not been taught previously.

7. Ability to remember longer what has been learned.

8. Flexibility in their thinking.

9. Ability to discover new principles from the principles they already know.

10. Ability to think and work abstractly and to enjoy working with abstractions.

11. High verbal comprehension and ability to communicate mathematical ideas to others.

12. Ability to objectively analyze the strengths and weaknesses in their own mathematical thinking.

13. Being bored with drill-type work. (See Riley and Carlson, 1984, National Council of Teachers of Mathematics, 1987.)

Should superior students be used to help the slower pupils? And if so, how? Probably the best answer to this question is "Sometimes." On occasion, both the fast pupils and the slow pupils can gain from working together. The fast pupil has to understand the mathematical content well enough to explain it clearly to the slower pupil, and often the thought processes the fast pupil goes through in verbalizing an explanation are helpful to the fast as well as to the slower pupil. If the "team-learning" approach is sometimes used in a classroom, there will be occasions on which the teacher can profitably team a slow student with a fast student.

This approach can be, and often is, overdone. The better student should not have the responsibility of being a tutor to a slower student. A rule of thumb might be this: use this technique in situations in which you believe both parties will derive benefit from the exchange.

What About Cultural Differences?

We definitely live in a multicultural society. Pick up any paper and you will find a news item relating to this phenomenon. Full participation of *all* the children in learning mathematics is a major goal in our democracy. How can this be accomplished? There is a growing body of evidence that indicates when teaching procedures such as those mentioned throughout this book and programs such as Cognitively Guided Instruction are used, children from diverse backgrounds learn. (Cognitively Guided Instruction is a program that is based upon four principles: teacher knowledge of how mathematics is learned by their students, problem solving as the focus of instruction, teacher access to how students are thinking about specific problems, and teacher decision making based on teachers knowing how their students are thinking.)

Some general ideas that need to be remembered on a daily basis are the following:

1. All children are more interested in mathematical problems that they can relate to than in problems that have no relevance to their lives.

2. Different cultures have placed greater or lesser emphasis upon mathematics achievement. We must help children and their parents to understand the variety and usefulness of mathematics.

3. Use the same standards for all children; do not insult children from special ethnic groups by giving the notion that they can't reach the "regular" standards.

4. Homogeneous grouping may discriminate against ethnic minorities.

5. Curriculum content should relate to the life of all groups in the classroom; get to know the interests, background, cultural activities, and home-life of all your students.

6. Believe that all of your children can achieve *if properly motivated.* (This is true.)

7. Check out the background of all your children. Then learn about the lifestyle and cultural pattern of all of the children. Often lack of knowledge hampers the teacher in dealing with children of a particular culture.

WHAT ARE SOME ORGANIZATIONAL PLANS FOR PROVIDING FOR INDIVIDUAL DIFFERENCES?

One Plan

Math as Problem Solving

A sixth-grade teacher found that many of the word problems presented in the textbook were not challenging the better students, and that the poorer students were experiencing extreme difficulty with these word problems. He devised a period-length problem-solving test made up of typical sixth-grade problems. The test was tape-recorded for the benefit of pupils with reading difficulty, and each pupil also received a duplicated copy of the problems. The test was administered and corrected by the teacher.

In the next class period, the teacher began by saying, "Yesterday we took a test in problem solving designed to help you gauge your present problem-solving ability and to serve as a basis on which to check the improvement you make. I've developed two sets of problem exercises. The problems on the yellow sheet of paper are the more difficult ones. Those on the white sheet are not so difficult. I am giving you each a white sheet to start with. Those who scored above the median (halfway score) on yesterday's problem-solving test may work three of the problems correctly and then try a yellow one. The rest of you should do all the problems correctly before you may try a yellow one. Each day we'll have both colors of sheets. After you've worked a while with the problems, we can more easily decide which color is best for you. Some of you may want to work with both sheets."

The first two problems were the same on both sheets. These were used as a basis for discussion and to acquaint the pupils with the materials. Pupils then began to work, with the teacher going about the room offering encouragement and help to those in need. After the pupils had been at work for a little while, the teacher called their attention to the fact that the last exercise, headed "How's Your P.Q.?" (problem quotient), was the most difficult on the page and was to be worked only if the pupil wished to do so. The teacher also suggested that when the students had finished all the exercises, they might compare their answers first with a companion and then with a check sheet on the teacher's desk.

During the weeks that followed, the teacher made use of the supplementary-worksheet plan when working on problem solving. At times, all the students were assigned a few problems from the text and from their choice of problem-solving sheets.

PROBLEM-SOLVING LESSON: USING DRAWINGS AND DIAGRAMS (ABOVE-AVERAGE STUDENTS)
Read the problem carefully, and then make a drawing or diagram to use in solving the problem. Try to check your answer by using another method of solution.

1. Two people both depart from one place and both go the same road; the one travels 12 miles every day; the other, 17 miles every day. How far are they distant the 5th day after departure? (Taken from *The Scholar's Arithmetic,* by Adams, 1812.)
2. Mr. Kramer and Mr. Black are going to put a new fence around their farms. Mr. Kramer's farm is in the shape of a square that is 1 mile long and 1 mile wide, and Mr. Black's farm is a rectangle 1 mile long and $\frac{1}{2}$ mile wide. How many times as much fence will be needed by Mr. Kramer than by Mr. Black?
3. Mary is cutting 4-inch-by-5-inch cards to use as tickets for the school play. How many cards can she cut from a sheet of cardboard that is 12 inches by 20 inches?
4. A circular fish pond has a border of red and white bricks. If it has 20 red bricks spaced evenly around the edge and follows a pattern of two red bricks, one white brick, two red bricks, etc., how many white bricks are there?

HOW'S YOUR P.Q.?
5. If a brick balances evenly with a $\frac{3}{4}$ lb. weight and $\frac{3}{4}$ of a brick, what is the weight of the whole brick?

PROBLEM-SOLVING LESSON: USING DRAWINGS AND DIAGRAMS (BELOW-AVERAGE STUDENTS)
Read the problem carefully, and then make a drawing or diagram to use in solving the problem. Try to check your work by using another method of solution.

1. Alice wants to divide 3 candy bars equally among 4 people. What fraction of a candy bar will each person's share be?

2. Clyde and his father set out for the mountains. In 3 hours they had gone 140 miles. They still had 28 miles to go. How far was it to the mountains?

3. One Friday George rode his bicycle $\frac{3}{10}$ mile to the store, $\frac{7}{10}$ mile to the YMCA, and $\frac{9}{10}$ mile to school. How far did he ride that day?

4. In the morning the snow behind Rachel's house was $6\frac{1}{2}$ inches deep. It snowed during the day, so that in the evening the snow was 12 inches deep. How much had it snowed during the day?

HOW'S YOUR P.Q.?

5. Jack said to his friend Bill, "I met a group of boys practicing marching. There were 2 boys in front of a boy and 2 boys behind a boy and there was a boy in the middle. How many boys did I see?" Try using a drawing to help you answer Jack's question.

Several features of the approach suggested can be noted:

1. Materials on the same topic but with varying levels of difficulty were provided. Note that the "How's Your P.Q.?" problem provided an opportunity for both the fast student and the slow student to work with challenging supplemental problems.

2. The introductory test demonstrated to the pupils who were having difficulty a need for the study of problem solving. One of the most important aspects in improving a pupil's achievement is to have the pupil see a need for an intensive study.

3. The pupils were allowed leeway in choosing material of varying levels of difficulty. Teachers using such materials have found that pupils who are experiencing some difficulty with problem solving will often ask to work both sets of materials. They are encouraged to answer correctly the majority of exercises on the easier sheets and to feel a sense of achievement if they are able to answer correctly any of those on the more difficult sheets.

4. The opportunity to check answers upon completion of the work provided for a correction of errors while the material was still fresh in the pupil's mind.

5. Class unity was still maintained because the class discussed some of the problems worked in common. Class discussion also gave the pupils a chance to hear the explanations from their classmates. Often, another pupil is able to explain an idea in a manner that is understandable to the

slow learner. These explanations also allow the able pupil to clarify in his or her own mind his or her method of solution.

6. The procedure provided the teacher with an opportunity to work with individual pupils. During this time, the teacher can also suggest materials for individual class members. In such cases, one or two pages from a supplementary book or worksheet may help to correct difficulty experienced by only one pupil.

7. A program such as the one described allows for a study in depth by the above-average pupil. This procedure has applications in all areas of the mathematics curriculum. The fact that pupils with varying degrees of mathematical ability can work on materials at several levels of abstractness allows the class members to move from topic to topic together. Some pupils will use concrete materials, some drawings, and some the standard algorithms, and some will work beyond the level of the standard form. Examples of pupils working at these levels are given in the chapters that follow.

Using Stations

Many teachers have found that the use of the "station" approach for a portion of each mathematics unit is helpful in making provisions for individual differences.

The station approach involves providing one to five sets of materials that may be at various levels of difficulty. Each station provides the challenge and the materials necessary to complete the work. Children often work at stations in pairs.

Classroom Organization

Assume that you have four groups of learners needing specific skill help. These groups have been formed on the basis of their lack of success in performing adequately on the pretests for some skill. You are planning to provide each individual group with 15 minutes of direct instruction. Your task is not only to plan the four skill lessons but also to plan activities that can be used by the learners not directly involved in the groups you are teaching.

While the teacher gives the 15-minute lesson on a particular skill to the first group of children needing it, the other children are occupied by working with individual materials (laboratory or otherwise). In addition, corrected papers and special assignments can be used as a part of the independent activities to be carried out by each child when he or she is not involved in a skill group. A bulletin board might list specific directions regarding independent activities that the children can perform. Recreational reading, listening activities, or practice-material packets based on mathematics skills taught previously are other ideas for independent tasks.

The most effective classroom organization cannot take place overnight; it will involve several weeks of careful planning. The following issues will need careful consideration: administering of the pretests for the skill objectives, recording pretest performance on your record-keeping device, and planning for independent activity that will involve the rest of the class meaningfully while you are working with the skill groups.

Enrichment and Remedial Laboratories

Some schools provide special instruction once or twice a week for pupils above or below average in mathematics achievement. These special sessions are usually 30 to 50 minutes long. Although the pattern or organization varies, usually some form of team teaching is used. For example, in a school containing 4 fifth grades with a total of 120 fifth-graders, one teacher may work on enrichment materials with the top students, a second teacher on remedial work with students in need of a particular kind of remedial aid, and the other two teachers with the average achievers on an appropriate topic. In other schools, a special mathematics consultant may work with enrichment materials with all classes. Still another pattern is for a teacher with a special interest in mathematics to work with gifted children from several rooms during the period in which music or art is taught in his or her homeroom. The success of such programs has varied with the enthusiasm and capabilities of the teachers involved.

Cooperative Learning

Math as Communication

On occasion, the idea of "cooperative learning" may be employed. In this situation, two or more children work on materials as a team (see chapters 1 and 3). The children study the materials together or work with the teacher.

This procedure has a great deal of merit if used wisely. There are many laboratory lessons, game situations, and practice materials that can be handled effectively through the team-learning approach. It should be noted that the pupils are able to make their own discoveries.

Some teachers have found that it is effective to begin some lessons with children working individually and then move into a cooperative-learning situation in which the children compare their findings.

Individualizing Instruction

Occasionally, some educators call for almost complete individualizing of instruction. If this means that the children are to be working on materials that are appropriate for their level of maturity and interest, this idea is very good. If, however, the goal is to have each child in a classroom working on a different set of materials, the idea is probably unrealistic, since only highly self-motivated pupils can maintain interest in mathematical study without the stimulation of discussion, arguments, and other exchange with peers and teachers.

Plans aimed at total individualization, often called *individually prescribed instruction*, have yet to produce consistently better achievement than "typical" large-group and small-group instruction. This may be due to a lack of superior teaching materials or a lack of sustained interest in working alone on the part of the children.

Another danger in complete individualization is the lack of direct attention that the child would receive from the teacher. In a class of 30 children, how much time would each child receive if the class lasted 40 minutes?

It should be noted, however, that materials designed for complete individualization can be very effectively used at points in the program where working individually is appropriate and necessary.

Variations

It should be remembered that there is no *one* perfect procedure for providing each child with the mathematics he or she needs. The teacher's role is somewhat like an orchestra conductor calling on almost all the various procedures for dealing with individual differences. Too often in the past, teachers or school systems have settled upon one procedure as a panacea, only to completely reject the program a few years later.

The flow chart and table in Figure 2-2 are designed to give the teacher an idea of the decisions that must be made for each unit of mathematics instruction. The teacher must consider the content to be developed, the materials that can be used for instruction, and the best approach to teaching that particular topic, all in the light of the individual children. With these variables in mind, the teacher then decides which mode of instruction (large groups, small groups, individual) will be best for the lesson, group of lessons, or unit.

How Can All Children Have Enrichment Mathematics?

Not only must the mathematics program be appropriate in difficulty for all children, but it must also provide in-depth or enrichment experiences for all children, including the mentally retarded and the handicapped as well as the gifted child. Enrichment can be thought of as a combination of *breadth and depth* experiences: breadth in that the materials used for enrichment will be broader in scope than the typical textbook program while being related to the program, and depth in that enrichment materials may be designed to

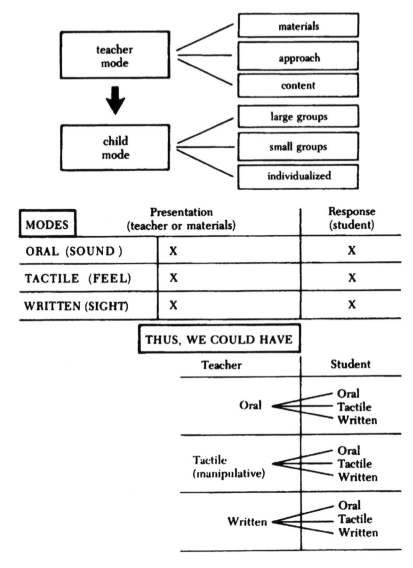

MODES	Presentation (teacher or materials)	Response (student)
ORAL (SOUND)	X	X
TACTILE (FEEL)	X	X
WRITTEN (SIGHT)	X	X

Figure 2-2   Teaching Decisions

"dig deeper" into the mathematical ideas than is typical of basic instructional materials. Several breadth and depth suggestions follow:

1. Emphasize the possibility of multiple solutions to number operations and verbal problems. The inventive pupil may develop several alternate solutions to an exercise while the slower student is developing one. Such a procedure not only enriches the learning situation for the inventive pupils, but it is also a valuable use of the time needed by the rest of the class to finish the basic work.

2. Use small groups with a laboratory strategy. This provides an opportunity for the teacher to work with other groups on specific difficulties.

3. Use a mathematics corner which contains appropriate manipulative materials, project cards, and work space as a great aid in organizing for group instruction.

4. Make use of historical materials. Such materials help to reveal the number system as a human invention and to develop cultural appreciation of it.

5. Make use of a mathematics bulletin board. This should act as a motivator for a unit. In addition, the bulletin board should always include several challenging problems, puzzles, or exercises developed at several different levels of difficulty so that every pupil can work at least one.

6. Provide supplemental worksheets containing challenging material. It should be noted that for many years supplemental puzzle-type exercises have been used by the better teachers. It is suggested that a somewhat different emphasis be placed on these exercises: that is, not only should finding an answer be stressed, but the pupil should also be directed to figure out what mathematical principle is involved in the solution.

7. Provide books and booklets that emphasize the use of mathematics in various careers (for example, National Council of Teachers of Mathematics, *Careers in Mathematics*). Pupils are often amazed at the need for mathematics in apparently nonmathematical occupations.

8. At the end of units, make use of "review study questions." In addition to providing a general review of understanding, some of these questions should encourage investigation and exploration. Here are examples of such questions:

   Grade Three (addition). How could you rename one of the 8s in $8 + 8$ so that a friend who knew only addition combinations with sums of 10 or less could probably understand? [Answer: $8 + (2 + 6) = 10 + 6 = 16$] (use of the associative principle)

   Grade Five (multiplication of fractions). What is the smallest number and the largest number that could be the product of a little less than 3 times a little more than 4? *Note:* A little less than 3 would be $> 2\frac{1}{2}$ but < 3; a little more than 4 would be > 4, but $< 4\frac{1}{2}$ [Answer: 10 plus to $13\frac{1}{2}$ minus] Smallest: $2\frac{1}{2} \times 4 = 10$. Largest: $3 \times 4\frac{1}{2} = 13\frac{1}{2}$.

SELF-TEST—HOW WOULD YOU RESPOND TO EACH OF THESE STATEMENTS?

- _____ Children are easily categorized by their learning problems.
- _____ Individualization of instruction has proven to be the best means of providing for individual differences.

- _____ Children with specific learning disabilities are almost always placed in special classes.
- _____ Motivation is probably the single most important variable for improving achievement in mathematics.
- _____ A station approach does not require many special materials.
- _____ Only very standard materials should be used with slow learners.
- _____ When dealing with a child who is having difficulty in mathematics, the teacher should have the attitude that if one approach does not work, another should be tried.
- _____ The calculator is a good device for use with EMR students.
- _____ Acceleration is the best method of providing for the gifted.
- _____ The slow learner can engage in the "breadth" type of mathematical experiences.
- _____ You cannot have a good mathematics program if you have a poor textbook.
- _____ The role of parents should be an important part of your planning.

THINK ABOUT

1. Find a school, college, or university that has several elementary mathematics textbook series. Study them for the scope and sequence of the material taught and the provision for individual differences.

2. Design a letter to a parent explaining one phase of the elementary mathematics program.

3. Why do we group pupils for instruction according to their chronological age (typical first-grader is 6 years old) when we know that the ability to learn is more closely related to mental age than to chronological age? Think of reasons for and against.

4. To provide suitable content for study by the superior pupils in a fifth-grade class, sixth-grade textbooks must be used. What are the chief objections to such a procedure?

5. If content from the upper grades (see question 4) is not to be used, what is to be the source of the arithmetic content for superior pupils?

6. Why has within-class grouping for instruction in arithmetic not been as popular as it has been in reading?

7. What features of the developmental method of instruction in arithmetic make it desirable as a method of providing for individual differences in ability within a class?

8. Should fifth-grade pupils who are doing remedial work be left with the class or put into a separate class? For what reason?

9. How much of a problem is the grade placement (assignment to grades) of exercises in an arithmetic enrichment program?

SELECTED REFERENCES

Ashman, A. F., & Conway, R. N. F. (1989). *Cognitive strategies for special education.* London: Routledge, p. 91.

Bell, A. Swan, M., Shannon, A., & Crust, R. (1996). Pupils Awareness of Their Learning. *Mathematics Teaching,* 154 March 6–9.

Baratta-Lorton, R. (1977). *Mathematics: A way of thinking.* Menlo Park, CA: Addison-Wesley.

Barone, M. (1996). Peer Tutoring, with mathematics manipulative: a practical guide. *Teaching Children Mathematics,* Sept. 8–15.

Baroody, A. J. (1987). *Children's mathematical thinking.* New York: Teachers College Press.

Garafalo, J. (April, 1986). "Metacognitive knowledge and metacognition processes: Important influences on mathematical performances." *Research in Teaching in Developmental Education:* 34–39.

Garafalo, J. (May, 1987). "Metacognition and school mathematics." *The Arithmetic Teacher,* 22–23.

National Council of Teachers of Mathematics (1978). *Developing computational skills, 1978 yearbook,* chap. 1–5 and 14. Reston, VA: National Council of Teachers of Mathematics.

National Council of Teachers of Mathematics (1982). *Mathematics for the middle grades (5–9), 1982 yearbook.* Reston, VA: National Council of Teachers of Mathematics.

National Council of Teachers of Mathematics (1986). *Estimation of mental computation, 1986 yearbook,* chapter 19. Reston, VA: National Council of Teachers of Mathematics.

National Council of Teachers of Mathematics (1987). *Providing opportunities for the mathematically gifted.* Reston, VA: National Council of Teachers of Mathematics.

National Council of Teachers of Mathematics (1991). *Professional standards for teaching mathematics.* Reston, VA: National Council of Teachers of Mathematics.

Riley, J., & Carlson, N. (1984). *Help for parents of gifted and talented children.* Carthage, IL: Good Apple, Inc.

Riley, J., & Carlson, N. (1987). *Providing Opportunities for the Mathematically Gifted.* Reston, VA: National Council of Teachers of Mathematics.

Schoenfield, A. H. (1988). "What's all the fuss about metacognition?" In A. H. Schoenfield (Ed.), *Cognitive Science and Mathematics Education.* Hillsdale, NJ: Lawrence Erlbaum Associates.

Trentacosta, J. (Ed.) (1997). *Multicultural and Gender Equity in the Mathematics Classroom: The Gift of Diversity, 1997 Yearbook.* Reston, VA: National Council of Teachers of Mathematics.

Zambo, R. & Hesss, R. K. (1996). The Gender Differential Effects of a Procedural Plan for Solving Mathematical Word Problems. *School Science and Mathematics:* 58, 362–363.

3 The Teacher— The Classroom Leader

LOOKING AHEAD

The role of the teacher of mathematics is undergoing a drastic change as greater knowledge about how children learn mathematics becomes available. Traditionally, the children have asked for explanations and the teacher has provided them. Today this is often reversed: the excellent mathematics teacher has the children explain their thinking and discuss why mathematical procedures work. Traditionally, children were taught how to do a mathematical procedure in a large group, and the teacher followed this with independent practice and individual help for students who needed it. Today, teachers use large group settings for posing problems. This is often followed by work in small groups. This small group work is typically followed by a large group discussion of the findings of the groups.

In addition to his or her role as manager of lessons, today's mathematics teacher must be able to make prudent decisions regarding technology. Calculators and computers have entered the classroom, and now teachers are faced with the responsibility of evaluating and guiding the uses that are being made of these tools.

Assessment of learning is another area where today's mathematics teacher must be knowledgeable. A variety of methods of assessing student learning are available. The teacher must know what his options are and when each of these options is appropriate. This implies an understanding of the strengths and weaknesses of the various assessment methods.

The mathematics teacher of today is faced with the need to continue to grow professionally throughout her career. Knowledge of mathematics, knowledge of pedagogy, knowledge of how children learn, and an assortment of other skills should be constantly improving. Various methods of self-evaluation aimed at professional growth are needed.

Always remember: One of the most important roles of the teacher is to motivate the children by showing enthusiasm, by supporting them, and by developing interesting materials.

CAN YOU?

- Define the three organizational components to a developmental mathematics lesson?

- Distinguish between a "group discussion" and a "community of inquiry"?

- Suggest ways of dealing with individual differences within a class of mathematics learners?

- Give at least three reasons for using cooperative learning to teach mathematics?

- Identify several roles for the teacher of mathematics?

- Describe appropriate and inappropriate classroom uses of calculators?

- Describe and evaluate three different categories of uses of microcomputers in the classroom?

- Describe and evaluate four methods, other than tests, of assessing children's growth in mathematical understanding?

- Describe two frameworks in which assessment of mathematics teaching skills can occur?

- Compare self-evaluation and peer evaluation as components of professional growth in teaching?

PLANNING FOR LARGE GROUPS/SMALL GROUPS/INDIVIDUALS

The Elevens Problem

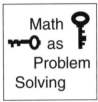

Math as Problem Solving

A classroom that reflects today's approaches to teaching mathematics will be examined as a way of introducing the various roles of today's mathematics teacher.

The children in Ms. Lopez's class have been working on the following worksheet in small groups (**see Homer's Elevens Problem**). She has called them back together for a large group discussion of their findings.

Ms. Lopez: As you were working in your groups I noticed that different groups were finding different patterns. I'd like a representative from each group to tell us one of the patterns that you found. Let's begin with Lee's group.

Lee: We found that they kept going up by elevens. Then, to do the ones ending in nines, you had to jump up by five elevens at once.

Barry: But, that wouldn't work for the last group . . . the ones with hundreds!

Lee: We know. The last ones had a different pattern. The two middle numbers were going up one each time, but we didn't figure out the last one yet.

Ms. Lopez: All right, Lee, maybe the findings of the other groups will help your group. Esteban, what did your group find?

Esteban: Well, its sort of hard to explain. May I come up to the board and show you?

Esteban goes to the board and shows that his group added the two digits of the bottom factor and used that as the middle digit in a three-digit answer. The right digit of the answer was the same as the right digit of the bottom factor, and the left digit of the answer was the left digit of the bottom factor.

Sue: Wow! That's neat! Does it always work?

Nic: What happens with the ones that have nines?

Esteban: Well, those were hard. At first we thought it didn't work, but . . .

Ms. Lopez: Excuse me for interrupting, Esteban, but instead of telling us how it works, why not let us try to figure it out. Maybe the other

HOMER'S ELEVENS PROBLEM

Homer Price's donut machine produces eleven donuts every time he presses the "START" button. Homer has been making a chart to tell him how many times he needs to press the button to fill various-sized orders. Can you use the calculator to complete the chart? Can you find a pattern that will help you figure out the number of donuts faster than you could with the calculator?

Presses	Donuts
1	11
2	22
3	33
. . .	
9	
. . .	
21	
22	
23	
. . .	
29	
. . .	
111	
121	
131	
. . .	
191	

groups can figure it out together right now. Let's look at them . . . 11 × 19 is 209, 11 × 29 is 319, 11 × 39 is 429 . . .

The lesson progressed with the children discovering that the pattern found by Esteban's group even "worked" with the nines. Ms. Lopez was not satisfied, however, with finding procedures that worked. For homework she asked the children to spend some time trying to figure out why the procedures worked. Her plan was to devote the following day's lesson to developing an understanding of why this worked. She also planned to have the children explore other multipliers in a similar way to have them find out if more general patterns exist.

Analysis of the Elevens Problem

The Elevens Problem illustrates many principles of effective planning of small-group and large-group activities. For the small-group portion of the lesson it is essential that each group has a specified problem area in which to work. In this case the worksheet provided a structure that was specific, yet a context that was somewhat open-ended. The open-ended nature of this exploration increased the probability that the various groups would approach the task somewhat differently. This variability between groups is important for the ensuing large-group portion of the lesson.

In the large-group portion of the lesson the teacher's goal is to create a community of inquiry. A community of inquiry is much more rich than a group discussion. Although Ms. Lopez provides a structured format for the discussion, it is not unusual, uncommon, or disrespectful for children to contribute to the discussion without being specifically called upon to speak. Interruptions, as in the case of Ms. Lopez's interruption of Esteban, are allowed if they are handled with politeness.

The community of inquiry is used for children to put forth conjectures about mathematics that they believe to be true. Other children who don't understand or who don't accept those conjectures are expected to probe and question until they do understand or until the conjecture is modified. In this process, the teacher attempts to communicate to the children that she is not the ultimate authority when it comes to mathematical thinking. The children learn through this process that some ways of thinking will withstand examination by the group, and that group examination is helpful in locating flaws in thinking.

Math as Communication

A community of inquiry takes time to develop. The type of interaction between children that is illustrated in the Elevens Problem and others like it throughout this book cannot be expected to occur spontaneously the first time an attempt is made. Teachers who are trying for the first time to develop a community of inquiry will need to try a variety of questions designed to get children to explain their strategies and to interact with each other. Even the teacher who is experienced with using a community of inquiry usually finds that the first few weeks of the school year are difficult. The children need to learn that giving explanations, thinking aloud, and reacting to classmates' thinking are essential elements of the learning process. If children have not experienced this before, they will find it highly unusual at first. However, after they become accustomed to what is expected, they will find the community of inquiry exhilarating and stimulating. The teacher, also, will find the community of inquiry to be an exciting and rewarding experience as she listens to and guides the children's reasoning. See the "A Problem-Focused Lesson Template" for a format you can usually use.

> **A PROBLEM-FOCUSED LESSON TEMPLATE**
> - Pose a realistic problem that can be solved using the math you intend to teach.
> - Give students time in small groups to solve the problem in whatever way makes sense to them. (Sometimes you may wish to have the children work individually.)
>   - As some groups find a solution, challenge them to find another way to solve the problem.
>   - As some groups find an alternative solution, challenge them to find as many ways as possible to solve the problem. (By this time it is likely that some groups are still working on finding a solution, some on finding an alternative solution, and some on multiple solutions.)
> - Bring the class together as a group to share their various ways of solving the problem.

Questioning and Problem Posing

A key role for teachers learning to guide and expand children's thinking is the role of problem-poser. Compare the following questions that may be posed for children:

> What are the key words in this word problem that will help us decide whether to add, subtract, multiply, or divide?
>
> Can we think of some other problems that might be similar to this one before we try to solve it?

The first question is closed and leads to specific answers. It is the sort of question that communicates to children that there are specific rules or formulas that need to be memorized in order to have success in math. The child who knows the "key words" will succeed, whereas the child who cannot remember the key words is handicapped.

In contrast, the second question is open-ended and gives children an opportunity to think of a variety of responses. Responses can be created by the children as a result of analysis of the structure of the problem that they are considering. A child is not dependent on his memory for success, but rather on his ability to think. Furthermore, in answering the second question the child will certainly be dealing with key words, but in a more implicit and functional way than would be the case if she were answering the first question.

This principle of asking open-ended questions can be expanded to include problem posing. The goal of problem posing is to make use of the child's natural sense of wonder. (See the Problem Solving chapter for the characteristics of a Good Problem.)

Cooperative Learning

What Is It?

Today there are a variety of meanings for the term *cooperative learning.* In general, cooperative learning refers to a classroom management technique in which small groups of children, normally about four to a group, work together on a project. Normally, this small-group work is followed by a summarizing activity involving the entire class. Some forms of cooperative learning involve specific guidelines for assignment of children to groups. These guidelines usually involve forming groups that are mixed in regard to ability, gender, and cultural background. Some forms of cooperative learning depend on each group being given responsibility for a different part of a large overall task. This way, no small group can fully appreciate the entire picture until each group has made its individual contribution.

Why Do It?

The vision of mathematics teaching implicit in the NCTM *Standards* cannot be implemented by children working in isolation. If children are to formulate their own ideas, express their thoughts about mathematics, articulate reasons for thinking the way they do, and come to agreement about the truth of mathematical notions, there must be a great deal of interaction. Cooperative learning in small groups has proved to be an ideal way of managing a classroom that is consistent with these goals.

In addition to the enrichment of mathematics learning that is possible with small cooperative groups, this management tool can be helpful in developing positive social attitudes and skills. Cooperative learning, with appropriate involvement from the teacher, has been shown to aid in fostering cooperation and sensitivity to races and cultures different from one's own.

CALCULATORS

Appropriate Use

Technology

One of the philosophical issues facing today's elementary mathematics teacher concerns the role of calculators. As calculators have become commonplace in our society, elementary teachers have become concerned that their use would hinder children from learning arithmetic. Parents, too, have often expressed concern, sometimes even forbidding children from using calculators. Partly as a result of this type of response to calculators, children sometimes have the belief that using a calculator constitutes cheating.

In spite of these concerns, the reasonable teacher will realize that calculators are a fact of modern life, and their correct and appropriate use must be taught. Defining and developing ideas about correct and appropriate use requires imagination and careful consideration of goals on the part of the teacher. An astute teacher will also attempt to deal with harmful beliefs and attitudes that children and parents sometimes have toward calculators. Certainly correct and appropriate use does not include using the calculator as a substitute for knowledge of basic facts. Correct and appropriate use should also imply something more powerful than using calculators to check computations done by traditional pencil-and-paper algorithms.

One of the issues that has been debated is the question of the use of calculators on tests. Makers of standardized tests have recently developed alternative sets of norms for scoring the tests. These alternative norms are used for scoring tests of children who were permitted to use calculators while taking the test. Typically school administrators decide whether their school will use the noncalculator or the calculator norms. The teacher should find out administration policy early in the year so that his children can be appropriately prepared for whatever format is expected in a given school.

Calculator Uses	
CORRECT AND APPROPRIATE	**INAPPROPRIATE**
To explore number patterns and relationships	Substitute for knowledge of basic facts
To do computations for complex applications that arise in real-world problem solving	Checking pencil-and-paper computations
To answer "what-if" questions that require laborious computations	Solving problems that could easily be estimated
When problem-solving processes rather than computations are the focus of instruction	Whenever other means (e.g., mental computations; computer) can provide a quicker answer
To explore relationships between fractions, decimals, and percents	For games or activities that manipulate the calculator display without any attention to meaningful mathematics

Types and Their Uses

Many types of calculators are available to children in the elementary school. They range from simple four-function calculators to calculators that can display information in graphic form. Some calculators have a memory and others do not. One of the newest products is a calculator that can perform operations on fractions as well as give division answers with remainders.

| A calculator should help a child develop an understanding of mathematics. |

Many calculators offer features far beyond the needs of elementary children. Scientific calculators and graphing calculators are so sophisticated that they pose a danger of intimidating a young child. One of the teacher's roles is to help her children obtain a calculator that is appropriate for their conceptual developmental levels. A basic guiding principle is that a calculator should help a child develop an understanding of mathematics. Because of the wide variety of calculators available, it is advisable for schools to provide appropriate class sets for each of the grade levels.

COMPUTERS

CAI

Technology

When computers first began to make an appearance in schools, the idea of programmed learning in work-texts had already been in existence for some time. Programmed learning was conceived as a form of individualized branching of instruction based on the unique responses of each learner who engaged in the tasks. Computers provided an electronic format for programmed learning that promised to mechanize almost all of the cumbersome administrative and logistical chores of programmed learning. Therefore, the earliest use of computers in educational settings was in this category, which came to be known as Computer Assisted Instruction (CAI).

The vast majority of computer programs available for microcomputers are of the CAI variety. Typically they provide an interesting context for presentation of information or drill and practice of basic facts. Many of these programs fail to provide the kind of learning environment envisioned by the *Standards* and illustrated here. Philosophically, many of the software designers continue to view mathematics as something that can be transmitted to children rather than as something that must be constructed by children.

| Many programs fail to provide the kind of learning environment envisioned by the *Standards*. |

Games and simulation programs that have a more constructivist orientation can sometimes be found. *The King's Rule*™, by Sunburst Communications, is a game that engages the child in making and testing conjectures about arithmetic and number patterns. The computer environment is a nonthreatening place to experiment and receive immediate feedback about the accuracy of conjectures. Simulations allow the child to experiment with cause and effect as they manipulate variables. Learning with this type of program can occur as a result of engaging in the activities. In order for learning to be optimal, the teacher must present questions that help the child to reflect on the activities of the game and form mathematical abstractions as a result of those reflections.

Another category of program gives the learner more control of the resources of the computer. These programs might be termed *tool* programs. *Elastic Lines*™, by Sunburst Communications, is an example of this type of program. It allows children to use the computer as an electronic geoboard to explore and illustrate geometric concepts. Again, the full success of a program of this sort depends on wise and timely intervention from the teacher.

> **With any uses of computers . . . , the teacher must guard against children becoming isolated.**

With any uses of computers in the teaching of mathematics, the teacher must guard against children becoming isolated. This is because of the fact that computers lend themselves to single-user settings, and the fact that many computer programs are highly engaging. Children who lack interpersonal skills are especially susceptible to becoming isolated with the computer. This can be prevented by setting computer tasks that require children to work together and develop a dialog about their interactions with the computer.

The Internet

Technology

There are a wide variety of activities available on the internet. One must evaluate their usefulness. The **PBS Mathline** is one teacher source worth checking out. It provides teacher evaluations of a number of new mathematics projects. You can use this service by either calling 703-739-5071 or email: mathline@pbs.org. The web address is http://www.pbs.org/learn/mathline. The elementary school projects are:

The Elementary School Math Project (ESMP)

The Middle School Math Project (MSMP)

The overview of the material suggests that anytime . . . anyplace . . . whenever you need it, you can receive materials on the following projects that are designed by teachers for teachers to support standards-based learning and teaching. Each profile provides:

Online, ongoing, learning community of peers facilitated by an experienced classroom teacher.

A series of video lessons featuring teachers and students engaged in standards-based instruction and assessment.

Printed Guides with comprehensive lesson plans and suggested ideas for online discussion.

Flexibility to allow local adaptation of national, state, and district standards.

Logo and "Microworlds"

Technology

Logo is not strictly a program, but could more accurately be called a programming language. Unlike other computer-programming languages, Logo is designed for extremely easy entry-level use by children. Logo has been adapted for use by children who are in kindergarten and first grade. By pressing single keys they can manipulate a "turtle" on the screen and explore the paths made as they move the turtle around. Geometry, measurement, number, and arithmetic concepts are built by the children as they work in this environment.

LOGO IN ACTION: AN EXAMPLE

To Triangle
  FD 75
  RT 100
  FD 75
  RT 100
  FD 75
End

The children have been trying to teach the turtle to draw a triangular roof for a house they are making. Their initial attempt had an incomplete triangular path that was not oriented correctly. Their first correction attempted to correct the incomplete path problem.

Joe: I think we just need to make that last FD longer. Maybe we should try 100.

Steve: But if we do, it still won't be right. Look, it will go down below where we started, and it will look crooked.

Joe: Let's try it anyway.

They change the last line to FD 100.

Joe: You were right. Maybe we need to keep the sides all the same. But then how will they ever meet?

Steve: The only other thing to change is the angles. Look, if the turtle turned a little more at that last turn, maybe he'd reach that first side in FD 75. It isn't as far to the first side if you turn a little more.

Math as Reasoning

The philosophy behind the development of Logo was one of providing children with "tools to think with." Seymour Papert (1980), one of the original designers of Logo, envisions electronic "microworlds" where children can manipulate dynamic representations of objects and abstract mathematical concepts from those manipulations. Logo has been used successfully to help children make intuitive geometric concepts explicit. This enables children to examine their own ideas and find out specifically where those ideas are inaccurate. In the example of the boys trying to correct their triangles, they have made their ideas about a triangle explicit to the computer. Now they are in the process of examining their own ideas in order to solve a problem that is important to them.

Although some valuable exploration of Logo might occur without structure provided by the teacher, maximum usefulness of the tool can be obtained by providing interesting tasks and challenges. *Logo Geometry*™, by Clements and Battista (1991), contains many tested ideas for teachers wishing to make good use of Logo. The teacher who is interested in using computers to facilitate children's construction of meaning in mathematics should keep abreast of new developments and extensions of the features of Logo.

Hypermedia

Technology

The newest concept in educational technology is hypermedia. Hypermedia combines the power of microcomputers with audio CDs, videodiscs, and CD-ROM. Although most of the early work with hypermedia in education has been in social studies and science applications, it is reasonable to expect that mathematics applications will be more widely available soon. The teacher who wishes to tap the power of hypermedia for teaching mathematics should read current issues of *Academic Computing, Journal of Research on Computing in Education, Educational Technology,* and *The Computing Teacher* to stay informed of current developments.

MANIPULATIVES, GAMES, AND BULLETIN BOARDS

Why Use Manipulatives, Games, and Bulletin Boards?

Learning theorists such as Piaget and Bruner have given us compelling reasons to depend on manipulatives, games, and bulletin boards in teaching mathematics to children. Mathematics, by definition, is abstract. For children, abstractions require tangible physical models as referents. Manipulatives can be used to provide those physical models of mathematical ideas. As children manipulate objects in the context of solving problems, they are setting the cognitive stage for making mathematical abstractions. In conjunction with the activities associated with the use of manipulatives, children must be given opportunities to reflect on those activities in order to construct meaningful mathematics understandings. It is the role of the teacher to select appropriate manipulatives, engage the children in meaningful mathematics tasks, and provide opportunities for reflection.

Games provide another means of helping children learn mathematics. The primary purpose of using games is to provide a motivating context in which the need for mathematical knowledge is embedded. Children quickly learn strategies that depend on mathematical knowledge when they realize that these strategies will help them win a game. It is not uncommon for a child to decide for herself that quick recall of basic facts is necessary if she wants to win a particular game consistently. This provides the motivation needed by that child in order for her to commit the basic facts to memory.

Bulletin boards have a unique function in the teaching of mathematics. Since bulletin boards are primarily a visual medium, they can provide a connection between manipulative work and abstract symbolic work. Pictures, drawings, graphs, and other visual representations are ideal for bulletin boards. A teacher who wishes her bulletin boards to be consistent with an overall philosophy of helping children find meaning in mathematics will highlight a question in each bulletin board. A bulletin board built around a question compels the children to become actively involved with the material of the bulletin board.

Evaluating Manipulatives, Games, and Bulletin Boards

There is no inherent value in the use of manipulatives, games, or bulletin boards. In order for any of these tools to have the desired effect, the teacher must make effective use of them. Since the connections between manipulatives and the mathematics that they represent are not transparent to children, it is necessary for the teacher to make these connections explicit. For example, it is not unusual for a child to be able to use manipulatives to represent a subtraction task but be unable to use the numeric symbol system to perform that same subtraction task.

A second concern with the use of these tools is the question of distractions. Some manipulatives are made to be commercially attractive at the expense of their pedagogical usefulness. It is possible that bright colors make it more difficult for some learners to focus on the relevant attributes of the manipulatives. Games that are more entertaining than pedagogical should be avoided. Bulletin boards that have distracting eye-catching pictures might overpower the mathematical message.

A third issue to consider in the use of manipulatives, games, and bulletin boards is the question of justification: Why is this topic better taught with a manipulative, game, or bulletin board? Single-digit multiplication can be sensibly introduced through manipulative devices. Such devices have questionable value for demonstrating three digit multiplication.

Finally, the wise teacher will consider alternative approaches when making decisions about manipulatives, games, and bulletin boards. If one of these tools is selected as the most powerful or the best way to represent a particular concept for use with particular children at a particular time, this is preferable to using a given tool automatically every time a particular topic is taught.

USE MANIPULATIVES, GAMES, OR A BULLETIN BOARD IF
1. the connections to more abstract mathematics can be made explicit.
2. the manipulative, game, or bulletin board is without unnecessary distractions.
3. the reason for using the manipulative, game, or bulletin board is clear to you.
4. alternatives have been considered.

ASSESSMENT

Assessment of Students

At least two reasons exist for assessing students' learning of mathematics. One reason would be to determine whether or not teaching has been effective. Traditional pencil-and-paper tests were designed with this in mind. A more basic reason for assessment, however, is to guide instruction. If a teacher's goal is to provide instruction that is at an appropriate level, it is necessary to make assessment an ongoing and continuous component of teaching. In the past few years a wide variety of materials have been developed to extend assessment well beyond the typical teacher made and standardized tests. Because of limited space we have just touched on the variety of approaches. Check carefully the **Selected References** at the end of the chapter for many resources that can be used in teaching.

One-Half?: An Example of Ongoing Assessment

Mr. Conrad is working with his class on understanding the concept of fractions and various ways of representing fractions. He has presented the following diagram on the overhead projector and the class has begun discussing ways of shading "one-half."

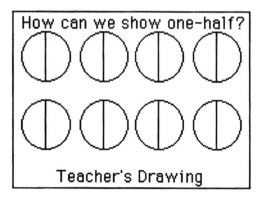

Julie: I think we should shade all the ones on the left. Like this:

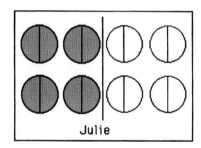

Bob: That would be OK, but you could do it another way. You could shade all the ones on top. Like this:

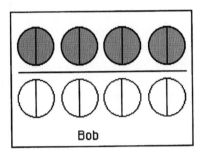

Curt: I think we should use those lines in the circles. They cut the circles in half. We should do it like this:

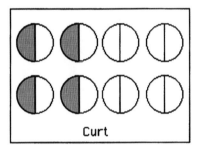

Sue: I don't think that comes out to be the same as the other ways. It looks like you've got less shaded than Julie or Bob.

Curt: No, look. . . .these lines cut the circles in **half,** so all you have to do is shade the left halves.

Sue: It just doesn't look right.

Mr. Conrad waits to see if anyone can clarify the discrepancy before he asks the following: How many whole circles did Julie and Bob shade? (4) If we put Curt's shaded portions together into whole circles, how many whole circles would be shaded? (2)

Curt: Oh, I see! I meant to shade the left halves of **all** the circles, not just the ones **on** the left!

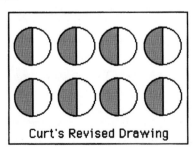

Interview and Observation

By listening to his children as they were thinking aloud and debating with one another, Mr. Conrad was able to tell much about the thinking levels of the various children. His guess about Curt's misconception suggested a line of questioning intended to help Curt correct that misconception. Mr. Conrad's teaching was inextricably linked to assessment; he could not have decided what questions to ask if he did not have some idea about what Curt was thinking.

At times it becomes necessary for a teacher to undertake a more comprehensive look at a child's thinking. Perhaps a child has been unable to consistently correct a misconception, despite repeated interventions by the teacher. At a time like this it is helpful to conduct a private, task-based interview in order to probe the child's thinking. A task-based interview is semi-structured, but somewhat informal. The task chosen for a task-based interview must be chosen carefully so that it involves the child in the fundamental aspects of the area of mathematics that the child is having difficulty with. An example of such a task for a child showing a lack of understanding of subtraction requiring regrouping follows. A full and complete treatment of the topic of task-based interviews, however, is beyond the scope of this book.

A TASK FOR A TASK-BASED INTERVIEW
Given sets of base-ten blocks representing ones and tens, the child is asked to represent the number 15. From this he is asked to subtract 7. If he succeeds, he is then asked to use pencil and paper to subtract 7 from 15. If he did not succeed on the original task, the teacher provides help in the form of suggestions that the ten-block can be traded for ten one-blocks. A follow-up question would be to ask the child to make up a story problem to go along with the 15 minus 7 task.

Portfolio

In addition to the information that can be gained by listening to and talking with children, portfolios of the children's work provide an important means of assessment. Written work has the advantage of being more permanent than classroom interaction. The teacher can examine and reflect on a child's written responses after school or between classes. In addition to this, written work provides a longitudinal view of the child's changing understandings.

Group Response (Immediate Feedback)

Sometimes during instruction with a group it becomes necessary for the teacher to gain an immediate idea of how many of the children are making sense of the instruction. At times like these the teacher can call for a group response to specific questions. There are a variety of ways that the teacher can require the children to respond. The important feature of group response assessment is that each member of the group must provide some response that is visible to the teacher but hidden from the other members of the group. The teacher then quickly notes which children have given an incorrect response, and she uses that knowledge to tailor her teaching to match the group.

Assessment of Teaching

The teacher who grows as a professional tends to view assessment of teaching in an educative framework rather than in an evaluative framework. An evaluative framework is one in which any criticism of teaching performance is taken as a negative factor, and a record is kept for comparison against future assessments. Teachers who are evaluated within this framework are expected to eliminate the negative factors from their teaching performance in order to achieve tenure or maintain career growth. Evaluative teacher assessment typically focuses more on management issues than on pedagogical issues. Evaluative teacher assessment tends to serve the purposes of administration more than it serves to improve instruction.

An educative framework for teacher assessment, on the other hand, interprets assessment as a means of improvement of instruction. Educative teacher assessment fosters dialog among professionals as a primary means of improving teaching. Assessment in this framework lacks the competitive aspect of evaluative assessment; in its place is cooperative goal sharing and brainstorming for innovative ways of meeting those shared goals.

Self-Assessment

A necessary component of educative teaching assessment is self-evaluation. Self-evaluation can be done informally, but is more effective if it is done with a certain degree of structure. Daily, weekly, or monthly schedules of self-evaluation are helpful in providing some of the needed structure. Further structure can be provided through the use of some form of written or computer-presented instrument for self-evaluation. In either format, these instruments focus a teacher's examination of his or her teaching by posing questions about student behaviors, teacher responses, teacher goals, and teacher knowledge. A formal analysis arising from self-scoring of the responses to these questions provides a teacher with suggestions for improvement.

Peer Assessment

Although self-assessment is necessary for professional growth, it is not sufficient. A companion to self-evaluation is peer evaluation. Like children, teachers grow when they are confronted with ways of seeing and ways of thinking that are different from their own. Peer evaluation and peer dialog about teaching are ideal settings for this to occur. As teachers share their goals, frustrations, and ideas together, they find that they are not alone in their need for improvement. Ideas from one person provide new ways of thinking for another person. Through cooperative brainstorming, teachers arrive at new possibilities for improving their teaching. In short, the constructivist view of learning that is seen throughout this book applies to teachers' learning as well as to children's learning.

WORKING WITH PARENTS

Several views of mathematics are commonly held by large numbers of parents. The first is that mathematics is only about numbers and arithmetic, unbending accuracy, and infallible rules. The second is that children should first know the basic computational rules and have a great deal of practice.

The third is that mathematics is an innate ability (whereas adults in other countries are much more likely to believe that success in mathematics depends on effort). A related belief is that mathematics is difficult, and so children should not be expected to do well. Textbooks in this country have reflected this view by introducing topics later than in other countries.

Finally, some parents believe that mathematics is not important. It is acceptable to not know mathematics. Parent to child: "Don't worry, I never understood math either."

Research has shown that parental attitude plays an important part in children's achievement. Thus, it is very important for the parent, the teacher, and the child to work together—they all have the same goals. Here are some ways that parents and teachers can work together.

1. If possible, have parents help in the classroom.

2. Hold short classes for parents, "How to help your child in mathematics."

3. Work with the children and develop a monthly newsletter to parents dealing with the mathematics program.

4. Develop handouts of games, problems, and puzzles that parents can do with their child.

5. Help parents to select computer software and supplemental books that are useful for the child.

SELF-TEST—HOW WOULD YOU RESPOND TO EACH OF THESE STATEMENTS?

- ____ Interruptions should not be permitted if a teacher is trying to lead a class discussion.

- ____ Children can arrive at mathematical truth as a result of arguing about their ideas.

- ____ An example of an open-ended question would be "How far do you walk in a day?"

- _____ More difficult problems should be posed for the brightest children, and less difficult problems should be posed for the slower children.

- _____ For cooperative learning to succeed, the teacher should not get involved in the group work because the children will figure things out for themselves.

- _____ Positive social outcomes can be expected as a result of proper use of cooperative learning.

- _____ Calculators are not appropriate for children in the primary grades.

- _____ Calculators cannot help children work with fractions.

- _____ Computer microworlds can be used to help children explore mathematical ideas.

- _____ A key concern in the use of manipulatives is helping children make connections to symbolic mathematics.

- _____ Interviews are a valuable way of gaining information about a child's mathematical thinking.

- _____ National teacher exams are a valuable way of stimulating professional growth in teaching.

SELECTED REFERENCES

Assessment Standards for School Mathematics Working Group (1995). *Assessment Standards for School Mathematics.* Reston, VA: National Council of Teachers of Mathematics.

Burns, M. (1996). What I learned from teaching second grade. *Teaching Children Mathematics.* November, 124–127.

Clarke, D. J., Clarke, D. M., & Lovitt, C. J. (1990). Changes in mathematics teaching call for assessment alternatives. In T. J. Cooney (Ed.), *Teaching and learning mathematics in the 1990's* (pp. 118–129). Reston, VA: National Council of Teachers of Mathematics.

Clements, D., & Battista, M. (1991). *Logo geometry.* Morristown, NJ: Silver, Burdett, and Ginn.

Cooney, M. P. (1996). *Celebrating Women in Mathematics and Science.* Reston, VA: National Council of Teacher of Mathematics.

Davidson, N. (1990). Small-group cooperative learning in mathematics. In T. J. Cooney (Ed.), *Teaching and learning mathematics in the 1990's* (pp. 52–61). Reston, VA: National Council of Teachers of Mathematics.

Gitlin, A., & Smyth, J. (1990). Toward educative forms of teacher evaluation. *Educational Theory, 40,* 83–94.

Jianjun, W., Wildman, L., & Calhoun, G. (1996). The relationship between parental influence and student achievement in seventh grade mathematics. *School Science and Mathematics,* 96(8).

Kaplan, R. G., Yamamoto, T., & Ginsburg, H. P. (1989). Teaching mathematical concepts. In L. Resnick & L. Klopfer (Eds.), *Toward the thinking curriculum: Current cognitive research.* Association for Supervision and Curriculum Development.

Karp, K. (1997). Portfolios as Agents of Change. *Teaching Children Mathematics,* January, 224–228.

Lambdin, D. V., Kehle, P. E., & Preston, R. V. (editors) (1996). *Emphasis on Assessment.* Reston, VA: National Council of Teachers of Mathematics.

Lynes, B. (1997). Mining Mathematics through the Internet. *Teaching Children Mathematics,* March.

Papert, S. (1980). *Mindstorms: Children, computers, and powerful ideas.* New York: Basic Books.

Schwartz, J. E. (1992). How can we evaluate ourselves? *Arithmetic Teacher, 39*(6), 58–61.

Stenmark, J. K. (Ed.), (1991). *Mathematics assessment myths, models, good questions, and practical suggestions.* Reston, VA: National Council of Teachers of Mathematics.

Webb, N., & Briars, D. (1990). Assessment in mathematics classrooms, K–8. In T. J. Cooney (Ed.), *Teaching and learning mathematics in the 1990's* (pp. 108–117). Reston, VA: National Council of Teachers of Mathematics.

4 Problem Solving—The Key Element of the Mathematics Program

Perhaps no facet of elementary mathematics instruction has received more attention than has problem solving. Properly understood, problem solving can be the key to meaningful change in the way mathematics is taught to children. Teachers must stop thinking of problem solving as a topic to be covered after the basic skills of mathematics have been mastered. Instead, they must view problem solving as the engine that drives the mathematics education curriculum.

LOOKING AHEAD

Whole Mathematics?

In recent years a ground swell of support has occurred among teachers of reading and language for immersion of children in literature. The basic philosophical and pedagogical position inherent in this movement is that children learn to read and appreciate language by reading and using language. Although not without its critics, the "Whole Language" movement has dramatically changed the way elementary reading and language arts are taught in the United States.

> **Problem solving is now seen as the heart of the mathematics curriculum.**

During the last two decades, ideas about problem solving in school mathematics have undergone a similar dramatic change. Once viewed as a skill to be taught along with skills of addition, subtraction, and so on, problem solving is now seen as the heart of the mathematics curriculum. As the twenty-first century approaches, mathematics educators are redefining the mathematics curriculum using problem solving as the basis for a "Whole Mathematics" movement.

Importance of Problem Solving

Evidence from NAEP

Recent data from the National Assessment of Educational Progress (Kouba, et al., 1988) in mathematics indicate that children in grades 3, 7, and 11 have limited problem-solving capabilities. On a recent assessment, children were successful on problems involving a single calculation, no extraneous information, and depicting familiar and simple everyday settings. However, non-routine problems, problems with extraneous information, and multi-step problems posed great difficulties, especially for the youngest children. Furthermore, children were not successful on problems requiring logical reasoning.

The strategies used by children to solve word problems tended to be nonmathematical in nature. A common strategy was to add all the numbers of a problem if there were more than two numbers in the problem statement. A guess-and-test strategy was most common when multiple choice answers were provided. According to Kouba, et al. (1988),

> Many more students were able to identify the correct response for an item worded in such a way as to allow students to work back and forth between the item stem and the answer choices than could identify the correct response for a similar or easier problem that did not allow for a guess-and-test approach. (p. 19)

Strategies such as using graphs or drawings or evaluating the reasonableness of answers were not widely used by children.

Two Perspectives

The nation's America 2000 plan for restructuring American education places a strong emphasis on mathematical problem solving. A report prepared by the U. S. Department of Labor (1991) identifies three foundations upon which solid job performance competencies are built. One of these foundations is "Thinking Skills: thinking creatively, making decisions, solving problems, seeing things in the mind's eye, knowing how to learn, and reasoning" (p. vii). This report goes on to stress that these foundations are not the end goals of education, but the beginnings. Throughout the report, problem solving is placed in the context of real situations. This report was derived from many interviews with business leaders, and reflects the concerns of the workplace for which schools must prepare children.

The NCTM *Standards* describe a mathematics curriculum in which children "use problem-solving approaches to investigate and understand mathematical content." This implies that problem solving is the engine that drives the mathematical investigations in school. The *Standards* emphasize finding mathematical investigations in everyday situations. Written by educators, the *Standards* reflect the concerns of those who are familiar with recent research about how children learn.

CAN YOU?

- Explain the difference between a problem and a word problem?
- Provide a simple definition of "problem solving"?
- Suggest an alternative to the traditional view of placing problem solving as the final activity of a unit?
- Defend the idea of introducing new material through problem solving?
- Suggest ways of helping children to realize that problem-solving process is more important than correct answers?

- Develop a comparison between the way American teachers tend to treat problem solving and the way Asian teachers tend to treat problem solving?

- Explain what is meant by "problem posing" and suggest how it may be used in teaching school mathematics?

- Suggest ways in which computers may assist with problem-solving instruction?

- Describe several problem-solving strategies that may be taught to children?

- State at least two cautions to keep in mind when teaching children problem-solving strategies?

- Describe a way to teach Polya's four-step problem-solving model without having it become a hindrance to children's thinking?

- Explain what is meant by the term *metacognition* and suggest some implications of recent research on metacognition for teaching practice?

- Explain what the role of algebraic thinking is in the problem-solving program?

CLASSROOM TEACHING OF PROBLEM SOLVING

Definitions

What Is a Problem?

> **A problem may be considered to be a situation in which things are perceived to be not as they should be . . .**

At one time, problem solving meant doing computation exercises presented in narrative sentence format. Problems were "word problems" found at the end of a chapter in a child's mathematics text. A much more comprehensive meaning for the term *problem* is necessary, however. Operationally, a problem may be considered to be a situation in which things are perceived to be not as they should be, with no known way to correct them. Under this definition of a problem, an initial state of confusion is presumed to exist. Furthermore, an initial state of discomfort is implied. Clearly, using this definition, many of the word problems that children solved in the past were not actually problems. On the other hand, much of what teachers have presented as "instruction" may have been a "problem" to children.

What Is Problem Solving?

Broadly conceived, problem solving can be seen as the process of locating and removing the sources of confusion and discomfort. In this sense, problem solving does not need to be taught: children of all ages are skilled at locating and removing sources of confusion and discomfort.

The job for the teacher of mathematics is to help children find and value increasingly abstract and sophisticated *mathematical* methods of solving problems.

A Good Problem . . .

1. . . . is one that can engender responses on multiple levels.

2. . . . can form the context in which many mathematical explorations occur.

3. . . . is one in which the specific questions that need to be answered are open for negotiation and definition.

4. . . . will not be solved immediately, and, in fact, may take one entire class session or more to explore fully.

5. . . . can be expected to spawn several other good problems.

One of the important features of good problems is their potential for engendering responses on more than one level. It is inevitable that the classroom teacher will be faced with a wide range of abilities among the children in her class. In the past teachers have tried to deal with this variability in many ways. Some teachers have attempted to individualize instruction so that everyone had instruction at his or her appropriate level. This was found to be unmanageable and inefficient. Another attempt at meeting individual differences was the formation of different ability groups. Unfortunately, this resulted in lower-ability children becoming trapped in a slow moving group with low expectations. If children managed to make important mathematical discoveries and increase their mathematical power in a slow-moving group, it was impossible to move them into a faster-moving group because of the ever widening gap between the groups.

Problems that allow for responses on multiple levels are a good way to meet individual needs without the unfortunate byproducts caused by ability-grouping. Another technique that has great potential for addressing individual needs is cooperative learning.

Math as Problem Solving

A Good Problem: How can we see what a million looks like?

The Question of a Skills/Applications Hierarchy

Tradition in mathematics education teaches that children must learn the basics before they can apply their knowledge to solving problems. This firmly held belief is, unfortunately, not pedagogically sound. In practice it results in children being taught isolated "skills" separate from each other and separate from any real-world requirement for those skills. Teachers often delay problem solving further and further because they feel their children need more and more time to master the basics. The result is poorly learned basic skills, an inability to use those skills in solving problems, and an attitude that mathematics is meaningless drudgery.

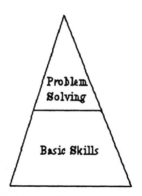

Traditional View: Problem
Solving Built on Basic Skills

The alternative to this is to reverse the process entirely. Instead of viewing problem solving as the final phase of a lesson sequence, we recommend introducing new material in the context of a rich problem. If a problem situation is presented to children, and they find that mathematics helps them to solve it, then mathematics is likely to be perceived as meaningful, situated, and valuable. If children lack a component of a "basic skill" necessary to the solution of a problem, they can be helped to invent that basic skill in the context of solving the problem. Research has indicated that children do, in fact, invent mathematics before they begin school, in the context of trying to make sense of the world. If school lessons in mathematics can be patterned after this "natural" process by which children learn mathematics, perhaps children will learn more and enjoy mathematics more.

New View: Problem Solving as
a Context for Skills

Process/Product Balance

There are two aspects to problem solving: the solution to the problem, and how that solution was obtained. The solution is sometimes referred to as the *product*, and the method of obtaining the solution is sometimes referred to as the *process*. Although both the product and the process are important, it is the process that should be the focus of school instruction. Children often develop the misconception that the only thing that matters is getting the right answer. Teachers can avoid contributing to that misconception by making it a habit to focus discussion on how answers were obtained and why the procedures worked or did not work. The questions and prompts in the box can be helpful in getting children to focus more on the process than on the product in problem solving.

Sometimes teachers go too far and suggest that correct answers are not important. But stop and think about it. If correct answers weren't important, then the process for obtaining answers would not be important either. Excellent teaching stresses both the process and the product *in balance*.

How do you know?
Can you show me that you are right?
Why does that work?
Can you solve it in another way?
Explain.
Will that always work?
Tell me more.

The Asian Comparison

James Stigler and Harold Stevenson (1991) have recently reported on a comprehensive comparison between education in the United States, Taiwan, and Japan. Among their findings are several comparisons in the way teachers treat mathematical problem solving. The following table compares Asian treatment of problem solving with the traditional American treatment of problem solving. Many of the procedures reported have been advocated by mathematics educators in the United States for many years.

ASIAN PROBLEM SOLVING	AMERICAN PROBLEM SOLVING
Teachers lead children in thoughtful interaction and discussion.	Teachers tell and explain mathematical ideas and procedures.
Lessons center on extended practical problems: one or two problems to a forty-minute lesson.	Problems follow work on basic skills. A problem-solving lesson will "cover" many problems.
The problem provides the lesson introduction, the setting for teaching mathematical mechanics, and the summarizing focus.	Lessons tend to lack continuity and coherence. Procedures are taught and children practice them.
A variety of solution strategies are sought and discussed.	The focus is more on right answers than on process.

ASIAN PROBLEM SOLVING	AMERICAN PROBLEM SOLVING
Errors form the focus of a fruitful discussion leading to insight.	Errors are glossed over to avoid embarrassing children.
Questions are carefully posed to stimulate thought.	Questions evoke simple, one-word or one-sentence responses.

Role of Problems

Problem Posing

Although we typically view problems only in the sense of problem *solving,* there is much more educational value to be found in problems. Problem *posing* offers some exciting possibilities beyond problem solving. When a problem is presented to children fully specified by the teacher, an implicit assumption is made that the children will accept that problem as their own. While this is often necessary for the efficient accomplishment of the goals of schools, it runs the risk of ignoring the human characteristics of children.

Problem posing is not just allowing children to make up their own word problems. Rather, problem posing is a means of tapping into the child's natural curiosity and sense of wonder in order to launch mathematical investigations. A problem-posing attitude needs to be developed and nurtured through specific structured questions and techniques.

Any fully specified problem is composed of elements that may be systematically varied. Variation of these elements, or elimination of certain constraints, can lead to new problems as children begin to wonder, "What if . . ." An example may help to clarify this. Suppose we were given the following problem: "A salesman needs to visit his four accounts. Use the following map to determine how far he must go."

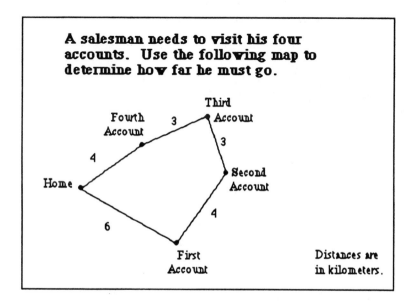

The problem, as stated, has the following constraints:

- He makes all the visits on one trip.
- He travels on the routes marked.
- He visits the accounts in the order marked.

Other constraints could be listed as well. Problem posing can begin when children begin to wonder what would happen if changes to these constraints were allowed. Young children might wonder what would happen if he traveled the route backwards; would the total distance be the same? What if he tried a different route; is this route the shortest? What route is the longest route possible if you visit every account once and only once? Many other interesting investigations could be conceived. The important point is not how many different problems could be derived, but rather, that children can develop fluency in posing their own problems. When they do this, they have a personal motivation for finding the answers.

Problems as Motivators

Much attention has been given in recent mathematics education literature to the role of intuition in learning mathematics. The prevailing view is that formal mathematics instruction should be built on children's intuitive understandings. While this is sensible, and should be done whenever possible, there is another side to the educational use of intuition.

Many of our intuitive notions about mathematics are wrong ideas. Many people, for instance, have incorrect intuitions about probability. If a coin has been tossed four times and comes up "heads" all four times, many people think that there is a higher than 50 percent chance that the succeeding toss will be "tails." Even after a mathematics lesson that would prove a 50 percent chance of tails on any toss of a coin, many people find themselves in a position where intuition conflicts with evidence. It simply feels like the next toss is more likely to be tails.

The existence of erroneous intuitions presents some exciting implications for mathematics teachers. If an erroneous intuition can be seen as an opportunity rather than as a liability, then it can be exploited in the teaching of mathematics. For example, if a teacher uses the coin toss problem to confront students with a conflict between reasoning and intuition, then the problem itself becomes only the doorway to deep thinking, questioning, and exploring.

Beginning with Piaget, researchers studying the cognitive development of children have found that this cognitive conflict is a necessary component of meaningful new learning. If a person does not notice any conflict between evidence and intuition, then erroneous intuition can cause a misinterpretation of evidence. On the other hand, if the conflict is noted, then the person must adjust his ideas in order to accommodate the evidence at hand.

Math
as
Problem
Solving

This general mechanism of meaningful learning can be used as a potential motivator. Problems can be sought which, when "solved," will leave the students puzzled, confused, or otherwise dissatisfied. This uncomfortable state of affairs can then serve as an opportunity for students to undertake their own investigations. Of course, this is not meant to imply that teachers should try to confuse their children, nor should teachers leave their children in a state of confusion. Rather, this state of disequilibrium can be used by a skilled teacher to motivate children for further investigation.

SITUATIONS FOR PROBLEM SOLVING

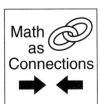

In order for problem solving to become significantly more than solving simple word problems at the end of a chapter, teachers must begin to use new contexts for problem solving. Many interesting mathematical problems can be generated in the course of completing class projects. A class play in which scenery must be prepared is a setting for exploring geometry and measurement concepts. A school store can provide a context for many interesting economic explorations. School sports and professional athletics generate great quantities of statistics that can be used for problem solving. Raymond Zepp (1991) reports on a project undertaken by several businesses and the Board of Education in Pinellas County, Florida, in which fifth-graders are given an opportunity to practice mathematics skills in a simulated economic community.

A promising new setting for problem solving is the microcomputer. The increasing sophistication of computer equipment available for classrooms enables these machines to present simulations in which children can explore data, make decisions, develop strategies, and test ideas about problem solving. Computer simulations of this sort include *Math Shop*™ and *Math Shop Jr.*™, from Scholastic; *Parking Lot: Time and Money*, from Queue; and *Conquering Percents*, from MECC. This genre of software makes good use of a computer's capabilities, and the software itself is being improved as the cost of computing power declines.

USING STRATEGIES IN PROBLEM SOLVING

In order for students to learn to solve problems, it is helpful for them to learn specific problem-solving strategies. These strategies should be viewed as resources to try when seeking a solution, rather than as procedures that must be followed to solve any and all problems. Choosing a promising strategy from among a variety of different possibilities is itself a skill that requires learning and practice.

Estimating

In daily life, most people routinely solve fairly complicated problems by using estimation and mental mathematics. For most circumstances, estimation is the most appropriate way of finding solutions. Children are sometimes surprised to find that estimation can be faster than using a calculator to find an acceptable answer.

If children have been exposed to an overemphasis on exact, correct answers, then getting them to rely on estimates may be difficult. It is not unusual for children in this condition to carry out a complicated computation and then round the answer, instead of using estimation. This, of course, circumvents the purpose in estimating: to provide a quick approximation of an answer. Sometimes children who are reluctant to rely on estimates can be shown the value of estimation through the use of games in which speed is important. If these children can see, through a game format, that estimates can be obtained very quickly and with a sufficient degree of accuracy for many situations, then they may become more willing to rely on them.

Problems without Numbers

Math as Reasoning

Although they are rarely, if ever, taught to do so, children sometimes "solve" word problems by noting the size and number of numbers in a problem and applying an operation according to a rule. If there are more than two numbers in a problem, children assume that addition is required. A problem with two numbers and the word *difference* somewhere in the problem will evoke a subtraction response. Partly to counter this pseudo-strategy, and partly to focus children's attention on problem-solving processes, teachers sometimes present problems without numbers. The children are then asked to describe how they would solve the problem if the numbers were supplied. This activity is ideal as a language activity if children are required to write sentences explaining how they would solve the problem.

Polya-like Thinking

Polya's Problem-Solving Model:
1. Understand the problem.
2. Devise a plan.
3. Carry out the plan.
4. Examine the solution obtained.

For many years, the influence of George Polya, one of the master teachers of problem solving, has been observed in the mathematics education literature. Polya's four-step model has been included in an NCTM yearbook, several elementary mathematics textbooks, and many teaching methods books. (See Polya, 1945, 1973.) Although the model has much to offer to mature individuals who wish to improve their ability to solve problems, it has had little impact on helping children learn to solve problems. In the past the model has been used as a suggested way to solve the majority of elementary school mathematics problems. However, to be effective, the problems to be used have to be complex. For example, "I'm going to build a house— What should I do? How should I handle my finances?"

Part of the reason for this limited effectiveness may be in the way the model has been presented to children. Perhaps teachers have led children to believe that this model will function as a fool-proof, systematic way of bringing a solution to a problem situation. Rarely are problems simple and straightforward enough that children can apply the model in a step-by-step way. Typically, one step flows almost imperceptibly into the next. Children become confused as they try to monitor which step of the process they are on. Management of the model becomes a problem in and of itself, compounding the original mathematics problem.

This does not mean to imply that the Polya model has no usefulness in the teaching of elementary mathematics. Teachers will benefit from practicing using the model on problems they face themselves. After teachers find that they have internalized the basic structure of the model, they are in a stronger position to informally guide children in its use. A teacher's questioning is an appropriate means for introducing elements of the model to children. When a problem is first presented, a teacher's questions should focus on helping children understand the problem. When the teacher has evidence that the problem is understood by the children, her questions can begin to focus on helping children devise and carry out a plan. When an answer is obtained, the teacher can ask questions that focus children's attention on evaluating the answer.

Such a use of the Polya model places the teacher in the role of a mentor, and places the children in the roles of apprentices. In this mentor/apprentice relationship, the teacher knows the steps of the problem-solving model and provides executive control over how these steps influence children's thinking. This relieves the children from the responsibility of memorizing a procedure and monitoring their own implementation of that procedure. As this process occurs repeatedly in the solving of many different problems, children will internalize the process, and will begin to take over aspects of the monitoring process themselves. Finally, as they approach maturity as problem solvers, the formal Polya model can be taught to them to enable them to use explicit labels of the steps and make their use of the process more efficient.

Mathematical Sentences

A mathematical sentence expresses a relationship between numbers. The relationship may be the equality relationship, as in $5 + 4 = 9$, or it may be an inequality, as in $5 + 4 > 8$. Mathematical sentences sometimes have variables or place holders in place of one or more of the elements in the sentence. Referred to as "open sentences," these sentences imply that a solution can be found that makes the sentence true. An example of an open sentence would be $5 + 4 = ?$. A more difficult open sentence would be $? + 4 = 9$. Some open sentences allow for more than a single answer, as in $N + 5 > 10$.

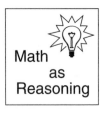

Math as Reasoning

Once children have developed an understanding of a set of generalizations such as the associative property and the commutative property, they can use mathematical sentences in a pre-algebraic manner. Suppose a child knows that addition and subtraction are inverse operations. Further, suppose that she has derived the sentence $? + 7 = 15$ from a word problem. She is now in a position to be able to reason that $15 - 7 = ?$. If the sentence was not solvable in its original form (and researchers tell us that problems that begin with an unknown are more difficult than others), the new sentence will be more easily solved.

In order to use mathematical sentences as a strategy in problem solving, children must already have a good grasp of the structure of the problem. In fact, if a child can write a correct mathematical sentence, the problem is nearly solved. For this reason, the use of mathematical sentences should normally be viewed as a relatively sophisticated strategy.

Drawings and Diagrams

Many people find that drawing a diagram is a helpful problem-solving strategy. Although, for many adults, the idea of drawing a diagram seems to be a natural approach to solving problems, children need to be taught the value and the skill of doing so. A recent investigation into the effectiveness of using Logo to teach geometry found that children who had received Logo Geometry™ instruction were more likely than the control group to use a diagram to solve problems. Unfortunately, the diagrams drawn by these children were often incorrect. These results indicate that there are two aspects of drawing diagrams that teachers should be concerned with: the choice of whether or not to use a diagram, and how to make a correct diagram.

Relevant to both concerns is the issue of the degree of detail that a drawing or diagram should provide. If children are simply instructed to draw a diagram to help them solve a problem, they are likely to become encumbered with the artistic detail of the task. This will circumvent any mathematical benefit that they could have derived from the diagram. To prevent this it is necessary for the teacher to stress the representational or symbolic function of a good problem-solving diagram. Consider the cycling problem outlined below in the box, for example. This is a very difficult problem to draw. Children might attempt to draw bicycles, and the detail of drawing them would be likely to distract them from the problem at hand. The teacher in this case might suggest that a simple dot be drawn to represent each bicycle. This simplifies the artistic demand but preserves the mathematical value of using a diagram.

Draw a diagram to help you solve this problem:
A circular track is 1000 yards in circumference. Cyclists A, B, and C race around the track: A at the rate of 700 yards per minute, B at the rate of 800 yards per minute, and C at the rate of 900 yards per minute. If they start from the same position at the same time and cycle in the same direction, what is the least number of minutes it must take before all three are together again?

Restatements and Analogies

Related to Polya's first stage of problem solving, understanding the problem, is the strategy of restating the problem or stating an analogous problem. When a teacher asks a child to read a problem orally and then describe in his own words what is being asked, this helps the child direct attention to understanding the problem.

If the problem uses large or complex (decimal or fraction) numbers, the teacher may ask the child to substitute smaller or simpler numbers in the same problem. Often this approach enables the child to realize the structure of the problem, which then enables him to find a successful problem-solving process. The teacher would ask the child to describe this process verbally or symbolically; she would then suggest that the process might be the same for the larger or more complicated numbers.

Eventually, after a number of experiences of this sort in which the teacher poses the guiding questions, the child will begin to take over the role of asking these questions of himself.

Oral Problems

In the development of literacy, there is interaction between reading, writing, listening, and speaking. In the same way, mathematical literacy develops from a variety of sources of input. Children grow in their problem-solving abilities as they solve problems presented orally. The following suggestions are intended to guide the teacher in using orally presented problems.

- Use the small blocks of time that might otherwise be wasted for orally presented problems (lining up for lunch, waiting for students to return from gym, waiting for a late guest to arrive . . .).

- Give children verbal chains of computations to follow and compute mentally: "6 plus 5 minus 1 divided by 2. . . ." As children become more skilled, you can present longer chains, and you can present them faster and faster. (If you get lost, just include "times zero" to start over.)

- Provide oral presentation of problems that are more easily solved by compensation or other transformations than by standard algorithms. (An example would be 1003 minus 697.) After the first few children have solved it, ask them to explain how they got it so quickly. The oral explanation of the process is as valuable an activity as the solving, and it benefits the listeners as well as the speakers.

- Each child can use a small (8" × 10") whiteboard to record answers. This whiteboard can be kept at the child's desk along with a dry-erase marker and a rag for erasing. When problems are presented orally the children can write their answers on the whiteboard, show them to the teacher, and hide them from the rest of the class. This gives the teacher a very quick assessment tool.

- Pupils can be told to write only the operation or mathematical sentence needed to solve a complex problem presented orally.

- Keep the pace brisk, and spend only short (5 to 10 minutes) spans of time on orally presented problems.

Tables or Charts

Many problems, particularly those that contain extraneous information, can be solved most efficiently when the data are put into table or chart format. Below is a portion of a table that was used to solve the problem "How many different amounts of money could someone make if they had 4 pennies, 2 nickels, 1 dime, and 1 quarter?"

PENNIES	NICKELS	DIMES	QUARTERS	TOTAL
4	2	1	1	$ .49
3	2	1	1	$ .48
2	2	1	1	$ .47
1	2	1	1	$ .46
	2	1	1	$ .45

When the children completed this much of the table one of them noticed that the totals were declining by one cent each row. She made the conjecture that this would continue all the way down to zero, and that meant that there were 49 different amounts of money that could be made. This hypothesis generated a great deal of discussion as children disagreed about whether it was possible to make every amount. Eventually, at the insistence of several of the children, they continued the chart and verified the conjecture.

Tables and charts are especially strong heuristics when statistical data are involved in a problem. Unorganized, "raw" data often conceal information that becomes evident when the data are systematically organized into a table. The ability to impose an order on unorganized data, and the realization that alternative orders are possible, are two understandings that children can construct as a result of using tables and charts to solve problems.

Technology

The increasingly sophisticated power of microcomputers makes them an ideal tool for extending the heuristic of using tables and charts. Most spreadsheet programs today can translate tabular data into a variety of graphic presentations. Often patterns in the data that are hard to detect become obvious when presented graphically. The ease with which computer software can accomplish these transformations makes it possible for elementary students to explore their use.

Choosing Appropriate Strategies

Even if children succeed in learning a variety of strategies for solving problems, they face the added difficulty of deciding when to use a given strategy. Clearly, not every strategy is equally helpful for every problem. Certainly children should not be taught to use all strategies for each problem. Choices and evaluations must be made about the likelihood of a given strategy to unlock a given problem. As children gain experience with several strategies, the teacher should begin to pose questions about the type of problem that lends itself well to each of the strategies. Lists of characteristics of problems might be generated to describe problems that fit well with a given strategy. As this is undertaken, the teacher should be careful to communicate that even under the best of conditions, true problem solving involves a degree of uncertainty and artistry.

THE ROLE OF ALGEBRA IN THE PROBLEM-SOLVING PROGRAM

The NCTM *Standards* suggest that the curriculum should include explorations of algebraic concepts and processes so that children can do the following:

> Understand the concepts of variable, expression, and equation.
>
> Represent situations and number patterns with tables, graphs, verbal rules, and equations, and explore the interrelationships of these representations.
>
> Analyze tables and graphs to identify properties and relationships.

Develop confidence in solving linear equations using concrete, informal, and formal methods.

Investigate inequalities and nonlinear equations informally.

Apply algebraic methods to solve a variety of real-world and mathematical problems.

For much of the elementary school program algebraic thinking is
useful in problem solving. It is only one of the tools that children use
in a multiple solution of a problems. Often it is the end approach. For
example:

Ms. James presented this problem to her second grade with the directions to solve the problem in as many ways as they could think of.
**Jimmy wants to buy a pencil at the school store that is on sale for 15
cents. He has 9 cents. How much does he have to borrow from a friend
to buy the pencil?**

The children worked on the problem for a time. Then the teacher asked
the children to share their findings. The children had used several methods.
Among those were the number line moving from 9 to 15 and giving an answer of six; using a row of circles to stand for pennies; drawing 15 circles
and then marking out 9 to arrive at an answer of 6.

Ms. James then asked, "Could you state the problem in a short form?"

Joe: How much does it take to get from 9 to 15?

Jenny: Nine and what number are 15?

Ms. James: Both are good answers. Now can we put them into numbers?

The children tried Joes's method and found it hard to put into numbers.
However, they found Jenny's rather easy.

Nine + N = 15

The children were then asked to make up problems that would fit the
format of the pencil problem. They developed problems such as "Nan has
5 apples. How many more must she buy to have an apple for 10 friends
and herself?"

Herbert and Brown report on a National Science Foundation sponsored
curricular program that uses a teaching sequence similar to that we have
suggested throughout the book. In a Patterns in Number and Space unit the
students encounter a problem in context, and then work in pairs or small
groups to act out the story whether kinesthetically, visually by drawing pictures, or by modeling the situation with physical objects. Their investigative
process involves: (1) seeking out a pattern in the story, (2) recognizing the
pattern and describing it using different methods, and (3) generalizing the
pattern and relating it to the story.

CHARACTERISTICS OF GOOD PROBLEM-SOLVERS

Characteristics of good problem-solvers can be derived from studies that have compared expert and novice problem-solvers. Schoenfeld (1985) has shown that expert problem-solvers are more efficient and are more likely to notice when an attempted strategy is not working. This work also showed that experts spend more time planning a strategy than do novices.

Other studies suggest that a deeper knowledge base of specific subject matter is responsible for expert problem-solving behavior. Experts evidently have more highly organized knowledge structures that enable them to use abstractions or representations of knowledge more easily in problem solving. If this is the case, then the implication is that general problem-solving strategies should be taught in the context of subject matter about which the children are knowledgeable. Problem-solving strategies, themselves, are not a substitute for a problem-solving context.

SELF-TEST—CHILDREN'S ACTIVITY CARDS

At the end of this and each of the following chapters there will be two or more children's activity cards—how would you use these?

SCHOOL SUPPLIES
You have $1.00, and you are going to buy one or more pencils, erasers, and paper clips at a stationery store. Pencils cost 10¢, paper clips are two for 1¢, and erasers cost 5¢ each. How much of each item will you buy if you have 100 items when you leave the store?

HOW MANY COWS?
A farmer did not want his neighbor to know how many cows he had, so when the neighbor asked, he replied, "I have 35 cows and chickens. They have a total of 78 legs." How many cows did the farmer have?

SPEEDY BIKES
Sarah and Janice rode their bicycles to school one morning, and when they saw each other at the bicycle rack, they both checked their bike computers to see what their average speeds were. Sarah's computer said she averaged 12.6 miles per hour. Janice's said she averaged 20.5 kilometers per hour. If a kilometer equals about .6 miles, who rode faster?

FAST TRACKS

Nancy and Tanya both like to run, but they live in different cities and can't run together. In order to see who runs faster, they each agree to run the length of the straight track at their schools and have their teachers time them. Tanya runs the length of her track in 11.5 seconds, and Nancy runs the length of hers in 14.2 seconds. If Tanya's track is 90 meters and Nancy's is 110 meters, who ran faster?

SELF-TEST—HOW WOULD YOU RESPOND TO EACH OF THESE STATEMENTS?

- ____ Word problems may or may not be problems to children.

- ____ Children arrive at school with an ability to solve problems.

- ____ Children need to learn "the basics" before they can be expected to learn to solve problems.

- ____ New skills can be learned in the context of solving problems.

- ____ Unless they are specifically taught otherwise, many children will believe that problem-solving process is more important than correct answers.

- ____ Asian teachers tend to stress memorizing and speed in the teaching of mathematics.

- ____ Conflict between intuition and reason can be used to motivate mathematical investigations.

- ____ Computer simulations are available in which problem solving is given a situated context.

- ____ Locating key words in a problem is a recommended strategy for problem solving.

- ____ Children need to be taught to evaluate problem-solving strategies for their appropriateness in solving any given problem.

- ____ Children find Polya's four-step problem-solving model difficult to use.

- ____ Metacognitive abilities appear to be inborn characteristics of a person's intelligence, and, as such, cannot be improved through instruction.

SELECTED REFERENCES

Bird, E. (1992). Guess My Rule, *Creative Classroom,* Jan/Feb 82–94.

Brown, S. I., & Walter, M. I. (1983). *The Art of Problem Posing.* Hillsdale, NJ: Erlbaum.

Carpenter, T. P., & Moser, J. M. (1982). The development of addition and subtraction problem-solving skills. In T. P. Carpenter, J.M. Moser, & R. A. Romberg (Eds.), *Addition and subtraction: A cognitive perspective* (pp. 9–24). Hillsdale, NJ: Erlbaum.

Clements, D. H., & Battista, M. T. (1991). *The development of a Logo-based elementary school geometry curriculum (Final Report: NSF Grant No.: MDR-8651668).* Buffalo, NY/Kent, OH: State University of New York at Buffalo/Kent State University.

Day, R., & Jones, G. A. (1997). Building Bridges to Algebraic Thinking. *Mathematics Teaching in the Middle School.* 2(4) 208–212.

DeCorte, E., & Verschaffel, L. (1987). The effect of semantic structure on first graders' strategies for solving addition and subtraction problems. *Journal for Research in Mathematics Education, 18,* 363–381.

Duckworth, E. (1987). Some depths and perplexities of elementary arithmetic. *Journal of Mathematical Behavior, 6,* 43–94.

Herbert, K., & Brown, R. H. (1997). Patterns as Tools for Algebraic Reasoning, *Teaching Children Mathematics,* Feb 340–345.

Kenney, P. A. & Silver, E. A. (1997). Probing the Foundations of Algebra. *Teaching Children Mathematics,* Feb 268–274.

Kouba, V. L., Brown, C. A., Carpenter, T. P., Lindquist, M. M., Silver, E. A., & Swafford, J. O. (1988). Results of the fourth NAEP assessment of mathematics: Number, operations, and word problems. *Arithmetic Teacher, 35*(8), 14–19.

National Council of Teachers of Mathematics (1989). *Curriculum and evaluation standards for school mathematics.* Reston, VA: National Council of Teachers of Mathematics.

National Council of Teachers of Mathematics (1990). *Reaching Higher: A Problem Solving Approach to Elementary School Mathematics.* Reston, VA: National Council of Teachers of Mathematics.

Polya, G. (1945, 1973). *How to solve it: A new aspect of mathematical method.* Princeton, NJ: Princeton University Press.

Schoenfeld, A. H. (1985). *Mathematical Problem Solving.* Orlando, FL: Academic Press.

Schoenfeld, A. H. (1989). Teaching mathematical thinking and problem solving. In L. Resnick & L. Klopfer (Eds.), *Toward the thinking curriculum: Current cognitive research* (pp. 83–103). Association for Supervision and Curriculum Development.

Silver, Edward A. (1997). "Algebra for All." *Mathematics in the Middle School, 2*(4), 204–207.

Stigler, J. W., & Stevenson, H. W. (1991). How Asian teachers polish each lesson to perfection. *American Educator,* Spring, pp. 12–20, 43–47.

U.S. Department of Labor (1991). *What work requires of schools.* Washington, DC: The Secretary's Commission on Achieving Necessary Skills.

Zellermayer, M., Salomon, G., Globerson, T., & Givon, H. (1991). Enhancing writing-related metacognitions through a computerized writing partner. *American Educational Research Journal, 28,* 373–391.

Zepp, R. A. (1991). Real-life business math at enterprise village. *Arithmetic Teacher, 39*(4), 10–14.

Number Concepts

LOOKING AHEAD

Children's understanding of numbers and the number system are the foundation upon which most of their mathematical abilities are built. While these fundamental concepts are taken for granted by adults, their development in children is not a simple matter. The teacher who wishes to help children develop these important concepts must take a close look at the cognitive demands involved in learning them.

CAN YOU?

- Distinguish between meaningful and rote counting?
- Suggest ways of using visual images and geometry to aid children in learning to count?

3 • Identify the benefits of using ten-frames in helping children learn to count?

4 • Describe the importance of viewing numbers as wholes that are composed of parts?

5 • Define and distinguish between base, place value, and positional notation?

6 • Argue in favor of the use of bases other than 10 in chip-trading activities?

7 • Explain the importance of connecting conceptual work with written symbolic work in teaching place-value concepts?

8 • Tell how you might use Dienes Blocks in teaching decimal concepts?

9 • Tell how you might use chip-trading activities in teaching decimal concepts?

NUMBER FOUNDATIONS AND BASIC FACTS

Basic Number Properties

Counting

Doing It

Long before children enter school most of them are able to say the sequence of words that constitute the beginning counting numbers. This does not, however, signify counting as the meaningful ordering and one-to-one matching of the counting numbers with the items to be counted. The ability to match items sequentially with the counting words in a meaningful way begins to occur sometime around the time children are in kindergarten.

A common activity undertaken by children who are beginning to construct meaning for counting is the verbalization of the counting words while pointing to items in a haphazard manner.

These children arrive at a count that is incorrect, but they are pleased and certain about their ability to "count." A helpful activity is to have children who have arrived at different counts of the same set of items try to resolve their difference by discussing their divergent results.

Understanding It

The ability to understand counting is undoubtedly brought about by many experiences where counting is desirable and valued. Families that value counting and understanding of numbers generally have children who are

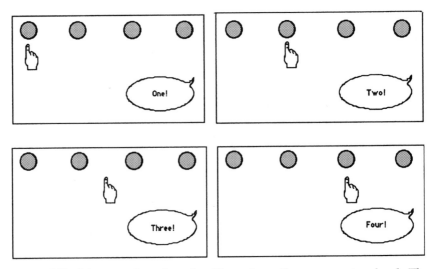

more skilled in counting than families where these are not valued. The teacher of children from impoverished families will need to provide many and varied informal experiences in which counting is valued and rewarded.

Ordering

Using counting to determine how many items are in a set is referred to as finding the *cardinality* of the set. Another use of counting is to determine which item in a series (first, second, third, and so on) is being referred to. This use of counting is referred to as finding *ordinality*.

Patterns (and a connection to geometry)

A part of the development of number sense is the development of an ability to recognize sets of small numbers of items without counting. For example, even very young children can identify a set of two or three items without counting the items.

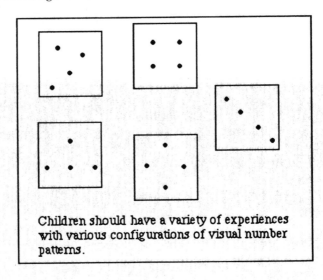

Children should have a variety of experiences with various configurations of visual number patterns.

As children gain experience with numbers, this ability to identify sets without counting can be extended to sets of four, five, or six items. Beyond six or seven items it is doubtful that children can identify the number of items without counting.

Ten-Frames

A way of representing numbers between 1 and 10 that has proved helpful for many early number concepts employs ten-frames. Ten-frames represent numbers in two horizontal rows of five blocks in each row. Numbers from 1 to 5 are represented by filling the boxes in the top row. Numbers from 6 to 10 are represented by filling the boxes in the bottom row.

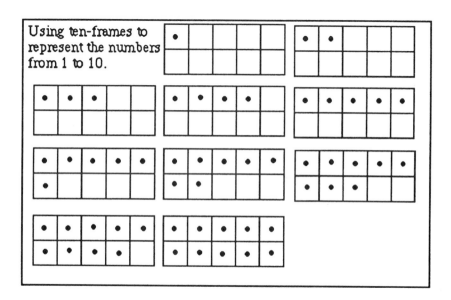

Through the use of this exact format in many contexts, teachers can provide children with a consistent visual representation of the basic counting numbers. This visual representation can be internalized by children, and can become for them a tool to think with.

Reading and Writing Numerals

Math as Communication

Children who have begun to develop a conceptual understanding of number can extend that knowledge to include communication about number. Written numerals, and the process of reading and writing numerals, should initially be presented to children in the context of a need to communicate.

Teachers who are implementing a whole-language approach to literacy, and those who are interested in employing writing across the curriculum, will look for every opportunity to have children recognize a need to communicate numerical information. Within the context of a perceived need, the teacher can structure lessons on the proper format for writing and reading numerals.

IN THE CLASSROOM

Dear Ms. Heath:

Somehow the books that your children took out of the library did not get written down. Later today I'll come to your classroom and make a list of what books were taken. But for now I need to know how many books were taken out. Would you send me a note telling me how many library books your class took today?

Thank you,

Mr. Fromme

Ms. Heath read a note that the school librarian had written to her. She decided to use this as an opportunity to show her children the need to use written numerals for communication.

Ms. Heath: Children, Mr. Fromme has written me a note asking me how many library books you took from the library this morning. He wants me to write a note back to him telling him how many. Let's begin by counting the books. Would anyone who got a new library book out today put it on his or her desk? Now I want each of you to count the books.

Ms. Heath gives the children time to count the books. She also guides them in working out the disagreements about the number of books. They agree that there are eight new books.

Ms. Heath (writing on the board): We need to write to Mr. Fromme that we took out eight books this morning. This is the word "eight." Does anyone know how to write the number "8"?

Several children volunteer. Ms. Heath lets one child come to the board and write the numeral.

Ms. Heath: That's great! Can you all point to the number 8 on our wall chart? Now, would you take your slates and write this number so I can see how nicely you write? Very nice! Wonderful!

Ms. Heath then writes Mr. Fromme a note and sends it to him with one of the children.

This vignette provides an example of a teacher who used a naturally occurring situation to provide instruction in writing numerals. Children saw the need for written communication, and they had a purpose for their activity. The teacher does not need to simply wait for situations such as this to occur. This particular situation could have been planned ahead of time between Ms. Heath and Mr. Fromme. Many such situations should be planned and used to help children develop abilities in reading and writing numerals.

More and Less

Another basic concept that is closely tied to counting is the development of an understanding of relationships between numbers. "One more" and "one less" are important relationships that help a child develop number sense. "Two more" and "two less" are further important relationships. Many activities and problems should be used to help children become comfortable with these relationships. They should be able to use these special relationships in mental math exercises.

Part-Part-Whole

The idea that any given number can be broken down in various component parts is fundamental to addition and subtraction concepts. A child who has learned to flexibly think of 9 as $4 + 5$, $6 + 3$, $7 + 2$, and $8 + 1$, is in a much stronger position mathematically than someone who lacks this ability. Some writers refer to this concept as the part-part-whole concept of numbers.

Different Ways of Naming the Same Amount

Teachers should encourage children to think of numbers as having many names. "Eight" is the name of a certain number; "8" is another name for the same number; "5 + 3" is yet another name for this same amount. Children are used to being called by different names and nicknames, and this analogy may be used to help them understand the use of several names for the same number.

Partitioning into Tens and Ones

In order for children to come into an understanding and appreciation of the place value number system, they must become comfortable with partitioning larger numbers into tens and ones. They must be helped to develop the idea that groups of tens are countable items. In order to facilitate this, the teacher should design many situations where numbers larger than ten can be partitioned into tens and ones.

Hundred Chart

1	2	3	4	5	6	7	8	9	10
11	12	13	14	15	16	17	18	19	20
21	22	23	24	25	26	27	28	29	30
31	32	33	34	35	36	37	38	39	40
41	42	43	44	45	46	47	48	49	50
51	52	53	54	55	56	57	58	59	60
61	62	63	64	65	66	67	68	69	70
71	72	73	74	75	76	77	78	79	80
81	82	83	84	85	86	87	88	89	90
91	92	93	94	95	96	97	98	99	100

A tool that can be extremely helpful in facilitating children's ability to partition numbers into tens and ones is the hundred chart shown on page 89. This chart not only sets up natural divisions that reinforce the idea of tens and ones, but it also presents families of numbers based on each of the counting digits. Children can visually explore the similarities between the two's family (the column headed by the two), and the three's family, for example.

After a group of children has become comfortable with the fact that each row contains ten items, they can be helped to see the value in counting rows as a shortcut to counting ten each time a row is referred to. For example, a child referring to the number 34 in the chart may say, "Ten, twenty, thirty (while pointing to the appropriate rows), thirty-one, thirty-two, thirty-three, thirty-four." Alternatively, another child may say, "One, two, three rows of ten, thirty-one, thirty-two, thirty-three, thirty-four."

PLACE VALUE WITH WHOLE NUMBERS

Perhaps the most crucial set of ideas in elementary mathematics are the ideas of base, place value, and positional notation, upon which our numeration system is built. These highly efficient concepts took centuries to invent and develop, and yet we expect all children to learn them by the time they leave elementary school. A child's difficulty with operations on whole numbers, fractional numbers, and decimal numbers can often be traced to a lack of understanding of base, place value, and positional notation.

Since these fundamental concepts are so important to the teaching and learning of elementary mathematics, it is of utmost importance that the teacher have a deep understanding of them. Due to the elegance and genius of the numeration system, these concepts have the deceptive appearance of simplicity. For this reason, it is recommended that the teacher actually obtain the materials described in the following sections and try the activities that are detailed before using them with children.

Foundational Ideas

Base
Much of the simple elegance of the Hindu-Arabic numeration system comes from the fact that when we count, we make groups and count the groups. The number of items that comprises a group is kept consistent throughout the system. That number is the *base* of the numeration system. The same base number is used repeatedly to make groups, groups of groups, and so on. In the Hindu-Arabic numeration system, the base is 10, but a numeration system can be built around any base other than 1. In this section, activities using bases other than 10 will be used to aid the teacher in constructing his or her own understanding of the use of base in a numeration system.

Place Value

Our ability to express any numerical amount through the use of only 10 symbols (the digits 0–9) is due to the fact that we re-use those basic digits in counting groups. The idea that any given digit can represent a number of items, or a number of groups, or a number of groups of groups, and so on, is the foundational idea for *place value*. Ones, tens, hundreds, and so on, are the place values of the base 10 Hindu-Arabic numeration system.

Positional Notation

The writing side-by-side of the basic digits to tell us how many of each place value we have is referred to as *positional notation*. Positional notation is necessary for communication of amounts in our numeration system.

The three concepts of base, place value, and positional notation are intertwined and interdependent in our numeration system. The meanings of these three concepts, while they are overlapping, are actually quite distinct.

Although it is not necessary for children to be able to distinguish between these concepts in a formal way, it is essential for the teacher to be able to do so. The teacher's depth of understanding of these fundamental concepts must far exceed that of the children. This depth of understanding will enable the teacher to create accurate representations of the concepts in teaching them to children. It will also enable the teacher to diagnose the difficulties that children encounter with arithmetic.

> **Positional Notation**
> 3 8 7 4
> ↑
> **The position of the digit determines its value. The 3 denotes 3 thousands in this position.**

Chip Trading

Duckworth (1987) describes an experiment in teacher education that made use of several chip-trading activities designed by Walter and Manicom. That experiment, and those activities, form the basis for the chip-trading vignettes and suggestions here.

Non-proportional Chip Trading Objects

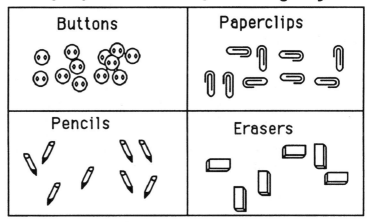

The basic principle behind chip-trading activities is that different types of chips or objects are used to represent the different place values. A base-amount grouping is chosen, and every time a person obtains that number of objects, a trade is made for one object of the next higher value. Chip-trading activities are most effective when the trading value is three, four, or five. Often teachers have asked us why we recommend chip-trading in bases other than ten. If base ten were used, many turns would involve only taking or giving back chips. There would be few trades of ten-for-one or one-for-ten. The learning occurs when the children are required to trade. The smaller base numbers ensure that more trading and more learning will occur than would be the case with a trading value of ten.

For adults and upper level elementary children, chip-trading activities can be undertaken with any sets of objects. Normally four different kinds of objects are used: one type to represent unit counters, a second type to represent the first base-amount grouping, and a third and fourth type to represent the third and fourth base-amount groupings. In the drawing, buttons are used as counters, paperclips are used for the first base-amount grouping, pencils for the third, and erasers for the fourth. If activities in base 3 were being conducted, three buttons would be traded for one paperclip, 3 paperclips would be traded for one pencil, and three pencils would be traded for one eraser. The use of everyday objects makes this an economical set of objects to use.

Proportional Chip Trading Objects
(shown with 3 as the base amount)

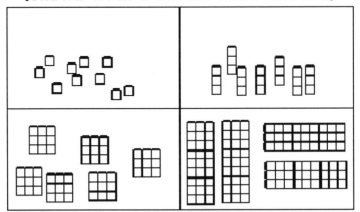

For younger children, Unifix Cubes™ are used in order to enable making proportional objects for each of the base-amount groupings. Single cubes represent the counters, interlocked groups of the first base-amount grouping are used as the second "objects," and so on.

In Bases Other Than 10

Trading Up

Joseph and Peter were playing the introductory chip-trading game. Joseph rolled the number cube (which had the digits 0 to 5 on its faces) and obtained a four. (According to the rules, this first roll must be greater than two. If a zero or one is rolled, the player must roll again.)

Joseph: OK. Four; we'll be trading every time we get 4.

Peter: I'll go first. (He rolls a 2 and picks up 2 buttons.)

Joseph: My turn. I rolled a five. Let's see, one, two, three, four, five. Now I trade the first four buttons for one paperclip. I've got 1 paperclip and 1 button.

Peter: I rolled a 4. That's the same as a paperclip. Now I've got a paper-clip and 2 buttons.

Joseph: Wait a minute! You didn't even take your four buttons!

Peter: I know. I just figured, why take four and then trade all four in for one paperclip. I did the same thing, but my way was quicker.

Joseph: Oh. Well I rolled a five again. One, two, three, four, five. The first four buttons are traded for one paperclip. Now I've got 2 paperclips and 2 buttons.

The game continued until one of the boys was the first to trade for an eraser. That person became the winner of the "trading-up" game.

A few things should be noted about the way the boys played the game. First, there was a large difference in the thinking levels shown by the two boys. Peter was apparently able to think in terms of the traded values while Joseph seemed to lack this ability. This is evidenced by the fact that Peter mentally translated his "four" into one paperclip. Joseph was initially troubled by this, and even after Peter justified his action, Joseph did not seem convinced of the reasoning behind it. Eventually Joseph would adopt a similar strategy, but until it is meaningful to him, the explicit counting and trading is adequate for his needs.

Secondly, the boys are operating within a trading system that parallels the Hindu-Arabic base 10 numeration system, but this fact is not made explicit. There is no converting between base 10 and base 4, and there is no comparison made between the two numeration systems. The goal of the activity is to cause the boys to think in terms of the trades and related values in an intuitive way. At a later time, during place-value instruction in base 10, the teacher will refer back to these activities as models and tools to think with. At that time, the trading system and relative values between the different types of chips will be made more explicit.

Finally, the boys were not required to translate trade values for objects that were not direct trades. In other words, they did not need to be concerned with the fact that one pencil was worth 16 buttons, or that one eraser was worth 64 buttons. Of course, had they been curious, they could have figured this out, and this would perhaps have led to some fascinating mathematical explorations, but this was not a necessary part of the play of the game.

Trading Down

Kim and Valerie each took one eraser from the tray. Valerie rolled the number cube to see what the trading value would be. She rolled a 1, so according to the rules, which state that trading values must be greater than 2, she rolled again. This time she rolled a five.

Valerie: OK, so 5 will be our trading value. Let's see, that means this eraser is worth five pencils.

Kim: Right; and I go first. (She rolls a 1 on the cube.) OK. I need to subtract one button from this eraser. First, I trade the eraser for five pencils, then I trade one pencil for five paperclips, then I trade one paperclip for five buttons, then I can turn in one button. So now I have 4 buttons, 4 paperclips, and 4 pencils.

Valerie: My turn. (She rolls a 5.) All right. First, five pencils for the eraser, then five paperclips for one pencil, then five buttons for one paperclip . . . wait a minute—I can just turn in one paperclip.

Kim: Have you ever noticed that whatever number is rolled for the trading value, that is the value of the paperclip? When we played trading up with 4 as the trading value, one paperclip was worth 4. Now we're playing trading down with 5 as the trading value, and one paperclip is worth 5. That's so cool!

Valerie: Well, if you think about it, that's the way it has to be. The first thing you trade for is the paperclip.

The girls continued playing until one of them traded in all her objects and was declared the winner.

Chip Trading to Model Operations

After each of the children had had an opportunity to play the trading-up game and the trading-down game several times, using different trading values, the teacher presented the following lesson to help them reflect on their experiences and draw some abstractions from them.

Teacher: I took some notes when Peter and Joseph were playing the trading-up game. At one point Peter had 2 buttons, and 1 paperclip. He had no pencils and no erasers. They were using four as the trading value. I wrote this chart to keep track:

ERASERS	PENCILS	PAPERCLIPS	BUTTONS
0	0	1	2

At this point, he rolled a 1. How could you show on my chart that 1 button was added to what Peter had?

(Carrie comes to the board and modifies the chart:)

ERASERS	PENCILS	PAPERCLIPS	BUTTONS
		1	2
			+1
		1	3

Teacher: Good! Now what if, on his next turn, Peter rolled a 2? (Steve comes to the board and modifies the chart:)

ERASERS	PENCILS	PAPERCLIPS	BUTTONS
		1	2
			+1
		1	3
			+2
		1	5

Denise: That's not right! He isn't allowed to have 5 buttons because the trading value is four.

Steve: Oh! I revise that.

ERASERS	PENCILS	PAPERCLIPS	BUTTONS
		1	2
			+1
		1	3
			+2
		2	1

Teacher: Try to remember that we're keeping track of numbers of paper-clips and numbers of buttons. If you remember that, you can keep it more clear. If you have one paperclip and three buttons, and you add 2 more buttons, you make a trade and end up with 2 paperclips and 1 button. Does that make sense?

Activities such as these, which begin to make a connection between the trading activities and a systematic way of writing or recording those activities, are helpful for developing an understanding of the addition and subtraction algorithms in the normal base 10 Hindu-Arabic system. If children have foundational activities with chip trading followed by tasks involving writing the results of those activities, these experiences can be referred to again and again as more complex mathematics is presented.

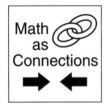

Chip-trading activities such as these can be returned to when whole number division and multiplication are being taught. In the middle of a trading-up game, at some arbitrary time, the partners can be directed to combine the objects they've collected and divide them equally among themselves. A more complex task would be to divide them equally among different numbers of people. Because it is difficult to know if a correct division has been accomplished, a further task is to develop a way of showing that you are correct. In most cases this leads to the invention of multiplication with chips.

Conversions (on paper)

Much of the value of these chip-trading activities derives from the activities and from abstractions made from the activities. However, full benefit does not occur until learners are faced with the task of recording on paper in systematic form what is done in the activities. The following table was developed to show that 1 eraser, 1 pencil, 3 paperclips, and 1 button (1131) in base 4 could be divided by 3 (distributed equally to 3 people) to obtain 133.

Source:

ERASERS	PENCILS	PAPERCLIPS	BUTTONS
1	1	3	1

First, **trade** 1 eraser for 4 pencils, since 1 eraser cannot be distributed to 3 people:

0	5	3	1

Next, **distribute** 1 pencil to each person. **Record** the results.

Person 1:

ERASERS	PENCILS	PAPERCLIPS	BUTTONS
	1		

Person 2:

ERASERS	PENCILS	PAPERCLIPS	BUTTONS
	1		

Person 3:

ERASERS	PENCILS	PAPERCLIPS	BUTTONS
	1		

Source:

ERASERS	PENCILS	PAPERCLIPS	BUTTONS
	2	3	1

Then, **trade** 2 pencils for 8 paperclips, since 2 pencils cannot be distributed to 3 people:

Source:

ERASERS	PENCILS	PAPERCLIPS	BUTTONS
		11	1

Next, **distribute** 3 paperclips to each person. **Record** the results.

Person 1:

ERASERS	PENCILS	PAPERCLIPS	BUTTONS
	1	3	

Person 2:

ERASERS	PENCILS	PAPERCLIPS	BUTTONS
	1	3	

Person 3:

ERASERS	PENCILS	PAPERCLIPS	BUTTONS
	1	3	

Source:

ERASERS	PENCILS	PAPERCLIPS	BUTTONS
		2	1

Then, **trade** 2 paperclips for 8 buttons, since 2 paperclips cannot be distributed to 3 people:

Source:

ERASERS	PENCILS	PAPERCLIPS	BUTTONS
			9

Distribute 3 buttons to each person. **Record** the results.

Person 1:

ERASERS	PENCILS	PAPERCLIPS	BUTTONS
	1	3	3

Person 2:

ERASERS	PENCILS	PAPERCLIPS	BUTTONS
	1	3	3

Person 3:

ERASERS	PENCILS	PAPERCLIPS	BUTTONS
	1	3	3

This systematic method of actions followed by the recording of those actions should be explored by the teacher prior to use with children.

PLACE-VALUE CONCEPTS EXTENDED TO DECIMALS

Dienes Blocks and Squared Paper

The concepts of base, place value, and base-amount grouping, along with basic fractional concepts, form the basis for understanding decimals. Dienes blocks, or place-value blocks, have proved to be quite helpful for representing decimal concepts. If the largest block is used to represent one counting unit, a face slice represents 0.1, an edge represents 0.01, and a corner represents 0.001. (Children who have used these blocks in the reverse order to represent ones, tens, hundreds, and thousands will need some time to adjust to this new way of looking at the blocks.)

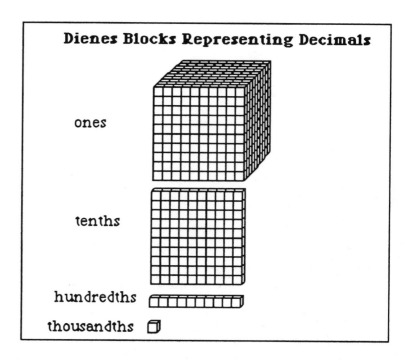

Dienes Blocks Representing Decimals

ones

tenths

hundredths

thousandths

An introductory problem situation in which the Dienes blocks are used to help represent decimal concepts follows.

KIDS IN ACTION

Ms. Martin: This large block represents one whole block of gold. It stands for the block of pure gold found by my great, great grandfather when he went prospecting for gold in California in 1849. When he found it he got so excited that he went running all around the camp shouting and showing it to everyone. This caused him some problems, because everyone became envious that he had found such a large piece of gold. The following day the camp foreman informed my great, great grandfather that he would have to collect the camp fee from the block of gold. My relative was unhappy, but he had agreed ahead of time to this, so he went along with it. The foreman also told him that the government was entitled to an equal share. My relative was greatly disappointed by this news. Furthermore, said the foreman, if the men in the camp did not receive an equal share to distribute among themselves, my relative's safety could not be guaranteed.

Ms. Martin then distributed sets of the various sizes of blocks to children in small groups and asked them to spend some time figuring out how to show the amount of gold that her great, great grandfather actually received from his discovery.

She spent about 15 minutes checking on the groups as they tackled this problem. When a group had come to a solution that satisfied all of the members, Ms. Martin gave them a sheet describing some additional challenging questions that caused them to focus on aspects of decimal fraction representations. She also asked them to explore how they might write down what they had done in solving the initial problem so that they could share it with others.

The solution of one of the groups is shown.

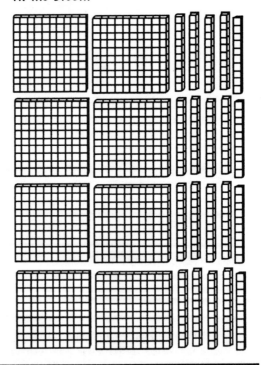

We made each share 2 flats and 5 talls.
The talls came from taking apart two
flats. Altogether there were ten flats
in the block.

Ms. Martin used Socratic questioning to help the children realize that each "flat" was $\frac{1}{10}$ of the original block, each "tall" was $\frac{1}{100}$ of the original block, and each share was $\frac{1}{4}$, or $\frac{25}{100}$, of the original block.

Chip Trading Revised

Since the foundational concepts for understanding decimal numbers depend on and are an extension of place-value concepts, the work described previously regarding chip-trading activities is applicable to decimal numbers. It is necessary to either redefine the basic trading items or obtain a new set of items to use to represent decimals.

Chip Trading Objects for Decimals

Nails	Old Keys
Styrofoam "Peanuts"	Buttons

In our example, nails will be traded for old keys, keys will be traded for Styrofoam peanuts, and peanuts will be traded for buttons. Note that buttons are common to this set of chip-trading items and the previous set of items. In the previous set, buttons were the items with the lowest value, but in this set they have the highest value. Buttons can be thought of as the unit counters in both sets of items. When we want to represent a count of anything, we can represent that count with buttons. When we want to think of an amount less than one whole button, we can think in terms of peanuts. Amounts less than one whole peanut are represented by old keys, and amounts less than one whole key are represented by nails.

One teacher introduced his class to the concept of parts of buttons with the following problem:

IN THE CLASSROOM

Four people were trading buttons, paperclips, pencils, and erasers on the basis of 4 as a trading value. They had a total of one paperclip and one button which they wished to share equally. They traded the paperclip for 4 buttons, which they distributed among themselves. They thought they were finished, and that the button was just a leftover. However, they didn't know they could trade that button in for Styrofoam peanuts. If they had known they could do that, what might they have done to finish sharing their original paperclip and button?

> Share one button and one paperclip equally among four people, using a trading value of 4.
>
>

Conversions (on paper)

Math as Connections

Understanding the concepts of place value, base, and base-amount grouping as they relate to fractional parts of wholes is only part of the conceptual framework necessary for a full understanding of decimal numbers. It is also necessary for children to build connections between these foundational concepts and the system of writing decimal numbers on paper. Here again, the previous work with chip trading using whole numbers provides a context that can be extended to decimal numbers. The previous problem of distributing one paperclip and one button could be recorded in tables as shown here.

Source:

PAPERCLIPS	BUTTONS
1	1

First, **trade** 1 paperclip for 4 buttons, since 1 paperclip cannot be distributed to 4 people:

PAPERCLIPS	BUTTONS
0	5

Next, **distribute** 1 button to each person. **Record** the results.

Person 1:

PAPERCLIPS	BUTTONS
0	1

Person 2:

PAPERCLIPS	BUTTONS
0	1

Person 3:

PAPERCLIPS	BUTTONS
0	1

Person 4:

PAPERCLIPS	BUTTONS
0	1

Source:

PAPERCLIPS	BUTTONS
0	1

Then, **trade** 1 button for 4 peanuts, since 1 button cannot be distributed to 4 people:

Source:

PAPERCLIPS	BUTTONS	PEANUTS
0	0	4

Next, **distribute** 1 peanut to each person. **Record** the results.

Person 1:

PAPERCLIPS	BUTTONS	PEANUTS
0	1	1

Person 2:

PAPERCLIPS	BUTTONS	PEANUTS
0	1	1

Person 3:

PAPERCLIPS	BUTTONS	PEANUTS
0	1	1

Person 4:

PAPERCLIPS	BUTTONS	PEANUTS
0	1	1

These results can be used by the teacher to point out a valuable ambiguity. The number of items received by each person is 1 1 (meaning one button and one peanut). In previous work, the number 1 1 represented one paperclip and one button. How can we communicate that 1 1 in this case means something different than it meant previously? Children can benefit from an opportunity to invent ways of clarifying this ambiguity and defending and justifying their inventions before being taught the conventional use of the decimal point.

CARDS

Materials: Deck of cards, face cards removed.

Place children in groups of two to four. Each group gets a deck of cards, which they place face down on the table. Each player takes a card. In turn, each student reads the number out loud and places the card face up on the table in front of himself. The player with the highest value takes the cards. Play continues until all the cards are gone. The winner is the player with the most cards at the end.

Extension: Make your own deck using symbols such as squares or happy faces to represent the numbers.

NUMBERS IN ORDER

Materials: Hundred board; numbers 0–99.

Working with a partner, students find the numbers 0 to 20. Ask them to place the numbers in order on the hundred board. As a class, talk about any patterns they might see.

Next have them put all the numbers in order on the hundred board. When they're done, ask if the patterns they talked about repeated for the larger numbers.

Have them empty the board and repeat the activity, as quickly as they can.

SELF-TEST—HOW WOULD YOU RESPOND TO EACH OF THESE STATEMENTS?

- _____ Children who can count can dependably find the correct number of items in a set.

- _____ Children can determine the number of items in a set without counting if they have learned to recognize visual patterns.

- _____ Ten-frames can help children learn to think of numbers in terms of parts and wholes.

- _____ Viewing numbers as composed of parts and wholes is confusing to children.

- ____ Base, place value, and positional notation are 3 terms that mean basically the same thing.

- ____ Chip-trading activities in bases other than 10 can help children learn foundational concepts of the base 10 number system.

- ____ Children can be taught place-value concepts either through hands-on activities or through written work.

- ____ Dienes blocks are primarily useful for teaching relationships between ones, tens, hundreds, and thousands.

- ____ Using the same objects for chip-trading activities to teach whole-number place value and decimal place value would be confusing to children.

SELECTED REFERENCES

Carpenter, T. P., & Moser, J. M. (1984). The acquisition of addition and subtraction concepts in grades one through three. *Journal for Research in Mathematics Education, 15*, 179–202.

Davidson, P. S. (1975). *Chip trading activities.* Fort Collins, CO: Scott Resources.

Duckworth, E. (1987). Some depths and perplexities of elementary arithmetic. *Journal of Mathematical Behavior, 6*, 43–94.

Hiebert, J., & Wearne, D. (1986). Conceptual and procedural knowledge. In J. Hiebert (Ed.), *Conceptual and procedural knowledge: The case of mathematics* (pp. 199–223). Hillsdale, NJ: Erlbaum.

Hiebert, J., & Wearne, D. (1988). Instruction and cognitive change in mathematics. *Educational Psychologist, 23*(2), 105–117.

Kuhns, K. L. (1997). Half-Time Day. *Teaching Children Mathematics*, Jan. 218–221;234.

Reys, B. J. (1994). Promoting Number Sense. *Teaching Mathematics to Children, f*(1) 114–116.

Wearne, D., & Hiebert, J. (1988). A cognitive approach to meaningful mathematics instruction: Testing a local theory using decimal numbers. *Journal for Research in Mathematics Education, 19*, 371–384.

6 Number Algorithms: Primary

LOOKING AHEAD

Traditionally, the greatest portion of time spent teaching elementary mathematics was focused on teaching children to perform basic addition, subtraction, multiplication, and division algorithms. These algorithms were first taught with single-digit whole numbers, then with multidigit whole numbers, and finally with decimals. Standardized tests reinforced this emphasis by devoting large numbers of items to the various algorithms. Teachers, parents, and administrators considered these skills to be the indispensable "basics" of elementary mathematics.

In order for children to gain fluency in all of the various number algorithms, great quantities of school time were needed. While virtually all educators acknowledged the desirability of teaching higher-level thinking skills in mathematics, the time required to perfect lower-level skills left little mathematics time for anything else. Many people felt that skill in these lower-level procedures was a necessary prerequisite for higher-level thinking.

Today's thinking on the teaching of elementary school mathematics places a different emphasis on number algorithms. The availability of calculators, combined with the growing need for mathematical thinking skills, has enabled a redefinition of what the basics of school mathematics really are. Today we realize that most of our precious school time must be spent on developing the higher-level thinking skills, and the time spent on teaching number algorithms should be devoted to understanding rather than to smooth, efficient, and flawless execution of procedures.

We do not recommend that teaching of number algorithms be eliminated; however, in agreement with the National Council of Teachers of Mathematics (1989) we recommend decreased attention to paper and pencil computation along with increased attention to meaning and number sense. In this chapter we present several suggestions for how this shift in emphasis can be carried out.

CAN YOU?

- Explain a single, underlying concept that relates addition and subtraction?

- Provide function-oriented definitions for addition and subtraction?

- Distinguish among three different definitions of multiplication?

- Distinguish between two different meanings of division?

- Tell why fractions are necessary answers for some division of whole-number problems?

- Describe the difference between memorized basic facts and derived basic facts?

- Explain why children can become proficient in addition without memorizing a great quantity of basic addition facts?

- Argue in favor of a specific limited role for drill and practice?

- Invent a problem situation appropriate for an introduction to multiplication in the primary grades?

- Invent a problem situation appropriate for an introduction to division in the primary grades?

MATHEMATICAL BACKGROUND

What Are Addition and Subtraction?

Addition and subtraction are two related operations that depend on a single underlying concept. That concept is the notion that things can be thought of as parts that comprise a whole. When we say that $2 + 3 = 5$, we are symbolizing the fact that a whole group of five items is formed when a group of 2 items is combined with a group of 3 items. Two small groups become parts of one large group. In reverse, the writing of $5 - 2 = 3$ symbolizes the fact that one large group of five items can be partitioned into a group of two and a group of three. Two small groups can be formed from one large group.

A more general definition of addition is that it is the function that maps every ordered pair of numbers on their sum.

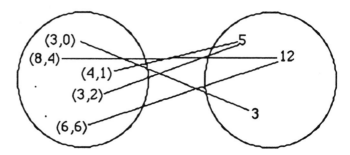

Addition: $(a, b) \rightarrow (a + b)$

A similar definition for subtraction is that subtraction is the function that maps every ordered pair of numbers on their difference.

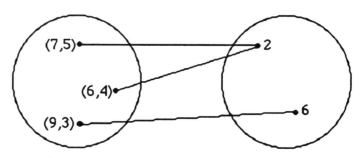

Subtraction: $(a, b) \rightarrow (a - b)$

Both of these function-oriented definitions display the underlying concept of the part-whole relation that is fundamental to both operations.

What Is Multiplication?

Multiplication, like addition, is an operation that maps (assigns) a pair of whole numbers (factors) to a unique whole number called its *product.* Thus, the pair of whole numbers 5, 4 is mapped to the product 20. We may write $(5, 4) \rightarrow 20$.

This idea may seem to be pure mathematics; however, there are many physical world situations for which multiplication is useful. An analysis of books concerned with mathematics for children and mathematics teaching reveals several different means of viewing the operation of multiplication. Here are a few:

1. Multiplication of whole numbers may be viewed as *a special case of addition* in which all the addends are of equal size. In set terms, 3×4 can be defined to be three sets of four elements each, since $3 \times 4 = 4 + 4 + 4$.

2. *The cross-product or Cartesian product of two sets* can be used to interpret multiplication. The cross-product is formed by pairing every member of one set with every member of the other. For example, if we asked four boys and three girls to form as many mixed dancing couples as possible, we would arrive at a product set of 12 elements (couples). Thus, the product of two numbers can be associated with a rectangular pattern or array.

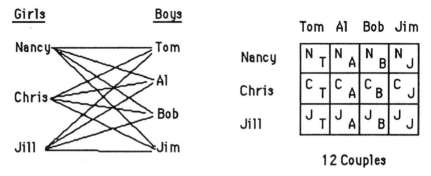

3. Multiplication may be thought of as *a mapping or a function*. Using a function machine, we could show multiplication in the following ways:

$$3 \times 8 = \square$$

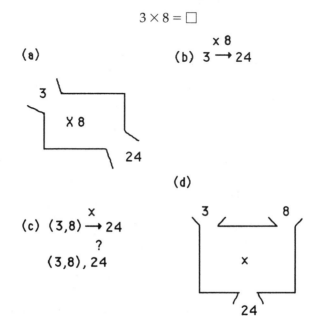

These three portrayals of multiplication differ greatly from one another. In order for elementary school pupils to develop a better understanding of the multiplication operation, they should be familiarized with the different multiplication ideas. A logical sequence for developing these ideas is found later in this chapter.

What Is Division?

1. The division of whole numbers is the inverse of the multiplication of whole numbers. If a and c are identified in the expression $a \times b = c$ and if they uniquely determine b, the operation of "finding" b is called division. Thus, if $3 \times b = 12$, then,

dividend		divisor		quotient
12	$\div$	3	$=$	b

    However, if $12 \times b = 3$, then b must equal one-quarter, and thus the division operation cannot be performed by using whole numbers alone. The student must remember that any time two whole numbers are combined by the operation of multiplication, the result (the product) is a whole number. This is not true for division. Thus, for the set of whole numbers, division is not closed; that is, division of one whole number by another whole number does not always result in a whole-number quotient; it may produce a fraction.

2. The addition of whole numbers and the multiplication of whole numbers may be related, because the multiplication of whole numbers may be viewed as a special case of addition, with the addends being of equal size. Division may be related to subtraction, because the division of whole numbers may be considered as a series of subtractions in which the subtrahends are the same size. For example, $12 \div 4 = X$ can be considered $12 - 4 = 8$, $8 - 4 = 4$, $4 - 4 = 0$; three subtractions have been made; therefore, $12 \div 4 = 3$. This thought process lends itself well to the question, "How many 4s equal 12?" Additional interesting investigations can arise from the questions, "Why did we stop at zero? What happens if this can't be done?"

3. Division by zero is said to be "undefined." The teacher can use a thought experiment to help children develop this idea for themselves. What happens when we divide a number, such as 12, by 6? (We get 2.) What happens when we divide 12 by a smaller number, such as 4? (We get 3, a larger answer than before.) What happens when we divide 12 by an even smaller number: 3? (We get 4, an even larger number.) What if we continue to divide by smaller and smaller numbers? (The answer gets larger and larger.) What is the smallest number you can think of? (If no one thinks of it, suggest the number zero.) What would happen if we

tried to divide by zero? How many times can you subtract zero from 12? (If you started, you'd never finish!)

4. As in the cases of the other whole-number operations, division may be viewed as a function. If the first component is a multiple of the nonzero second component, division is a function that maps an ordered pair of numbers on its quotient. (Note: The first number of the ordered pair is the dividend and the second number the divisor.) To develop this mapping for all pairs of whole numbers, fractions are needed.

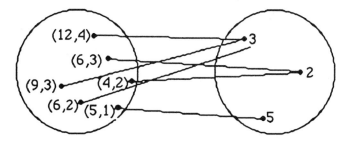

These interpretations are interrelated and should be developed from problems and laboratory activities that relate to the real world of the student.

There are basically two types of problem situations that lead to a solution by division: measurement and partition. The difference between the two can most easily be seen by analyzing two examples that make use of these concepts.

MEASUREMENT DIVISION	PARTITIVE DIVISION
• Total known	• Total known
• Number in Each Group Known	• Number of Groups Known
• **Number of Groups (or partial groups) Unknown**	• **Number in Each Group (or size of group) Unknown**
Example: You have 12 buttons. A shirt pattern calls for 3 buttons for one shirt. How many shirts could you make from this number of buttons?	Example: You had 12 buttons. From these you were able to make 4 shirts. How many buttons did you use in each shirt?

READINESS AND FOUNDATIONAL EXPERIENCES

Addition and Subtraction

Children develop informal methods of working out simple addition and subtraction problems on their own, and these methods need not depend on arithmetic that they are taught in school. Before children know any other methods, they can solve some types of addition and subtraction problems by directly modeling the problem using some type of counting objects.

An intermediate step in children's informal arithmetic development is when they are able to use counting-on from one of the numbers given in the problem to reach the answer. For example, if a child is solving a problem involving 4 + 5, he may be heard to say, ". . . four. Five, six, seven, eight, nine . . . the answer is nine." This child has abstracted the concept of four, and it is unnecessary for him to directly model the four. Furthermore, he has realized that counting numbers is a substitute for counting objects. When he says, ". . . five, six, seven, eight, nine . . ." he stops at nine because it is the fifth number that he has uttered. He must have been counting his utterances to know where to stop counting.

Another intermediate step in this informal development is when the child realizes that in addition the order of the numbers may be reversed, and if the count begins from the larger number, the job of counting is simplified. A child in this condition will solve the problem 2 + 9 by saying, ". . . nine. Ten, eleven . . . the answer is eleven."

The most sophisticated level of development is when children use addition and subtraction facts to solve problems. Some of the facts that they use are memorized facts, and others they are able to derive from the facts that they have memorized (Carpenter and Moser, 1984).

Basic Facts

An approach to teaching basic facts is presented in the context of the addition facts. This approach can be generalized to the teaching of other sets of facts, such as the subtraction facts and the multiplication tables. Full treatment of subtraction facts and multiplication tables is not developed here, and the reader is urged to use this presentation of the addition facts as a model for the others.

Concepts or Rote Memory?

For many years educators have debated whether children should learn the basic addition and subtraction facts by rote or through a meaning-centered approach. Those who advocate a meaning-centered approach argue that children should not have to depend on abstractions supplied by an outside agent or authority figure as they develop mathematical abilities. Those who advocate learning the basic facts by rote memory argue that meaning is built on the basis of certain foundational ideas that must be available in memory.

Math as Problem Solving

Research has shown that children who have been taught early addition and subtraction concepts through a problem-solving approach can perform as well on basic facts as can children who have been taught in a fact-memorization program. This comparable performance on basic facts was surprising in view of the fact that the children in the basic facts group spent considerably more time practicing basic facts than did the children in the problem-solving group. Furthermore, interviews with the children revealed that the problem-solving children had much richer understanding of numbers and mathematics than did the basic facts group (Carpenter, et al., 1989).

Developing Number Sense through Derived Facts
One of the goals of the NCTM *Standards* is that children of all ages should be helped to develop number sense. *Number sense* is a term that has been used to describe a flexible, creative understanding of numbers and mathematics that enables a child to manipulate numbers mentally. If the basic addition facts are defined as the 100 combinations possible by pairing all the digits from 0 to 9 in every possible way, number sense can be developed to reduce the memory load for these 100 "facts" considerably. Children can be taught a variety of strategies for deriving many of the basic facts from a few memorized facts.

Commutative Property   Because addition of two numbers is not affected by the order of the numbers, 45 of the 100 basic facts are redundant. By helping children learn the commutative property, a teacher reduces the memory load for learning basic facts by nearly 50 percent.

Ones   Addition of one generally presents no difficulties for children. It is not important whether they memorize these or use strategies to figure them out quickly; in either event, most children find addition of one to be nearly intuitive. Ones account for an additional seven basic facts.

Doubles and Near-Doubles   Of the basic facts involving addition of single digit numbers, some are easier to remember than others. The doubles $(1 + 1, 2 + 2, 3 + 3,$ and so on) are among the easiest for children to remember. Teachers who are helping children develop number sense will teach them to use the doubles as landmarks for figuring out other facts. If a child can remember that $8 + 8$ is 16, then she can use that knowledge to help her quickly determine $8 + 9$ (one more than $8 + 8$) and $8 + 7$ (one less than $8 + 8$). Of the 50 distinct facts, 10 are doubles and 9 more are near-doubles.

Tens   Five of the basic facts are combinations that sum to ten: $5 + 5, 6 + 4$, $7 + 3, 8 + 2$, and $9 + 1$. These pivotal facts should be learned by children as a special family of facts. The role of ten in many thinking strategies makes these facts especially important.

Partitioning into Ten-and-   The facts whose sums are above ten can be learned in terms of partitioning into ten-and-an amount above ten. For example, a child who has learned that $8 + 2 = 10$ can use that knowledge as a reference point for all of the facts above $8 + 2$: $8 + 3$ is one more than $8 + 2, 8 + 4$ is two more than $8 + 2$, and so on. The ability to use the 10-facts as reference points in this manner depends on a child's ability to think flexibly about the addends. The child who thinks of 3 as $2 + 1$ will be capable of understanding a partitioning strategy, but a child who thinks of 3 rigidly will lack this capability.

Zeros   Addition of zero proves to be surprisingly difficult for children. Addition of zero is counterintuitive for children beccause it is not easy to represent through a concrete action. For this reason we suggest that the zeros be the last set of facts studied.

A Distinction Between Drill and Practice

In a traditional program where memorization of facts was stressed, the terms *drill* and *practice* became synonymous. Both terms were used to refer to the activities of repetition of number combinations and their sums with the goal being instant recall. Frequently timed speed tests were given to provide children with an incentive to reach a level of mastery.

Increasing

Abstraction

In a program where strategies are taught for deriving unknown combinations from known combinations, the terms *drill* and *practice* can take on different meaning. *Drill* is a more appropriate term for work on memorization. *Practice* can be used to connote energy spent on bringing a performance toward greater fluency. The word *practice* is used in this sense by musicians. In this sense, the energy spent by children learning to make better use of strategies and inventing new strategies is a highly desirable form of practice.

Drill and Practice in Proper Perspective

Technology

In the type of program that we recommend, special roles are reserved for drill and for practice. Generally practice and drill should occur near the end of a learning cycle. After problem-solving work has been used to introduce a new concept and children have had many opportunities to reason together, make conjectures, and justify their thinking to one another, they need to acquire greater fluency with the concepts that they have developed. At this point in the learning cycle, practice is appropriate. As the very last step in learning a concept, children will need to have some drill in order to strengthen their ability to recall meaningful facts and procedures quickly. Games and computer activities that require speedy recall of facts are appropriate at this stage of learning.

Multiplication

As in the case of addition and subtraction, the use of laboratory exploration and orally presented problems provides developmental foundation work in multiplication. The two laboratory activities and the two problems that follow are representative of the type used by successful first- and second-grade teachers to develop background for the formal study of multiplication.

Lab 1. Groups of children were given plastic tiles (about 50). They were asked to make as many rectangles as they could with 20 tiles, with 12 tiles, and so on. They made drawings on squared paper of the various arrangements.

Lab 2. Groups of three children were given a picture of a house and were asked to find the number of panes of glass in the front of the house. On completion of the lab, the groups discussed the approaches they had used.

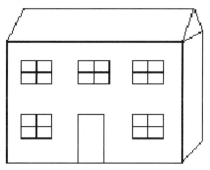

Problem 1. Joe bought three 9¢ stamps. How much did they cost?

Problem 2. How much will five pieces of candy cost if each piece costs 4¢?

Math as Problem Solving

To make full use of these laboratory activities and problems, the following approaches are suggested: (1) Provide children with actual objects so that they can use counting to find an answer; (2) use tens and ones blocks and Cuisenaire Rods™; (3) make use of the number line for solutions; (4) encourage the children to think of as many ways as possible to solve the word problems; and (5) solve the more difficult problems by means of total-class consideration.

When children have had experience with a variety of these problem situations, they usually have little difficulty in developing the "equal-additions" concept of multiplication. Recently, groups of children with background laboratory and problem-solving experiences but no formal multiplication study scored a median of 18 correct on a 21-item test that consisted of questions such as the following ones:

1. Alice is serving ice cream at her birthday party. If one package of ice cream serves four children, how many children will three packages serve?

2. Ann gets 2¢ each day for helping with the dishes. How much will she get for helping with the dishes for four days?

3. How many are 4 fives?

4. How many are 3 sevens?

5. How many are 5 fours?

Math
as
Reasoning

Pupils who have had an opportunity to explore number relationships will often demonstrate a grasp of numbers far beyond their level of study. One child who had not studied any multiplication heard her teacher read in *Little Women* that Amy could not think of the answer to 9 × 12. In about a minute, the girl asked the teacher, "Is 9 times 12 equal to 108?" The teacher answered, "Yes, how did you figure out that answer?" "I left out the twos and added all the tens. That was 90. Then I added all the twos. That was 18. I added 90 plus 18 for the answer of 108."

Such reactions are common in programs in which an emphasis is placed on a strong foundation of orally presented problems and laboratory activities.

Division

Many elementary school mathematics programs do little to develop any understanding of division until its formal introduction, which usually occurs in third grade. This practice is to be questioned. An important yearbook of the National Council of Teachers of Mathematics stresses the idea that learning fundamental mathematical ideas is a continuous process and is facilitated by a continual development of a topic from grade to grade (1959). To implement this procedure, foundation work in division should begin in kindergarten and grade 1. However, although it is of great importance to develop readiness for division early in the primary grades, it is usually desirable to delay the formal study of it until the child has a sound grasp of multiplication.

Foundation work dealing with division can make use of laboratory experiences and orally presented word-problem situations that can be solved by the use of objects, number lines, sets, counting, subtraction, and addition. Many situations at the readiness stage can be developed through class consideration of problems; in other cases, small-group laboratories are appropriate. The situations that follow are illustrative of the types of materials that can be used in the foundation program.

Laboratory sheets containing exercises such as those below can be used. A single child or several children can work to find the solution. (*Note:* The teacher must be sure that children's reading ability is not a hindrance. Thus, it is probably wise for the teacher to read the directions and the exercises to the children.)

1. Claudia is going to paste nine pictures on a sheet of construction paper. If she pastes three on each sheet, how many sheets of paper will she need? (The problem can be solved with pictures or drawings.)

2. Mother made 12 cookies for three children to share. How many will each get? (The problem can be solved by taking 12 objects and "counting them out" to three pupils.)

3. The teacher can use problems such as, "How many children do we have in the class? Right, 30. How many cars will we need for our science trip to the weather station if we put six of you in each car?" (The problem can be solved by the class's counting off by sixes, by the class's forming in groups of six each, or by class considerations of the number line.)

CATALOG

You are going to order some things from a catalog.

Materials: Catalogs of interest to the class.

Have the students flip through a catalog and find five things they would like to buy. They should write down the name and the price of each item, and then find out the total amount they would be spending. Then have them switch catalogs with a friend to do it again. You could modify the activity by setting a spending limit. For example, pretend they each got $25.00 for their birthday.

Extension: Have them figure out the shipping charges for each item, add them up, and then add them to the total. To check, add each shipping charge to the item; then add up the totals.

LOCKERS

These three side-by-side lockers have numbers that add to 66. What three side-by-side lockers have numbers that add to 135?

SELF-TEST—HOW WOULD YOU RESPOND TO EACH OF THESE STATEMENTS?

- _____ Addition and subtraction are both dependent on an understanding of part-whole relationships.

- _____ Addition is a function that maps ordered pairs of numbers onto their sums.

- _____ Equal additions and cross-products of sets are essentially very similar definitions of multiplication.

- _____ It is more difficult to find problem situations that require partitive division than it is to find problem situations that require measurement division.

- _____ All whole-number division problems have whole-number answers.

- _____ Children who do not have all their addition and subtraction facts memorized will be unable to solve more complicated addition and subtraction problems.

- _____ There is no role for drill and practice in a meaning-oriented mathematics program.

- _____ Since multiplication and division are more complicated than addition and subtraction, children should be taught the multiplication and division facts before they are expected to solve multiplication and division problems.

SELECTED REFERENCES

Ball, D. L. (1990). Prospective elementary and secondary teachers' understanding of division. *Journal for Research in Mathematics Education, 21*(2), 132–144.

Carpenter, T. P. (1986). Conceptual knowledge as a foundation for procedural knowledge. In J. Hiebert (Ed.), *Conceptual and procedural knowledge: The case of mathematics* (pp. 113–132). Hillsdale, NJ: Erlbaum.

Carpenter, T. P., & Moser, J. M. (1984). The acquisition of addition and subtraction concepts in grades one through three. *Journal for Research in Mathematics Education, 15,* 179–202.

Carpenter, T. P., Peterson, P. L., Chiang, C., & Loef, M. (1989). Using knowledge of children's mathematics thinking in classroom teaching: An experimental study. *American Educational Research Journal, 26,* 499–531.

Davis, R. B. (1984). *Learning mathematics: The cognitive science approach to mathematics education.* Norwood, NJ: Ablex.

Kaplan, R. G., Yamamoto, T., & Ginsburg, H. P. (1989). Teaching mathematical concepts. In L. Resnick & L. Klopfer (Eds.), *Toward the thinking curriculum: Current cognitive research 1989 ASCD yearbook* (pp. 59–82). Association for Supervision and Curriculum Development.

Lampert, M. (1986). Knowing, doing, and teaching multiplication. *Cognition and Instruction, 3,* 305–342.

National Council of Teachers of Mathematics (1959). *The Growth of Mathematical Ideas, Grades K–12*. Washington, DC: National Council of Teachers of Mathematics.

National Council of Teachers of Mathematics (1989). *Curriculum and evaluation standards for school mathematics*. Reston, VA: National Council of Teachers of Mathematics.

Pratt, N. (1997). Shielding children from mathematical danger. *Mathematics Teaching*, 158, March.

Tirosh, D., & Graeber, A. O. (1990). Evoking cognitive conflict to explore pre-service teachers' thinking about division. *Journal for Research in Mathematics Education, 21*, 98–108.

West, L. R. & Sturbaun, M. B. (1996). Need New Problems-Solving Ideas? Take a Trip! *School Science and Mathematics 96*(4), 187–191.

CHAPTER

7 Number Algorithms: Intermediate

computations of numbers

LOOKING AHEAD

In the intermediate grades children learn to extend their basic understandings of addition, subtraction, multiplication, and division to multidigit numbers. The teaching of whole-number multidigit algorithms has traditionally occupied most of the mathematics time available in the intermediate grades. The following suggestions are not meant to provide comprehensive programs for teaching multidigit algorithms. Instead, some general ideas are provided that will give the reader an idea of the type of activities that can be used to teach these algorithms meaningfully. It is our intent that these models will provide a springboard from which the reader will be able to develop his or her own approaches.

CAN YOU?

- Explain the importance of place-value concepts in the development of understanding of multidigit addition and subtraction?

- Justify the use of chip-trading activities for teaching multidigit addition and subtraction?

- Plan some chip-trading activities that may help children construct the necessary cognitive structures for understanding of multidigit addition and subtraction?

- Invent a problem situation that can be used to introduce multidigit multiplication to intermediate grade children?

- Identify some of the value that comes from having children solve multiplication problems in more than one way?

- Tell why renaming is such an important part of understanding multidigit multiplication?

- Suggest reasons that it may be wise to devote less time to long division in the intermediate grades than has typically been the case?

- Evaluate the use of the calculator as a tool for division readiness activities?

- Invent a problem situation that can be used to introduce multidigit division to intermediate grade children?

- Defend the use of alternative division procedures in the teaching of long division?

MULTIDIGIT ALGORITHMS

Addition and Subtraction

Place-value concepts are the crucial cognitive structures that are necessary in order for children to extend their understanding of addition and subtraction to include multidigit applications. If children have had many experiences with chip trading, of the sort described in chapter 5, these can be used to introduce multidigit addition and subtraction.

As the children were playing the trading-up chip activity, one teacher focused the class's attention on an interesting challenge. He suggested that in one game, one child had accumulated 2 paper clips and another child had accumulated 1 paper clip. Neither child had any buttons, and the trading value was five. The teacher asked the children what would happen if these two children combined their paper clips. After the children told the teacher that there would be 3 paper clips, he asked them how they could record this transaction. Most of the children were confident that this could be represented by 2 clips, 0 buttons + 1 clip, 0 buttons = 3 clips, 0 buttons.

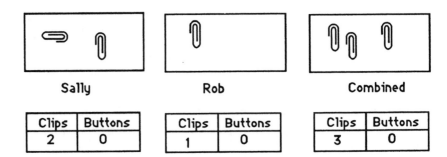

Clips	Buttons
2	0

Clips	Buttons
1	0

Clips	Buttons
3	0

Following this, the teacher wondered how they could show the combination of 2 clips, 2 buttons with 1 clip, 2 buttons. Again, after some discussion, the children agreed that this combination would be represented by 2 clips, 2 buttons + 1 clip, 2 buttons = 3 clips, 4 buttons. They recorded this as follows:

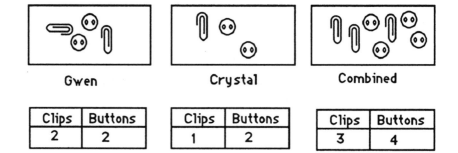

Clips	Buttons
2	2

Clips	Buttons
1	2

Clips	Buttons
3	4

As a final step before introducing children to addition in base 10, the teacher wondered if the children could figure out what to do with the combination of 2 clips, 4 buttons with 1 clip, 3 buttons. This challenge led to some rich discussion. Eventually the children agreed that five of the seven buttons needed to be traded for one more clip. Their final representation looked like this:

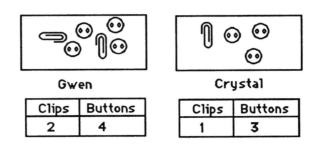

Clips	Buttons
2	4

Clips	Buttons
1	3

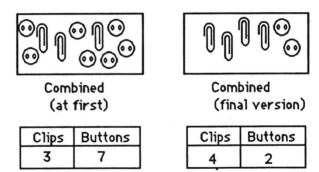

Combined (at first)			Combined (final version)	
Clips	Buttons		Clips	Buttons
3	7		4	2

Activities such as these can provide the children with "tools to think with."[2] The teacher used these mental models in introducing addition and subtraction with multidigit numbers in base 10. She was able to remind children many times of their work with chip-trading. The transfer of this conceptual framework to numbers in base 10 was meaningful and easy for the children.

Multiplication

The teacher began the study of multidigit multiplication with a problem sheet containing a number of problems involving multiples of ten such as, "How many wildlife stamps will Jane need to fill her book if there are three empty pages and each page holds 30 stamps?" After setting up a laboratory supplies table containing squared paper, duplicated number lines, and place-value frames, the teacher directed the children to think of the mathematical sentence for each problem and then independently solve the problems in several ways. The teacher's final comment to the group was, "While there are seven problems on the sheet, I'd rather have you solve three or four of them in several different ways than work them all by using only one method."

The responses shown below were given by the children:

Jim:

$$\begin{array}{r} 30 \\ 30 \\ +30 \\ \hline 90 \end{array}$$

Phyllis:

90 stamps

---

[2] Thanks to Papert, S. (1980), for this lovely phrase.

Kim:	**Pete:**	
$3 \times 30 =$	3 tens	30
3×3 tens $= 9$ tens $= 90$	$\times\ 3$	$\times\ 3$
90 stamps	9 tens	90
	90 stamps	

Joe:

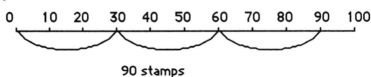

90 stamps

Matt:

tens	ones
I I I	
I I I	
I I I	

90 stamps

A discussion of the solutions to several examples like these should lead class members to formulate a generalization such as, "To multiply tens, you multiply the number of tens that you have ($30 = 3$ tens) by the multiplier and then you write a zero in the ones place to show that your product is tens." (3×3 tens $= 90$)

The next logical step is the multiplication of a two-digit number by a one-digit number in a situation that does not involve renaming (carrying). Some approaches that children use follow:

Ted:	**Jim:**	
23	tens	ones
23	I I	I I I
$+ 23$	I I	I I I
69	I I	I I I

May:

2 tens 3 ones	Twenty-three is 2 tens and 3 ones.
$\times\qquad 3$	Three groups of 3 ones equals 9,
6 tens 9 ones	and 3 groups of 2 tens equals 6
69	tens, or 60. Adding these, I got an answer of 69.

Fred: I used a squared-paper array.

John: I used the number line.

Helen: I made use of the "multiplying twice" (distributive principle) that we have used to check multiplication combinations.

$$3 \times 23 = 3 \times (20 + 3) = (3 \times 20) + (3 \times 3) = 60 + 9 = 69$$

or

$$\begin{array}{r} 23 \\ \times\,3 \\ \hline 60 + 9 \end{array} \qquad \begin{array}{r} 20 + 3 \\ \times\quad 3 \\ \hline \end{array} \qquad 60 + 9 = 69$$

After several days of experimental work, class discussion of the various approaches verified that the multiplying twice approach was the most effective, particularly when the computational shortcut was used. This shortcut was stated as

$$\begin{array}{r} 32 \\ \times\,3 \\ \hline 6 \\ 90 \\ \hline 96 \end{array}$$

or

"Think 30 + 2. Multiply 3 times 2; write the 6 in the ones place of the product. Think 3 times 30 equals 90; write 9 in the tens place of the product."

However, children were urged to experiment with various approaches.

Renaming

Renaming is one of the more important ideas whose understanding is necessary for success with multiplication. The idea of renaming was introduced in one classroom with the following problem: "The Girl Scout troop asked Alice to bake eight dozen cookies. Remember, there are 12 cookies in one dozen. How many cookies will she need to bake? Think of the mathematical sentence and solve the problem in as many ways as you can. Then work in groups of three to figure out other solutions to the problem." The pupils later reported the following means of working the problem:

Ned:

$$\begin{array}{r} 12 \\ 12 \\ 12 \\ 12 \\ 12 \\ 12 \\ 12 \\ +\,12 \\ \hline 96 \end{array}$$

Joan: 13 12 11 10 9 8 7 6 5 4 3 2 1 0   1 2 3 4 5 6 7 8 9

8 × 2 = 16

8 × 10 = 80

Jill: $8 \times 12 = X$

$10 + 2$

$\underline{\times \qquad 8}$

$80 + 16 \rightarrow 96$

Sally: $8 \times 12 = 8 \times (10 + 2) = (8 \times 10) + (8 \times 2) = 80 + 16 = 96$

Craig: You could use a number line, but it takes too long.

Jeff: Draw an 8-by-12 array. Then you can fold the array to make combinations that you know. For example:

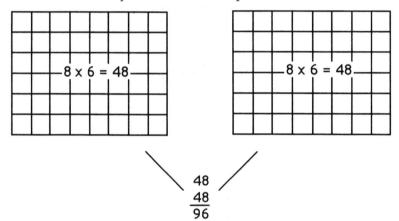

The class discussed the various approaches and decided that Sally's method and Jeff's method made use of the distributive property (studied earlier with single-digit work), as did Jill's. However, they felt that Jill's approach was easier. They also concluded that Joan and Jeff both used the distributive idea in marking off an array. Joan's method was preferred because of the ease with which they could multiply by tens.

Two-Digit Multipliers

To introduce multiplications such as 23×45, the teacher gave each child the laboratory sheet on the next page.

The teacher suggested that in addition to grids, several other methods could be used to help find the answer. Many children had cut out the grids and folded them in different ways to find the answer. Three of the methods used are depicted on the following pages.

EXPERIMENT:
Use squared paper.

How many floor tiles below?

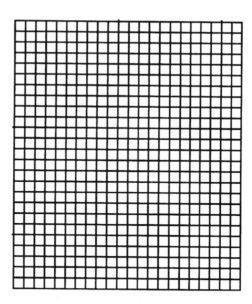

25 by 22

Find with squared paper (using larger sheets of squared paper):

32 by 19

12 by 16

Some solutions:

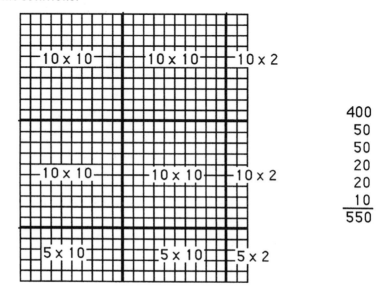

400
50
50
20
20
10
550

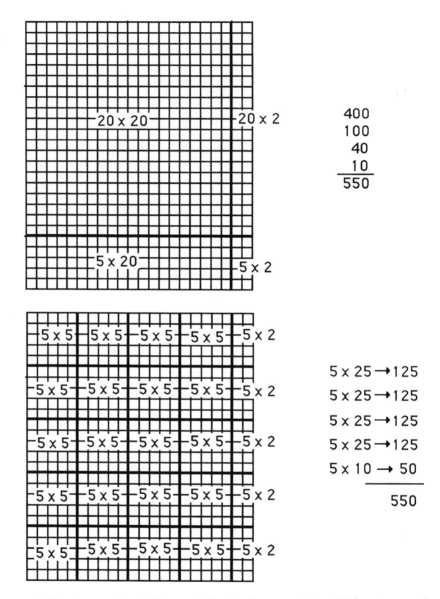

Following work of this sort, the teacher used the children's experiences with the various ways of partitioning the multiplicand and multiplier to obtain an answer. This concept became the foundation upon which the children constructed an understanding of the traditional multidigit multiplication algorithm.

Division

Multidigit division occupies a good deal of time in the intermediate grades. It is difficult to ascertain the amount of stress that should be placed on this topic. A distinguished group of scientists and mathematicians (Cambridge Conference on the Correlation of Science and Mathematics, 1969) has suggested a "downplaying" of the study of multidigit division:

> Most adults do not seem to use the long division algorithm very much. Moreover, the vast majority of interesting school units in science and mathematics do not require more than about two-figure accuracy in multiplication and division. The needed accuracy can be obtained by estimation, by rounding, by cruder and simpler algorithms, by use of arrays and grouping, or with the help of tables. . . . If the algorithms are to be learned, they should emerge from an investigation on the part of the students. Various useful forms they arrive at will suffice whether or not they are the most standard or the most compact.

The teaching suggestions that follow are designed to provide children with basic competence in division through procedures designed to foster mathematical thinking (Heddens and Lazerick, 1975).

Before undertaking an intensive study of multidigit division, the child should have

1. An understanding and mastery of multiplication and subtraction facts and the multiplication and subtraction algorithms.

2. An ability to supply missing factors for examples such as $3 \times \text{'} = 27$.

3. Facility with estimations such as $6 \times \text{'} = 8{,}248$ (either 10, 100, or 1000).

4. An understanding of measurement and partitive meanings of division.

5. Mastery of the basic ideas of place value through the thousands.

Readiness with the Calculator

A variety of orally presented "guess and test" calculator activities can provide understanding and motivation when beginning multidigit division. One teacher made use of the following type of exercises in this introductory work:

Technology

1. "Guess how many twenty-fours are in 350. Check with your calculator."

   Kim: That's about 25; 4 twenty-fives per hundred; about 14.

2. "Guess the value of 8500 divided by 385. Check with your calculator."

   Kent: About 400 in 8500; 5 four hundreds equal 2000; 20 four hundreds in 8000; about 21.

3. "Guess what number should be multiplied by 35 to get 630. Check with your calculator."

   Joe: Thirty-fives in 630; that's about 40 in 600; $10 \times 40 = 400$; $5 \times 40 = 200$; that's about 15. I checked with my calculator and got 18 for an answer. Fifteen is a good estimate.

When using the calculator, an important consideration is the remainder. Except for the newer calculators that can report division results with remainders, remainders will be expressed as decimals. One teacher introduced the concept by suggesting, "Divide 5 by 2 on your calculators. What do you get for an answer? Jill would you write it on the board?"

Jill: 2.5.

Teacher: What does the 2.5 mean? What do you get for an answer when you divide with paper and pencil?

Pete: 2 with a remainder of 1. That's $2\frac{1}{2}$. So .5 must be the same as $\frac{1}{2}$.

At this point the teacher introduced a decimal place-value chart, and, through group discussion, the children compared the tenths and hundredths to tenths of a dollar (dimes) and hundredths of a dollar (pennies). Use of experimentation helped the children to see the approximate value of each of the tenths numbers.

After the teacher felt the children had a grasp on the decimal leftover part (remainder), the teacher gave the children a number of multidigit numbers to divide. The children found that many of the answers had repeating decimals such as 5 divided by 3 = 1.666666.... Experimentation and discussion helped the children discover that .6666... is $\frac{2}{3}$; .3333.... is $\frac{1}{3}$; .125 is $\frac{1}{8}$, and so on. Then the children were given the instructions, "Use a calculator to divide the number 12 by each of the numbers from 1 to 12 in turn. Record all your calculations and answers, and then discuss what these results mean." The children worked in groups of three and later shared their findings with the entire class. Try this experiment yourself.

Teaching Multidigit Division

Multidigit division can be introduced through a situation involving a division such as 48 ÷ 4 = N. A group-thinking lesson is described below.

The teacher began in the following manner: "A class made 48 artificial flowers to sell at the carnival. If they tie them in bunches of four, how many bunches will they have to sell? Write the mathematical sentence you can use to solve the problem and then solve the problem in as many ways as you can. You will see an array diagram of the flowers at the top of the duplicated sheet I've given each of you. This may help with the problem." After a few moments, the teacher said, "I see that most of you have identified the mathematical sentence. What is the mathematical sentence?—Yes, 48 ÷ 4 = N ($\square \times 4 = 48$). Some of you seem to be having trouble starting out on the problem. How have we solved many division problems in the past?—Right, use subtraction. Go ahead and try to find an answer." While the pupils worked, the teacher moved about the room asking questions and giving aid. As the students completed various solutions to the problem, the teacher asked class members to illustrate their solutions on large sheets of lined paper (24 inches × 30 inches) with felt-tip pens or crayons. When discussion began, the teacher had the pupils explain their methods of solving the division problem, beginning with students who used the less mature solutions and ending with those who used the more mature solutions. The children's solutions and explanations follow.[3]

Sid: I used a number line made from squared paper. I cut out a 4-length and moved it along until I had counted the numbers of fours in 48.

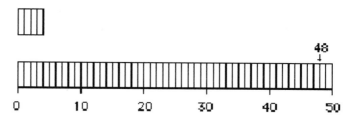

Lyle: I know that we can solve any division situation by a series of subtractions. I started to find "how many fours equal 48" by subtracting fours. Then I shortened it some by subtracting two groups of 4.

$$
\begin{array}{r r}
4\overline{)48} & \\
-4 & 1 \\
\hline
44 & \\
-4 & 1 \\
\hline
40 & \\
-8 & 2 \\
\hline
32 & \\
-8 & 2 \\
\hline
24 & \\
-8 & 2 \\
\hline
16 & \\
-8 & 2 \\
\hline
8 & \\
-8 & 2 \\
\hline
0 & 12 \\
\end{array}
$$

---

[3] If in a lesson similar to this the children do not think of the variety of approaches suggested, it will probably be wise to use Socratic questioning to bring them out. As was previously mentioned, the knowledge that there are many ways of finding an answer usually provides children with greater confidence when they undertake a new task.

Joan: I studied the array patterns and then circled groups of 4 in the pattern.

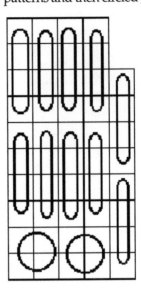

Jeff: I used the same method as Joan, but I cut a 4-strip pattern and fitted it on the squared-paper array.

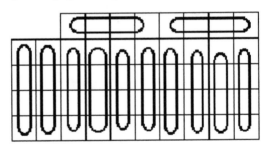

Mike: I also used the array pattern, but I shortened it some. I could see that by counting the row I could find the fours in 40. Then I partitioned the 8 into two groups of 4.

Kevin: I thought, "My question is what times 4 equals 48." I did some thinking and decided that a good first guess was 10. I knew that $10 \times 4 = 40$. Then I just knew that there were two more fours in the 8. So my answer was 12.

$$X \times 4 = 48$$
$$10 \times 4 = 40$$
$$\underline{2 \times 4 = 8}$$
$$12$$

Ann: I used subtraction. I know five sets of four equal 20, so I recorded 5 and subtracted 20. I still had another group of 5 fours, so I subtracted another 20. Two fours equal 8, so I recorded the 2.

$$\frac{12}{\begin{array}{r}2\\5\\5\\4\overline{)48}\\20\\\overline{28}\\20\\\overline{8}\\8\end{array}}$$

Charlie: I used the same procedure but a different form.

$$
\begin{array}{r}
4\overline{)48}\\
20\\
\overline{28}\\
20\\
\overline{8}\\
8\\
\end{array}
\qquad
\begin{array}{r}
5\\
\\
5\\
\\
2\\
\overline{12}
\end{array}
$$

Nancy: I shortened the procedure they used. I know that 10 fours equal 40, so I subtracted 10 groups of 4. I also know that 2 fours equal 8.

$$
\frac{12}{\begin{array}{r}2\\10\\4\overline{)48}\end{array}}
\qquad
\begin{array}{r}
40\\
\overline{8}\\
8\\
\end{array}
$$

Claudia: I wrote the division in a different way. Then I thought of another name for 48. It's 40 + 8. Then I went ahead and divided. I think that is a good way of solving the problem.

$$\frac{48}{4} \rightarrow \frac{40+8}{4} \rightarrow \frac{40}{4} + \frac{8}{4} \rightarrow 10 + 2 = 12$$

The representative procedures used by the children illustrate the wide range of approaches that may be used in early division study. The approaches taken by Nancy and Claudia are quite mature in their development and might well have occurred later in the sequence of division work. The procedure suggested by Kevin merits consideration. The use of multiples of 10 in finding a quotient is usually quite productive, since children can usually multiply easily by 10. Also, his suggestion of thinking what number can be multiplied by 4 to arrive at 48 is illustrative of thinking that is necessary for mature computation with division.

During the next several days, the teacher continued the study of similar division problem situations. Often, children worked in groups of three.

Normally, the task was to find as many ways as they possibly could to solve the division rather than working many division exercises in a single way.

Other procedures for solving division problems can be developed. Popsicle® sticks can be used effectively to solve partition division problems. For example, the teacher may give each child a number of bundles of 10 sticks and some single ones. They would then be given a laboratory-oriented sheet directing them to solve division computations by using the sticks. If they seemed to be having difficulty, the teacher could suggest working in small groups or she could make use of a Socratic questioning technique.

A portion of the laboratory sheet and two strategies for developing the division follow:

EXPERIMENT

Use: bundles of 10 Popsicle® sticks and single ones. Find the answers to these problems using sticks.

1. Their uncle gave Tom, Nancy, and Jill 36 stamps to share. How many stamps will each child get?

2. To make up laboratory kits, Joe has 44 pencils that he is to put in four boxes. How many pencils will he put in each box?

PROBLEM 1

Kate: I used 36 sticks to stand for the stamps. I thought, each child can have 10 sticks; I still have six left, I can give two to each one. My answer is 12 stamps for each child.

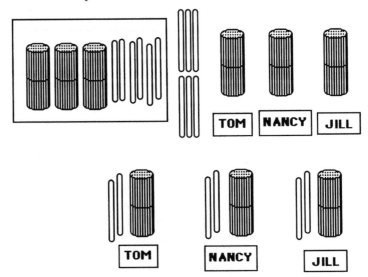

PROBLEM 2

Teacher: How could we use the tens bundles and single sticks to solve the problem?

Ken: First we'd set out 4 tens and 4 ones for the 44 pencils.

Lucy: We'd then need to divide the sticks into four piles. We could un-bundle the sticks and deal them out one at a time.

Pete: Wait. We could give each of the four boxes a bundle of 10.

Teacher: Fine; then what?

Mary: We'd have four sticks left. We could give one stick to each box. Then there would be 11 sticks in each box.

Teacher: Very good. Now let's see if we could write down what we did. [She wrote $^{44}/_4$ and $4\overline{)44}$ on the board.] Now, what did we do?

Jill: We looked at the tens first, so we really did this:

$$\frac{40 + 4}{4} \qquad \text{or} \qquad 4\overline{)40 + 4}$$

Then we divided.

The children went on to discuss and solve the other problems on the sheet. The teacher used discussion to stress thinking, "What number do I multiply by?" She also helped children realize that the dividend could be renamed to help in the division.

Further discussion and exploratory work helped the children to develop generalizations concerning the division of a multidigit dividend. Emphasis was placed on finding the multiples of 100 and 10 that could be subtracted from the dividend. The teacher was able to analyze each pupil's thinking by use of a mathematics theme in which each child was asked to explain the "how" and "why" of working a division situation. The selection that follows is representative of an acceptable development.

Math as Communication

What is the first step in finding "how many fives equal 582?" I have to think of renaming 582 so I can divide each addend by the known factor (5). I also want to use as large a multiple of 5 as I can. Looking at 582, I think that 500 can be used because it is the smallest multiple of 5×100 that can be used. Now I need to find the number of fives equal to 82. Using a multiple of 10, I know that $5 \times 10 = 50$, so I use this. The next question is, "How many fives equal 32?" or, "5 times what number equals 32?" I know from basic multiplication and division facts that $5 \times 6 = 30$. I continue to work. I subtract 30 from 32 to get 2. Since 2 is less than 5, it is considered to be the remainder. My answer is 116 r 2.

$$5\overline{)582}$$
$$(500 + 82) \div 5 = N$$
$$\begin{array}{r} 116 \\ 6 \\ 10 \\ 100 \end{array}$$
$$5\overline{)582}$$
$$\begin{array}{r} \underline{500} \\ 82 \\ \underline{50} \\ 32 \\ \underline{30} \\ 2 \end{array}$$

Multidigit Divisors

The teacher introduced the multidigit phase of division as follows: "Look at the division problems and exercises on the photocopied sheet. The first problem says,'Packing material for electronic parts comes off the assembly line in sections that contain 168 small parts. [See the array pictured.] How many sections that hold 12 parts each can be made from the section that contains 168 parts?' Use the array and other means to solve the problem. First identify the mathematical sentence that is needed to solve the problem."

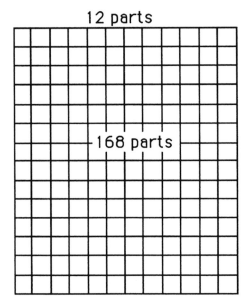

12 parts

168 parts

The work of the pupils on the problem revealed several solutions.

Nan: $168 \div 12 = N$. I knew there were 12 elements in each row, so I counted the number of rows: 14. This is the same as subtracting 12 from 168 fourteen times.

Phil: $168 \div 12 = N$. I used subtraction. I knew there were at least 5 twelves. Then I took 5 more, 2 more, and 2 more.

$$
\begin{array}{r}
12\overline{)168} \\
\underline{60} \qquad 5 \\
108 \\
\underline{60} \qquad 5 \\
48 \\
\underline{24} \qquad 2 \\
24 \\
\underline{24} \qquad \underline{2} \\
14
\end{array}
$$

Jean: I thought, "How many sets of 12 equal 168? Are there 10? Yes, 10×12 = 120. How many more? Two? Yes, more than two. Four? Yes, exactly $4 \times 12 = 48$."

$$
\begin{array}{r}
\underline{14} \\
4 \\
10 \\
12\overline{)168} \\
\underline{120} \\
48 \\
\underline{48}
\end{array}
$$

Jim: I tried to think of a way to rename 168. Since I am trying to find how many twelves in 168, I thought, $10 \times 12 = 120$. So I renamed 168 to be $120 + 48$. Then I went ahead and divided.

$$\frac{168}{12} \to \frac{120 + 48}{12} \to 10 + 4 \to 14$$

Kim: I used the same idea as Jim, but I wrote it differently.

$$12\overline{)168} \to 12\overline{)120 + 48} \to \overset{10 + 4}{12\overline{)120 + 48}} = 14$$

Then to direct pupil thinking toward ways to solve such division situations efficiently, the teacher used the following guided questions:

Teacher:	Pupil:
Let's look at this division situation: $568 \div 22$. Will the quotient be in the hundreds?	No, $100 \times 22 = 2{,}200$.
Will it be more than 10?	Yes, $10 \times 22 = 220$.
How about 20?	Yes, 20×22 would be $220 + 220$, or 440.
We'll try 20 as a starter. What next?	Let's try 5.
How does 5 turn out?	$5 \times 22 = 110$. Good.
Now what?	There will be no more sets of 22. Our answer is 25 r 18.

$$
\begin{array}{r}
\underline{25 \text{ r } 18} \\
5 \\
20 \\
22\overline{)568} \\
\underline{440} \\
128 \\
\underline{110} \\
18
\end{array}
$$

Reintroductions

There are many situations in elementary school mathematics that call for a review or further practice on a topic. At times, there has not been enough review on basics. Often a high school mathematics teacher states, "The pupils do not understand the basic principle of renaming in addition. They use 'carry the 1.' I wish the elementary teachers would teach them the basic ideas of mathematics." Such indictments probably arise not so much from a lack of teaching basic principles at an early grade as from a lack of reviewing them at an upper-grade level. Too often, the computational procedure is reviewed but the mathematical meaning is not.

To make reintroduction or review an active learning experience for the pupils, the material should be introduced in a new setting. Pupils who need further study on addition often attack reintroduction work with a lack of fervor. They feel, and justly so, "We had that in the same way last year; we're doing the same old thing." The situations that follow are illustrative of the type of reintroduction materials designed to vary the setting so that pupils may get further insights into addition and also be able to study "something new." Such material is also a valuable aid in diagnosing the level of the child.

Patterns (upper primary)
The teacher said, "I noticed a girl doodling with addition combinations. Can you tell what she did?" The teacher wrote on the board:

1	2	3	4
1 + 1	1 + 2	1 + 3	1 + 4
2	3	4	5
1 + 2	2 + 3	3 + 4	4 + 5
3	5	7	9
?	?	?	?
?	?	?	?
?	?	?	?

"See if you can complete her chart." The teacher then moved about the class and helped those pupils who had not discovered the pattern of computation. Other pattern-searching exercises can be used at higher-grade levels.

Front-End Addition (intermediate)
Adding the most important digits first is a method often used by people in business and can be a means of estimation or checking. It also provides a good review of place-value concepts.

An introductory statement that may be used is, "When I bought some clothing the other day, the clerk added my purchases on a sales slip. I've drawn the sales slip on the board. At first I wasn't sure how the clerk added the amounts. Can you find out what procedure was used?"

Sport coat	$95.75
Tie	6.25
Top coat	98.50
Shirt	15.95
Step 1	19
Step 2	24
Step 3	2.3
Step 4	.15
	$216.45

After a discussion, the teacher asked, "Would this method always work? What do you like about the method? What don't you like about it? Try using this 'front-end' arithmetic to solve the addition exercise in your text. Check using the regular method."

Lattice Multiplication
The jalousie or lattice method is an alternate multiplication procedure. This is one of the older methods of multiplying and is proving to be an effective introductory procedure for most children and a usable terminal procedure for the slow learner.

The teacher used a pattern-searching strategy, beginning by drawing figure a on the board, and then writing in the product (figure b). Using a "silent strategy" the teacher drew figure c on the board and handed one of the children the chalk. The child filled in the product (figure d). The teacher continued this procedure for several other examples. When a child made a mistake, another child took the chalk and corrected it.

The teacher drew figure e and gave the chalk to Tom. The multiplication was completed (figure f). The teacher then wrote $6 \times 23 = ?$ and gave the chalk to Mary. Mary wrote 138 in the box. From the expressions on the faces of the children, the teacher gathered that most of them had discovered the relationship between lattice multiplication and other methods.

Then the children were given a worksheet with several examples to be completed by using lattices. The teacher moved about the room, using leading questions to guide those who were having difficulty with the lesson.

The next day, the teacher gave a worksheet containing several lattice multiplication examples to be completed. The children worked in groups of three with the direction, "Discuss the multiplication and be ready to tell the other groups the reasons that lattice multiplication 'works.'"

A very valuable use of teacher workshop time is the search for new and varied methods for reintroduction of topics. Check local teacher centers and school materials stores.

PRIME NUMBERS
Materials: 1-inch square tiles.

Have the students make rectangles out of the tiles, making sure that they don't leave any space inside the rectangle unfilled. Suggest numbers such as 12, 16, 21, and 39. Ask them to make as many different rectangles out of a given number of tiles as they can, and have them record the lengths and widths of their rectangles. After they've found all the rectangles that they can make out of a number such as 12, ask them what the factors of 12 are.

Suggest a number such as 29. Let them work on it for a while and see if anyone can come up with a rectangle. This is a good time to see if they understand that a rectangle with a width of one is an acceptable rectangle. Ask them if they've heard of prime numbers before.

Without using the tiles, ask them how many rectangles they could make out of 13 tiles. 27 tiles? 37 tiles? 53 tiles? Then ask which of the above numbers are prime numbers.

Challenge: Have them find as many prime numbers between 0 and 200 as they can. See if they can come up with strategies for eliminating some numbers from the list of possibilities.

PEST CONTROL
One happy frog ate 200 flies in 5 days. Each day he got better at ambushing the unwary bugs, so he ate 6 more flies than the day before. How many flies did the frog eat on each of the 5 days?

THE 100-YARD DASH, OR HOW FAR CAN YOU RUN?
Take the class out to the track on a nice day to run the 100-yard dash. Divide them up into groups of four. Each group of four will race at the teacher's signal down to the finish line while another group of four times them (each timer is assigned to a different lane). A third group of four will record their runner's name and the time that their timer calls out. Rotate runners, spectators, recorders, and timers (probably in that order to give runners a chance to catch their breath) so that each student gets to be involved with each aspect of the activity. When all the results are in, have each student find his unit speed; that is, have the students divide the 100 yards or 300 feet by their time to get their speed in feet per second. Now have them convert this answer into miles per hour. For example, if a student ran the 100-yard dash in 15 seconds, that would be 300 feet ÷ 15 seconds = 20 feet per second, × 60 seconds in a minute = 1,200 feet per minute, × 60 minutes in an hour = 72,000 feet per hour, ÷ 5,280 feet in a mile =a running speed of 13.64 miles per hour. Finally, ask them if they could really go that many miles on foot in just one hour.

SELF-TEST—HOW WOULD YOU RESPOND TO EACH OF THESE STATEMENTS?

- ____ Place-value concepts are too confusing to children. If they are just taught to do the algorithms, they can understand the place-value concepts later.

- ____ Chip-trading activities can be extended to provide children with models for multidigit addition and subtraction.

- ____ Children using chip-trading activities will naturally come into contact with the concepts necessary for multidigit algorithms.

- ____ When children are allowed to solve problems in their own ways they naturally come to understand a variety of approaches.

- ____ If children can solve a multidigit problem using the traditional algorithm, they have no need for alternative approaches.

- • ____ Traditional multidigit algorithms gain their great efficiency from the use of place value and base-amount grouping.

- • ____ Because long division is so complex, children must spend a great deal of school time mastering it.

- • ____ Because calculators ordinarily do not provide whole-number remainders for division problems, they are of great value in helping children interpret division remainders.

SELECTED REFERENCES

Cambridge Conference on the Correlation of Science and Mathematics in the Schools (1969). *Goals for the Correlation of Elementary Science and Mathematics,* Education Development Center, Houghton Mifflin.

Carroll, W. (1996). Mental Computation of Students in a Reform-Bases Curriculum. *School Science and Mathematics* 96(9) 305–311.

Heddens J. W. & Lazerick, B. (1975). "So 3 'Guzinta' 5 Once! So What!!" *The Arithmetic Teacher* 22: 576–578.

Hiebert, J. (1988). A theory of developing competence with written mathematical symbols. *Educational Studies in Mathematics, 19,* 333–355.

Papert, S. (1980). *Mindstorms: Children, computers, and powerful ideas.* New York: Basic Books.

Riedesel, C. A., Schwartz, J. & Clements, D. (1996). *Teaching Elementary School Mathematics,* Chp 7.

The Secretary's Commission on Achieving Necessary Skills (1991). *What work requires of schools.* Washington, DC: U.S. Department of Labor.

8 Fractions and Decimals

LOOKING AHEAD

The meaning that most people associate with fractions, that of parts of a whole, is actually only one of many mathematically correct interpretations of fractions. The "parts-of-a-whole" meaning for fractions is one of the most easily modeled meanings, and is used extensively to teach children fraction concepts. If children are to gain mathematical power with fractions, however, teachers must know and teach many different meanings for fractions.

The Candybar Problem

One teacher presented groups of children with the challenge of equally sharing two candybars among three people. She gave each of the groups two rectangular pieces of oaktag to represent the candybars. She also provided scissors, glue, tape, markers, and crayons. She asked the children to attach each person's share of the candybars to a piece of notebook paper when they finished. As some groups finished the problem before others, the teacher encouraged them to try to show the solution in another way.

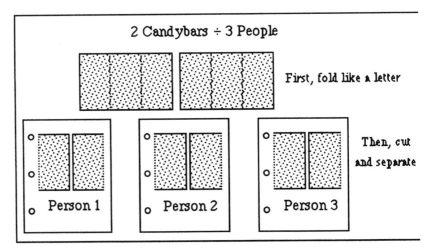

After each of the groups had found at least one way to show a solution, the teacher called them back together for a summarizing activity. One of the groups had decided to fold the oaktag pieces into three equal parts "like you fold a letter." They then cut them along the fold lines and gave each person two of the pieces. The teacher allowed other groups to show and talk about alternative ways of solving the problem before she returned to this method.

The teacher's next goal was to introduce the children to the correct symbols for writing fractions. She asked if anyone knew how to write the answer for the candybar problem. She allowed volunteers to offer different ideas of how the answer might be written. She was receptive to their ideas and praised them for their creativity.

Then she explained that, although their ideas were good and useful, the rest of the world had developed a certain system for writing fractions. Writing ⅔ below "Person 1," she asked the children if they had ever seen this fraction and if they knew how to read it. Most of the children had seen it, and one or two of them knew it was two-thirds. The teacher then asked if anyone could give suggestions for why this particular fraction might be written as ⅔. By building on the children's ideas, she showed them that the three represented the number of pieces into which each whole candybar had been cut. She also showed them that the two represented the number of pieces each person received.

This teacher continued the lesson by presenting several similar problems and asking the groups to solve them and write their answers using the standard method of writing fractions.

CAN YOU?

- Tell how fractions are like whole numbers and how they are different from whole numbers?

- Describe the relation between fractions and decimals?

- Describe three different meanings for fractional numbers?

- Provide a rationale for teaching children about Greatest Common Factors and Lowest Common Multiples?

- Find situations in which it is necessary to shift back and forth between different definitions of "one-whole?"

- Give a rationale for using multiple representations in the teaching of fractions?

- Represent common fractions by using number lines and geometric regions?

- Represent common fractions by using sets of objects?

- Develop a geometric representation of lowest common denominators?

- Identify a common subtraction-of-fractions error made by children who have learned whole-number subtraction well?

- Identify various structures of multiplication-of-fractions problems, and suggest a sequence in which they should be presented to children?

- Suggest a problem situation through which division of fractions may be introduced to children?

- Develop a geometric representation for "canceling" in multiplication of fractions?

FRACTIONS AND RATIONAL NUMBERS

How Are Fractions Like and Unlike Whole Numbers?

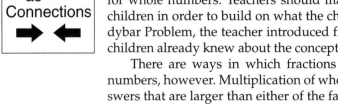

When children begin formally learning about fractions in school, they already possess considerable informal knowledge about fractions in their world. Common fractions such as one-half, one-fourth, and one-third are encountered frequently by children, and young children have some understanding of the meanings of these fractions. In addition to this, they also have had considerable formal and informal experience working with whole numbers. It is not surprising that children expect fractions to follow the same rules that they have learned in working with whole numbers. Properties, such as the associative property, the commutative property, and the identity property, for example, hold true for fractions as they do for whole numbers. Teachers should make these similarities explicit for children in order to build on what the children already know. In the Candybar Problem, the teacher introduced fractions by building on what the children already knew about the concept of division.

There are ways in which fractions operate differently from whole numbers, however. Multiplication of whole numbers always results in answers that are larger than either of the factors. Multiplication of fractions, however, often results in answers that are smaller than either of the factors. Division of whole numbers always results in answers that are smaller than the divisor or the dividend. But division of fractions often results in larger answers.

Even if children have not been explicitly taught these generalizations about multiplication and division with whole numbers, it is likely that they have formed them on their own. (Children may have formed these generalizations in a tacit way that they cannot articulate.) It is also likely that they will assume that fractions will follow these generalizations. The surprise that can result when children encounter this unexpected behavior of fractions can be a powerful learning tool. The teacher who allows children to discover this unexpected behavior of fractions, and who makes a point of leading children to explore it, will be more successful than a teacher who tries to teach this to children as facts to remember about fractions.

Relationship with Decimal Numbers

There are similarities between fractions and decimals. Children, however, often fail to make this connection when mathematics is presented as a series of compartmentalized procedures and algorithms. Because fractions and decimals are completely different symbol systems for communicating concepts, they are normally kept separate throughout most of the elementary curriculum. Children can learn, however, that they are just two different ways of representing numbers. In fact, middle school children who have been taught to look for alternative solutions will often convert a fraction problem into decimal format.

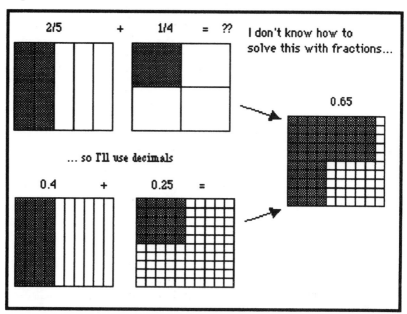

There will be times in a child's development when her understanding of fractions will help her to construct decimal concepts. There will be other times when her understanding of decimals will help her construct fraction concepts. A child who has explored the relationships between the two symbol systems will gain a deeper understanding of both.

Various Meanings of Fractions

> **Six cookies are to be shared equally by 3 children. How many cookies does each child get? Write this problem like we wrote the Candybar Problem. (6 ÷ 3 is written as ⁶⁄₃.)**

Division Meaning of Fractions
The Candybar Problem that introduced this chapter presented fractions in the context of a division problem. One of the uses of fraction notation is to denote the division concept. $^A/_B$ means A divided by B. In the Candybar Problem, $2 \div 3$ was seen to be $\frac{2}{3}$. A full appreciation of this concept cannot occur until a child can use the division algorithm with decimals in order to divide 2 by 3 to obtain 0.666 . . . , but problems that involve fractional notation used to represent division can be presented from the beginning of work with fractions. Improper fractions can be used for the type of problem on the left, and this offers an alternative to the use of decimals. Some of the children will solve this problem by physically manipulating the cookies; others will use division of whole numbers. The teacher's goal is to

make explicit the use of fractional notation to represent this division situation. Therefore, she will lead the children to notice that both $6 \div 3$ and $\frac{6}{3}$ can be seen to be representations of 2. This foundational work with improper fractions in a division context will make it easier for children to understand the division meaning of proper fractions.

Parts-of-a-Group Meaning of Fractions
Another use for fractions is to denote a select number of items to be considered as part of a group. We may speak of $\frac{7}{20}$ of the class being absent on a given day. In this case, the numerator refers to the select number of items to be considered, and the denominator refers to the number of items in the whole group. Although an adult may find this to be a trivial difference from the parts-of-a-whole meaning for fractions, the meaning is significantly different. Not only is the difference in meaning important, the difference must be made explicit for children. It is appropriate for the teacher to present a problem with this structure after having presented fraction work in another context. It is even advisable to design a problem that uses the same numbers that were used in a different type of fraction problem. This way the similarities and differences in the problem types are highlighted and can become the focus of a group inquiry.

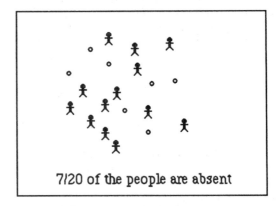

7/20 of the people are absent

Probability, Rate, Ratio, Proportion (see chapter 9)
There are many practical applications for fractions, including solving problems of probability, rate, ratio, and proportion. These topics are dealt with in detail in another chapter. The important thing to note regarding instruction in fractions is that fraction algorithms operate the same in all circumstances, but the problem contexts and meanings differ. This difference in problem contexts is crucial in a problem-centered curriculum. By finding fraction algorithms to be useful in different contexts, children will construct an understanding of the many meanings of fractions. The focus

Math
as
Reasoning

should be on reasoning about various problems, and the insight that we want children to develop is that fraction algorithms can be applied in different contexts.

GCF and LCM: What They Are and What to Do about Them

In recent years, much attention has been given in upper elementary mathematics programs to greatest common factors and lowest (or least) common multiples. Lowest common multiples (LCM) are useful when performing the addition and subtraction algorithms for fractions with unlike denominators. Greatest common factors (GCF) are useful for renaming fractions in their simplest form (lowest terms).

While both of these concepts are sensible and useful for mature mathematical thinkers, their utility must often be taken "in faith" by children. This is because much background instruction in factors, multiples, and procedures for working with them must be presented before children can use the GCF or LCM to make their own use of fraction algorithms more efficient. Adding to the difficulty is the fact that children often fail to see any importance, other than pleasing the teacher, to expressing fractional answers in simplest form.

The expert mathematics teacher cannot ignore the children's need to learn to use the GCF and LCM. Neither can he or she assume that the children will figure out their use on their own. The key to meaningful teaching of the GCF and LCM is to involve the children in tasks that can be performed without using the GCF or LCM, but which become dramatically easier when the GCF or LCM are used. Then, in this task-oriented context, the children can be led, through careful questioning, to invent procedures for finding the GCF or LCM as needed.

FUNDAMENTAL IDEAS ABOUT FRACTIONS

Intuitive Notions and Symbolization

Children arrive in kindergarten with primitive, intuitive ideas about parts of wholes and parts of sets. The challenge for the teacher is to come to an understanding of the ideas held by children and build on those ideas in presenting the formal, standard understandings of fractions. One of the notions that must be constructed by children is that words used for fractions, such as one-half, have a specific, non-arbitrary meaning. What do children have in mind, for example, when they say they want one-half of a cookie? Before they have had any formal instruction in fractions, any of the following representations would be acceptable representations for one-half.

"I want one-half of a cookie."

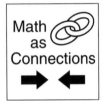

Math as Connections

As the Candybar Problem illustrated, it is quite possible to do sophisticated work with fractional concepts before the written symbol system for fractions is learned. Teachers of the primary grades can do much work with fractions in the process of teaching geometry. Studies of symmetry are an ideal context for early work with fractional concepts.

Another step in the construction of a mature understanding of fractions is learning the standard written forms for fractions. Since there are a variety of meanings for fractions, the teacher should avoid defining the terms of a fraction only in the narrow parts-of-a-whole context. It may be enriching to have children think of as many meanings as they can for the numerator and denominator of a common fraction.

NUMERATOR	DENOMINATOR
Number of pieces you have	Number of pieces in a whole thing
Number of items you have	Number of items in the whole group
Number of whole things you have	Number of parts into which to divide those whole things
(List continued by children)	(List continued by children)

Importance of Defining "One-Whole"

All of the various meanings and applications of fractions are dependent on an agreed-upon definition of "one-whole." If a geometric representation of fractions is being used, the geometric region that represents one-whole must be made explicit. If a group of items is being partitioned, it must be made clear how many items constitute the original whole group. Flexibility in redefining the unit whole can be gained through working with activities such as the following. The flexibility that can come from work of this sort will prove to be especially helpful for children developing an understanding of multiplication of fractions.

If ⁙ is one-whole, what is ⁚ ?

If ∷ is one-whole, what is ⁚ ?

If ∴ is one-whole, what is ⁚ ?

If ⁙ is one-whole, what is • ?

Partitioning

There is a vast difference between studying geometric regions that have been pre-partitioned into fractional regions and making those partitions yourself. Children whose sole experience with fractional regions is through prepared activities in which someone else has drawn the partitions will miss out on the opportunity to develop fractional concepts themselves. Activities involving paper folding, the use of sticks to manipulate various partitions on shapes, and the use of on-screen computer graphics objects are recommended as vehicles by which children can explore partitioning on their own. This exploration should be goal-directed, with the teacher providing the setting and initial goals. An example of one such goal-directed activity is provided by Pothier and Sawada (1990). They suggest that students can be asked to "prove" that areas of non-congruent parts of given shapes are equal. Children might be asked to find a way to "prove" whether or not the shaded portion of both of the squares below are equal. Activities of this sort have the potential to lead to rich investigations by the children.

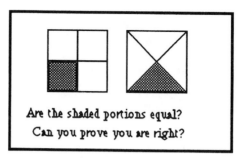

Are the shaded portions equal?
Can you prove you are right?

Equivalent Fractions

One of the most powerful ideas in working with fractions is the idea that any given fractional amount can be named in many different ways. The recognition that fractions with unlike denominators can be renamed as fractions with like denominators hinges on this important understanding. The concept of placing a fraction in its simplest form is dependent on the understanding that a fraction can have many names. Children who can re-name fractions in a number of different ways can quickly compare the sizes of two unlike fractions.

Fraction Chart

A chart such as the one above is extremely useful in helping children see the relationships between some common equivalent fractions with different names. With this chart to work from, children can be asked to find many fractions equivalent to one-half. A list of these fractions should be made. Children can then be led into a discussion of the possibility of finding a pattern in the various names for one-half. The same procedure can be followed for other fractions. The use of this chart will provide necessary scaffolding for children as they develop the idea that fractions often need to be renamed; a large copy of the chart should be posted in the classroom for a few weeks. Many questions for reflection can be posed, such as "How does $\frac{1}{6}$ compare in size with $\frac{1}{8}$?" The goal is to enable children to internalize the relationships shown on the chart so that they can produce a mental version of the chart whenever they might need it.

Multiple Representations

Number Lines and Geometric Representations

Early work with fractions should focus on finding and naming equivalent fractions. In addition to this, there should be an emphasis on the idea that there are various pictorial ways of representing fractions. The goal is to help children develop a flexible and multifaceted understanding of what fractions are. In our geometric representations of fractions, we recommend that teachers avoid using circular regions. Partitioning a rectangular region into fairly accurate representations of fractions is much easier than is partitioning a circular region. Extremely accurate representations can be generated if graph paper is used. Furthermore, partitioning a rectangular region can provide children with an opportunity to apply whole-number arithmetic reasoning skills. Partitioning circular regions does not so readily provide this opportunity.

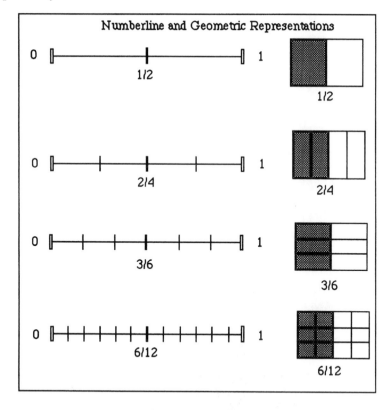

Representing Sets of Objects

Bethany and Emily were discussing the way Emily had arranged her box of 64 crayons. In one of the smaller boxes inside, she had placed all of the

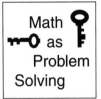

Math as Problem Solving

crayons that seemed to her to have some purple or blue in them. She grouped all the blue ones on one side and all the purple ones on the other side. They disagreed about what fraction of the crayons in the small box was blue. Emily thought that since there were 12 blues and 4 purples, that meant that $\frac{12}{4}$ of the small box was blue. Bethany thought it was $\frac{12}{16}$ of the small box.

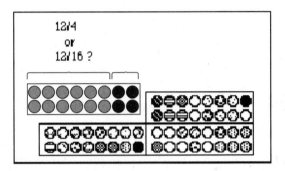

Emily: It's just like when we had parts of a group in school. The 12 is for the twelve blue crayons, and the 4 is for the four purple crayons.

Bethany: No! The 4 purple crayons are part of the total crayons . . . 16 in the little box. You have 12 blue crayons out of 16 crayons in the box. It's like in school when we had 7 out of 20 kids absent. It wasn't written as $\frac{7}{13}$!

Emily: But $\frac{12}{4}$ would make more sense. I've got 12 blue and 4 purple!

Bethany: Maybe there's another way to write that. That would be blues compared to purples, but we've been talking about blues to crayons in the small box.

Emily: I guess you're right. $\frac{12}{16}$ of these crayons are purple. I wonder what fraction of my **whole box** is purple . . .

ADDITION AND SUBTRACTION OF FRACTIONS

Common Denominators

If children have developed a deep understanding of the meanings of fractions, and if they have made the necessary connections between the various representations and the symbolic written form of fractions, addition and subtraction of fractions with like denominators will not be difficult for them. Teaching should begin with a problem situation presented verbally. After children show their solutions using various means of representation (number lines, geometric regions, dot paper, graph paper), discussion of the results should follow. Finally, the written form should be shown to children, and they should be guided to explain the meaning of the written form. This is not likely to be very challenging for children.

Unlike Denominators

Introduction

The real challenge occurs, and new learning can be expected, when children are faced with a problem involving addition or subtraction of fractions with unlike denominators. Instead of telling her children that "you can't add fractions with unlike denominators," Mrs. Long presented the following problem to her fourth-graders.

Mrs. Long: Two sisters were making sandwiches for lunch. One of them wanted a half of a sandwich, and the other wanted one-fourth of a sandwich. How much bread did they need for the top of the sandwiches? Work with your math partner to find out. Show the problem and answer in as many ways as you can.

As the children discussed the problem, Mrs. Long noted that some of them "just knew" the answer, and others of them had to use models or drawings to figure it out. Interestingly, none of the children used written forms of the fractions to figure it out. After a short time Mrs. Long began a discussion of the solutions.

Mrs. Long: Eric, would you explain what you and Marco did?

Eric: We drew the bread. We saw that one-half a piece of bread and one-fourth of a piece of bread together formed three-fourths of a piece of bread.

Mrs. Long: Well, your drawing does look like three-fourths of a piece of bread. What do the rest of you think? Can you prove to me that it is really three-fourths of a piece of bread?

Sonja: You can cut that half into two pieces. That's how you get fourths. Then you can see that it's three-fourths.

(Mrs. Long cuts the half, but not into two equal pieces.)

Sonja (and others):   No! You have to cut the half in half! The pieces have to be equal!

Mrs. Long redraws her partition, and everyone is satisfied. She then writes $\frac{1}{2} + \frac{1}{4} = \frac{3}{4}$ on the blackboard. She questions them about the meaning of this. Using the children's ideas, she rewrites it as $\frac{2}{4} + \frac{1}{4} = \frac{3}{4}$. Mrs. Long realizes that much work will need to be done to enable these children to work with less intuitive fractions, but she is happy with the way the children comprehended her introduction.

Advanced Work

In order for children to move beyond this initial level of converting fractions to like denominators, they must develop a more sophisticated way of finding common denominators. In cases where one of the denominators is a multiple of the other, children will be able to determine this by dividing the larger denominator by the smaller denominator. However, when neither denominator is a multiple of the other, a common multiple of both denominators must be found. Mathematicians use the lowest common multiple (LCM) in order to work with the smallest numbers possible. Children, however, are normally satisfied (initially) by using the product of the two denominators.

If children make the discovery that the product of the two denominators will work, then the teacher should not initially discourage children from using this procedure. However, the inefficiency of this procedure can be demonstrated to children by asking them to imagine using it for pairs of numbers that have a very high product (12 and 8 would be a good pair to use for this demonstration). A problem that can be submitted to a group inquiry is the question of whether an alternative procedure can be found that will give a lower common denominator than that which is obtained by multiplying the two denominators.

Since this group inquiry builds on the children's understanding that fractions sometimes need to be renamed, an appropriate beginning point is to ask them to generate several names for each of the fractions that they are dealing with. If the addition problem is $\frac{11}{12} + \frac{3}{8}$, the children can generate a few fractions equivalent to each of these. As the lists grow, someone will usually notice that both original fractions have been renamed with the number 24 as the denominator.

$$\frac{11}{12} = \frac{22}{24} = \frac{33}{36} = \frac{44}{48} = \frac{55}{60} \cdots$$

$$\frac{3}{8} = \frac{6}{16} = \frac{9}{24} = \frac{12}{32} = \frac{15}{40} \cdots$$

Once attention is focused on the greater efficiency of using 24 rather than 96 as the common denominator, the teacher should encourage the children to explore why 24 will work as a common denominator for 12 and 8. A geometric exploration of this phenomenon is shown.

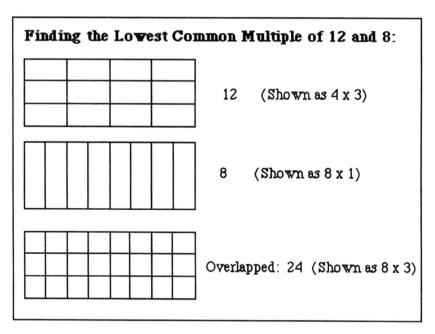

Although there are more sophisticated mathematical procedures for determining common denominators through finding the lowest common multiple (LCM) of any given numbers, elementary school children are generally happy with this procedure. Since calculators have made work with anything but common fractions rare, perhaps this is an adequate level of sophistication for elementary children.

Regrouping Difficulties in Subtraction of Fractions

Subtraction problems that do not involve regrouping are not significantly more difficult for children than are addition problems. However, when regrouping becomes necessary, such as in $3\frac{1}{5} - 1\frac{3}{5}$, children will normally experience some difficulty. Children who have meaningfully learned to subtract whole numbers with regrouping will often overgeneralize what they have learned and try to apply it to their work with fractions. That is, they will tend to rename the larger number in this example problem as $2\frac{11}{5}$. This is not a meaningless thing for children to do. It represents an attempt on their part to apply something that was meaningful in one context to a new context.

One approach to correcting this overgeneralization is to help children to become uneasy about what this regrouping procedure represents (and what it does not represent) for fractions. A child who has been observed to be making errors of this sort can be asked to use a model, such as Cuisenaire Rods™, to demonstrate $3\frac{1}{5} - 1\frac{3}{5}$. If he can correctly model the problem with

Read carefully!
What makes
the child think
3$\frac{1}{5}$ would be
renamed as 2^{11}/$_5$?

a manipulative device, he should then be asked to show how his written symbols represent what he showed with the manipulatives. Often this is sufficient to reveal to him that 3$\frac{1}{5}$ does not equal 2^{11}/$_5$. Once this discovery is made, the child can most likely find a way to rename 3$\frac{1}{5}$ correctly. Discussion can then focus on the general process involved in renaming mixed numerals.

Handling Mixed Numerals as well as Simple Fractions

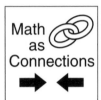

Once children have explored this common regrouping overgeneralization, the process of renaming mixed numerals as improper fractions or as different mixed numerals can be applied in many different contexts. Also, the reverse procedure, changing improper fractions to mixed numerals, can be used extensively. Children may need many experiences with drawings and physical models, in connection with written symbols, before they can perform these transformations automatically.

MULTIPLICATION OF FRACTIONS

Natural Language

If children have been taught multiplication of whole numbers in a way that makes use of natural language and meaning, transition to multiplication of fractions can be made meaningful too. A multiplication sentence that can be translated "number of times" to take "number of items" can be used for teaching multiplication of fractions. If the whole number sentence $3 \times 4 = 12$ can be read "three times of taking four items," then the fraction sentence $6 \times \frac{1}{3}$ can be read "six times of taking one-third of an item." Such use of natural language and meaning in teaching multiplication of fractions is strongly recommended in place of teaching the simple procedure of multiplying numerators and denominators.

A Sensible Sequence

In helping children develop an understanding of multiplication of fractions, it is sensible to consider three of the different problem structures and how they differ conceptually from multiplication with whole numbers. Multiplication of whole numbers by fractions, of the form $8 \times \frac{1}{2}$, is conceptually close to multiplication of whole numbers. This form should be used to introduce multiplication of fractions. Thought experiments, such as the following, can help children arrive at the new idea. "Consider 8 times 3 . . . taking 3, eight times. How many is that? Now, consider 8 times 2 . . . taking 2, eight times. How many is that? Now, consider 8 times 1 . . . taking 1, eight times. How many is that? Now consider 8 times $\frac{1}{2}$ . . . how would we use the same language to say that? How much would 8 times $\frac{1}{2}$ be?"

1st: Whole Number by Fraction
2nd: Fraction by Fraction
3rd: Fraction by Whole Number

Following an introduction using the structure of whole numbers times fractions, work can proceed with fractions times fractions. The example of the Blue Team is an example of work with this problem structure.

The Blue Team
Mr. Todd had formed teams for the class kickball game. Before leaving for the playground he decided to lay some groundwork for an introduction to multiplication of fractions.

Mr. Todd: Look everyone! On the blue team there are 12 members. What fraction of that team is made up of girls?

Bill: Well, there are 8 girls, so that's $\frac{8}{12}$. Right?

Sally: You could say that, but you could also say $\frac{4}{6}$ or $\frac{2}{3}$!

Mr. Todd: Good thinking! Both of you! Now, I want you to tell me something about those girls . . . something about that $\frac{2}{3}$ of the team. What fraction **of that $\frac{2}{3}$ of the team** is wearing glasses?

Juan: What? Four of them are wearing glasses. But is that supposed to be 4 out of 12, or is it 4 out of 8?

Isabel: He said, ". . . of that $\frac{2}{3}$ of the team . . ." so he's talking about 4 out of 8.

Emily: $\frac{4}{8}$ . . . That's $\frac{1}{2}$ of them.

Mr. Todd: One-half of what?

Juan: $\frac{1}{2}$ of the $\frac{2}{3}$ of the 12 team members!

Mr. Todd: Wow! That's some heavy-duty thinking. Let's go play ball now. This afternoon in math class we'll explore this some more.

Mr. Todd had used the naturally occurring situation of the fractions of the team to focus children's attention on the shifting definition of one-whole. In reference to the question about gender, "one whole group" referred to the blue team (12 members). But in reference to who was wearing glasses, "one whole group" referred to the group of girls on the team (8 members). This ability to shift the definition of one-whole is a necessary component for understanding multiplication of fractions.

After the kickball game, Mr. Todd made the following diagram on the board. He also passed out sets of different colored chips for the children to use to model their problem.

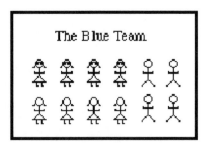

Mr. Todd: After you all get done laughing at my artwork, I want to use this diagram and those chips to go further with our discussion about the members of the blue team who are girls and are wearing glasses. Juan, you said that the glasses-wearers were $\frac{1}{2}$ of the $\frac{2}{3}$ of the 12 members of the team. Can you come to my diagram and explain what you meant?

Juan: Well, $\frac{2}{3}$ of the team are girls. That's like this:

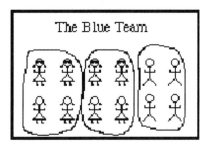

And $\frac{1}{2}$ of them wear glasses. That's like this:

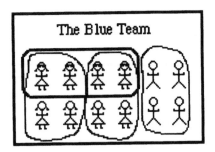

. . . so, $\frac{1}{2}$ of the $\frac{2}{3}$ of the team . . . are girls who wear glasses.

Mr. Todd: Great! Thanks! Now, I'd like you all to use the chips I've given you, and work with a partner to make a chip model of this situation.

Mr. Todd's work with this situation went on to include connections with manipulatives and symbolic written representations of the same problem. He also included work with different problems that had the same structure, and eventually different problems with a different structure.

Aside from problem situations, there is reason to believe that children who understand the first two structures for multiplying fractions can figure out this third structure on their own. Harry Bohan (1990) describes a case of a child spontaneously renaming 4 as $3\frac{3}{3}$ when attempting to solve $\frac{2}{3} \times 4$ for the first time. This child then went on to change $3\frac{3}{3}$ into the improper fraction $\frac{12}{3}$.

After working with these structures, children should be introduced to problems of fractions multiplied by whole numbers. If we continue to use the same language for multiplication, we would express $\frac{1}{4} \times 8$ as "$\frac{1}{4}$ of a time of taking 8 items." Clearly this is much less intuitive than the structures presented previously. As with other introductions, it is helpful to present a problem situation that provides a context for introducing this sort of problem.

Handling Mixed Numerals as well as Simple Fractions

Teaching children to multiply with mixed numerals does not involve teaching them anything new if they understand the relationship between whole numbers and fractions. The child who was able to "invent" $3\frac{3}{3}$ as a representation of 4 illustrates the kind of power that is available to children who have conceptual understanding of elementary mathematics. The difficulty in teaching multiplication of mixed numerals is finding a real situation through which to teach the concepts. It is much easier to use multiplication of whole numbers by mixed numerals to initiate an investigation, because real-life situations are readily available for this problem structure.

The problem $3 \times 2\frac{2}{3}$ can arise from a situation in baseball where three relief pitchers have each pitched $2\frac{2}{3}$ innings. The question of how many innings these pitchers pitched can be posed. Initially, children should be allowed to work with partners to find a solution in whatever way is sensible to them. In discussion of the various solution strategies, the teacher should help the children see the value of using the standard method of converting the mixed numeral to an improper fraction and multiplying.

After working with realistic problems of this structure, children can be challenged to find ways to solve multiplication of mixed numerals by mixed numerals. Their involvement with the invention of converting mixed numerals to improper fractions will enable them to figure out how to solve problems of this sort.

DIVISION OF FRACTIONS

Two Meanings of Division

As with division of whole numbers, division of fractions is used for solving two distinct types of problems: measurement problems and partitive problems.

MEASUREMENT DIVISION	PARTITIVE DIVISION
• Total Known	• Total Known
• Number in Each Group Known	• Number of Groups Known
• **Number of Groups (or partial groups) Unknown**	• **Number in Each Group (or size of group) Unknown**
Example: You have ½ of a cup of sugar. A cake recipe calls for ¼ of a cup of sugar. How many cakes could you make with this amount of sugar?	*Example:* You had ½ of a cup of sugar. With that sugar you were able to make 2 cakes. How much sugar went into each cake?

The first difficulty in teaching division of fractions is in presenting a realistic problem situation that calls for division of fractions. The meaning of division of fractions, and the rationale for the division of fractions algorithm, can be presented initially through a problem of dividing a whole number by a fraction.

The Hamburger Stand

The following problem was presented to a group of sixth-graders.

> Some children were preparing to sell hamburgers at the parade. They wanted to make each hamburger from ⅓ of a pound of meat. Sherry brought 4 pounds of meat. How many burgers could they make from this 4 pounds of meat? Work with your partner and find ways to show this situation. Solve it in as many different ways as you can.

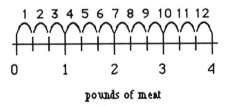

One of the groups used a number line to solve the problem. They explained that you just had to count the number of ⅓-pound jumps needed to get to 4 pounds.

After other groups had discussed their methods, the teacher modified the problem. She said that Jose brought 1½ pounds of meat. How many hamburgers of this size can be made from that? This modification led to a rich discussion of parts of a hamburger. Several of the children noted that only four full-sized hamburgers could be made. The question arose of how much of a hamburger could be made from the remaining meat. These considerations were, of course, at the heart of the teacher's modification of the problem.

In order for division of fractions to make sense to children, they must understand that the reference unit for one-whole changes depending on which number in the problem is under consideration. With the hamburger problem, $\frac{1}{3}$ refers to a unit of weight: $\frac{1}{3}$ of a pound. But at the end the children were considering a fractional unit **of a hamburger.** Eventually they would decide that the leftover meat was enough to make $\frac{1}{2}$ of a hamburger. This ability to redefine the reference unit to which a fractional amount refers is crucial to an understanding of division of fractions.

The Division Algorithm

After children have explored meaningful applications of division of fractions, attention can be focused on the division of fractions algorithm. It is not unusual for children to notice that in solving $4 \div \frac{1}{3}$, the answer, 12, is the product of 4×3. This observation should provide the springboard for a very powerful discussion. Why does multiplying the denominator by the whole number give us the answer? Does it "work" in other problems too? What is the relationship between $\frac{1}{3}$ and 3? Questions such as these can help the children construct meaning for the very obtuse division of fractions algorithm.

Handling Mixed Numerals as well as Simple Fractions

Teaching children to divide with mixed numerals need not involve teaching them anything new if they understand the relationship between whole numbers and fractions. The difficulty in teaching division of mixed numerals is that a large number of procedural steps are involved in any algorithm. For this reason, division of mixed numerals is best reserved for the middle school grades. Children of that age are more likely to be able to handle the complex procedures with understanding.

A problem of the sort "$4\frac{3}{8} \div 1\frac{1}{4}$" can arise from a situation in sewing where a piece of material $4\frac{3}{8}$ yards long is available, and pieces $1\frac{1}{4}$ yards long are needed to make a scarf. The question of how many scarves can be made can be posed. (Children should be made aware that fractions of a scarf are not normally made, but that the answer, $3\frac{1}{2}$, actually means that $3\frac{1}{2}$ scarves *could* be made.) Initially, children should be allowed to work with partners to find a solution in whatever way is sensible to them. In discussion of the various solution strategies, the teacher should help the children see

Math as Reasoning

the value of using the standard method of converting the mixed numerals to improper fractions before proceeding with the division algorithm.

SIMPLIFICATION OF MULTIPLICATION AND DIVISION

Multiplication and division of fractions with anything but the most simple fractions can quickly become unwieldy. Because of this, procedures such as "canceling" are often taught as ways of simplifying the process of multiplication. Teaching children to cancel without helping them understand the mathematics involved is not recommended. On the other hand, understanding the mathematics involved is not easy. For these reasons, teaching of cancellation is best delayed until a solid understanding of all operations with fractions has been achieved.

Although the mathematical basis for cancellation is not difficult, explanation of this mathematical basis becomes cumbersome. Consider the following:

$$\frac{2}{\cancel{3}_{1}} \times \frac{\cancel{3}^{1}}{5} = \frac{2}{5}$$

Cancellation-in-Action

$$\frac{2}{3} \times \frac{3}{5} = \frac{2 \times 3}{3 \times 5} = \frac{3 \times 2}{3 \times 5} = \frac{3}{3} \times \frac{2}{5} = 1 \times \frac{2}{5} = \frac{2}{5}$$

(commutative property)

(a name for one)

(identity element)

Cancellation "Explained"

This type of explanation makes sense to a mathematician, but would provide little or no help to a child trying to understand "why it works."

COMPUTATION WITH DECIMALS: ADDITION AND SUBTRACTION

Addition or subtraction with decimals presents nothing basically new to children who have mastered addition and subtraction of whole number and of fractions. Begin with several problems in which decimals need to be added such as: (1) John's bicycle shows that he lives .8 mile from school. How far does he ride going to and from school. (2) One day Jan rode her bicycle 3.6 miles in the morning and 5.1 miles in the afternoon. How far did she ride that day.

After the children worked these problems and "made up" several other problems they considered, they developed the idea, "You add tenths to tenths and carry just as you did with whole numbers. You use the decimal point in your sum to separate the fractions and the whole numbers."

The subtraction of decimals usually follows immediately after the teaching of decimal addition. Since there is basically little that is new to the pupils, little introductory work is need. The use of a few challenging problems is suggested. Fractions can be used as a check for both addition and subtraction with decimals.

COMPUTATION WITH DECIMALS: MULTIPLICATION AND DIVISION

With decimal multiplication and division the major problem is the placement of the decimal point. Children who have had experience with estimation will typically use this as the first method of decimal point placement. For example, with the problem, "A boy scout walks at the rate of 2.8 miles an hour. At that rate how far will he walk in 8 hours." The thinking is 2.8 is almost 3; 3 times 8 equals 24. Then 3 time 2.8 equals 224—that's 22.4 miles. After experimentation the typical adult algorithm usually emerges—"We save time by just counting the decimal places."

Division presents a more challenging problem. Again estimation can be used for a beginning. Over a period of time the following procedures can be discovered:

1. If you are dividing by a whole number the quotient is expressed in the same place as the dividend. For example, 23.56 divided by 6 the quotient is expressed in hundredths.

2. If the divisor is a decimal, multiply both divisor and dividend by a power to ten that will cause the divisor to be a whole number. For example, 24.65 divided by 2.2 become 246.5 divided by 22.

PICTORIAL FRACTION COMPARISON
Materials: Graph paper.

Draw five rectangles, one containing two blocks, one with three blocks, one with four blocks, one with five blocks, and one with six blocks. Shade in one block of each rectangle.

Below each rectangle, list what fractional part of the total is shaded.

QUESTION:
1. Are any of the above fractions identical?
2. If none of the fractions is identical, what is the major difference among them?
3. Which fraction above is the largest?
4. Which fraction above is the smallest?
5. Can you answer Questions 3 and 4 by looking at the rectangles?
6. Write the fractions for each rectangle if you shade two parts instead of one.

FRACTION BARS
Materials (per child): 4 construction-paper strips (3"-by-9") of 4 different colors.

Have children fold a blue strip into halves, mark the fold with a dark line, and write halves on the back.

Have them make fraction bars for thirds, fourths, and sixths in other colors in the same way.

Ask them to take the fourths bar and count the parts: "1, 2, 3, 4 fourths."

Now have them count the parts of the other bars.

In pairs, have children put two bars of the same color together and count the parts to see that, for example, 8 fourths is 2 wholes, 6 fourths is one whole and 2 fourths, and so on.

FRACTIONS AROUND YOU
Examples of fractions are all around you.
Materials: Blank index cards.

If there are 4 wastebaskets in the room and one of them is empty, we could say ¼ of the baskets are empty. Have the children find an example of fractions in their classroom and write a sentence to explain it.

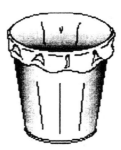

Have children work in pairs to find 8 other examples; then have them write a sentence about each.

Have each partner write 6 questions that can be answered with a fraction and then exchange questions and record answers.

WHEELS, LTD.

The rubber tread on your wheel is rated to last 800 kilometers. Your wheel bearings will wear out after 480,000 revolutions. Which will you have to replace first?

Materials: Wheels from a wagon or bicycle; cloth measuring tape.

In groups, measure the circumference of a wheel in centimeters. Then figure out how many times the wheel will go around in a kilometer.

Next figure out how many revolutions the wheel will make in 800 km.

Is this number greater than or less than the rating for your wheel bearings?

Which will you have to replace first?

GAS MILEAGE

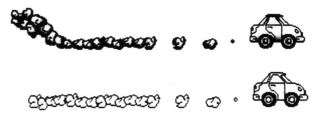

Fred's car can travel 322 miles on 17.5 gallons of gas. His friend Barney can travel 235 miles on 12.5 gallons of gas. Which car gets more miles per gallon (better gas mileage)?

SELF-TEST—HOW WOULD YOU RESPOND TO EACH OF THESE STATEMENTS?

- ____   What children know about whole numbers will be likely to confuse them when they first start learning about fractions.

- ____   Because fractions and decimals are completely different symbol systems, they should normally be kept separate so that children do not become confused.

- ____   One meaning for fractional notation is to express a division situation.

- ____   Children need to learn about Greatest Common Factors and Lowest Common Multiples in order to understand addition and subtraction of fractions.

- ____   In order to understand multiplication of fractions it is necessary to define and redefine the reference for "one-whole."

- ____   Teachers should only use rectangular regions to represent fractions.

- ____   Teachers should not stop children from multiplying two denominators in order to obtain a common denominator.

- ____   Children who rename $5\frac{3}{8}$ as $4\frac{13}{8}$ have probably developed a good understanding of whole-number subtraction.

- ____   A problem of the sort $4 \times \frac{3}{5}$ is probably more natural than a problem such as $\frac{3}{5} \times \frac{5}{8}$.

- ____   Real-life problem situations involving division of fractions are common.

SELECTED REFERENCES

Behr, M. J., Harel, G., Post T., & Lesh, R. (1992). Rational number, ratio, and proportion. In D. G. Grouws (Ed.) *Handbook of research on mathematics teaching and learning* (pp. 296–333). New York: Macmillan.

Bohan, H. (1990). Mathematical connections: Free rides for kids. *Arithmetic Teacher, 38* (3), 10–14.

Burns, M. (1987). *A collection of math lessons from grades three through six* (pp. 37–44). New Rochelle, NY: The Math Solutions Publications.

Carpenter, T. P., Corbitt, M. K., Kepner, H. S., Lindquist, M. M., & Reys, R. E. (1981). *Results from the second mathematics assessment of the National Assessment of Educational Progress.* Reston, VA: National Council of Teachers of Mathematics.

Cramer, K., & Bezuk, N. (1991). Multiplication of fractions: Teaching for understanding. *Arithmetic Teacher, 39* (3), 34–37.

Lindquist, M. M., Brown, C. A., Carpenter, T. P., Kouba, V. L., Silver, E. A., & Swafford, J. O.

(1988). *Results from the fourth mathematics assessment of the National Assessment of Educational Progress.* Reston, VA: National Council of Teachers of Mathematics.

Pothier, Y., & Sawada, D. (1990). Partitioning: An approach to fractions. *Arithmetic Teacher, 38* (4), 12–16.

Steffe, L., & Olive, J. (1991). The problem of fractions in the elementary school. *Arithmetic Teacher, 38* (9), 22–24.

9 Ratio and Proportion, Percent, and Probability and Statistics

LOOKING AHEAD

The topics of ratio, proportion, percent, probability, and statistics could just as well have been fitted into the problem-solving chapter of this book. Why? They are all applications of mathematics, and they occur widely in problem situations. It is impossible to be an informed consumer without a good working knowledge of these topics, and they are necessary for almost any mathematical application in science and social studies.

Every day the lives of both children and adults are affected by some application of these areas. Here are just a few decisions that are based on notions of probability:

- Should I take an umbrella? What is the probability of rain?

- Should I buy extra flight insurance?

- How many plants should I put in the garden? What is my experience with growth? What is the probability of germination?

- A TV commercial states, "The probability is that one of every three persons listening to me will have a stalled car at least once this winter." Another says, "Statistics show that brand X is an effective aid in the prevention of tooth decay." What do they mean?

Probability theory can be a highly abstract mathematical topic, and statistical ideas go far beyond the scope of the elementary school curriculum. Thus, the study of these two topics should be of an exploratory nature, with an emphasis on gaining insight, experimenting, and solving simple problems involving them rather than taking a formal look at probability and statistics. One of the continuing needs of the elementary mathematics program is the development of basic skills needed for life applications of mathematics and a basic understanding of these ideas. The level of the student will dictate the sophistication of computational skill obtainable in these areas.

In addition to the usefulness of these ideas themselves, they also (1) can be used to experiment, search for patterns, and generalize; (2) provide novel and interesting approaches to standard elementary school mathematics topics such as multiplication, fractions, ratio and proportion, and geometry; and (3) provide a means of practicing essential mathematical topics.

The National Council of Teachers of Mathematics *Standards* suggest close attention be given to probability and statistics. In this age of information there is an increasing need to understand and interpret data. Study a copy of *U.S.A. Today* or *The Wall Street Journal.* Note the number of charts, graphs, and statistical information. In truth, the average person encounters statistics much more in daily life than long division or computation with fractions.

The teacher should carefully consider the use of hand-held calculators in teaching these topics. It may well be that the study of ratio, proportion, and percent could involve a major emphasis on the calculator.

CAN YOU?

- Develop a group-thinking lesson on ratio by using a topic in science as the motivation?

- List four errors made in thinking about percent?

- Give reasons for the use of percent?
- Write a problem for each type of percent situation?
- Illustrate the solution to each of the problems you devised in the previous exercise by means of each of the following approaches:
   a. Decimal approach
   b. Ratio approach
   c. Unitary-analysis approach
   d. Equation approach
- Write a challenging problem using ratio and proportion?
- List five errors made in statistical interpretations?
- Develop a game for teaching one idea about probability?
- Suggest a role for calculators in application work?

RATIO AND PROPORTION

Mathematical Background

Pairs of numbers may be used to indicate a relationship between the numbers. One of the most useful relations is the ratio of one number to another. The ratio of the number 3 to the number 4 is the quotient $3 \div 4$. In former times this relationship was written 3:4 (three is to four). Today ratios are sometimes written in the form of a fractional numeral ($\frac{3}{4}$) or as an ordered pair (3,4). The concept of sets provides a helpful method of studying ratio. The ratio is considered to express a numerical property that exists between two sets. For example, if apples are sold at two for 5¢, the relationship between sets of apples and pennies may be shown in this way:

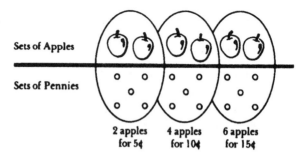

Sets of Apples

Sets of Pennies

2 apples for 5¢   4 apples for 10¢   6 apples for 15¢

The greatest use of ratios in problem solving involves finding the equivalent ratio or proportion. The statement $\frac{3}{4} = \frac{6}{8}$ expresses a proportionality relationship and may be read "3 is to 4 as 6 is to 8." An infinite set of equivalent ratios such as $\{\frac{1}{2}, \frac{2}{4}, \frac{3}{6}, \frac{4}{8}, \dots \frac{n}{2n}\}$ can be generated. This set is representative of a proportionality relationship.

Illustrated procedures for teaching proportions are developed later in this chapter.

TEACHING RATIO AND PROPORTION

Ratio involves matching sets in one-to-one, one-to-many, many-to-one, or many-to-many correspondence. A proportion is a statement of equality between two ratios. Primary-grade teachers can begin to develop pupils' understanding of ratio by using sets of objects, the flannel board, and the chalkboard. Several possible situations and their representations are shown in Figure 9-1.

Children should be provided with many laboratory activities involving the use of objects and/or graphs to find the solution to problems of ratio and proportion. Several such situations are described briefly next.

The children were given four or five small nut cups and a bag of large lima beans. They were given the tasks of (1) finding how many beans it took to fill a nut cup and (2) after agreeing on what they meant by "fill," finding the number it would take to fill two nut cups, three nut cups, five nut cups, and so on. The following chart was given to them to develop a pattern for solution:

Number of nut cups	1	2	3	4	5	6	7	8
Number of lima beans	7	14						

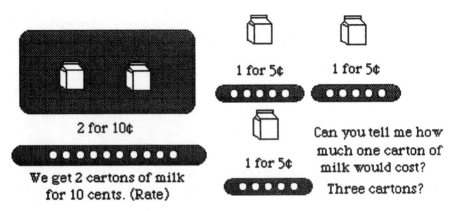

Figure 9-1   Depictions of Ratios

Then they were to find the information in as many ways as possible (working in groups of three).

JOE'S GROUP:

PHYLLIS'S GROUP: We used two number lines.

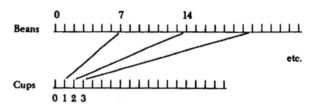

JANE'S GROUP: We used the number line to indicate 1 for 7. We marked off another 7 for two cups and still another for three cups. By this time, we had a pattern.

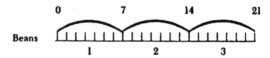

A teacher using these ideas may want to begin with a problem situation concerned with the planning for a party. The lima beans are about the same size as jelly beans, and the problem could involve the number of jelly beans needed to fill nut cups for the class and/or visitors.

Another teacher presented sticks 10 cm, 20 cm, 30 cm, 40 cm, and 50 cm in length. Each group of four or five children was provided with a set and was given a sheet of paper like that shown below. They went out on the playground on a sunny day and recorded their data. Then the teacher suggested that they use their pattern to determine the height of several taller objects; for example, a basketball pole, a high fence pole, a tree, the school building.

HEIGHT OF STICK IN CENTIMETERS	LENGTH OF SHADOW IN CENTIMETERS
0	
10	_____
20	_____
30	_____
40	_____
50	_____

Another teacher used a study of levers from the science book:

The Cross-Products Approach

Knowing that the cross-products of two equivalent ratios are equal can be a valuable tool in problem solving. In looking for an unknown such as N in $\frac{2}{3} = \frac{N}{21}$, the cross-products are $3N$ and 42. Written as an equation, this becomes $3N = 42$. Pupils can then find the value of N by dividing both sides of the equation by 3, since this does not affect the equality. Thus, $\frac{3N}{3} = \frac{42}{3}$, and $N = 14$.

The cross-products idea can be developed in the following manner. Pupils had been working on sets of equivalent number pairs:

$$\left\{\frac{1}{2}, \frac{2}{4}, \dots, \frac{N}{2N}\right\} \left\{\frac{2}{3}, \frac{4}{-}, \frac{6}{-}, \frac{-}{12}\right\}$$

$$\left\{\frac{5}{9}, \frac{10}{18}, \dots, \frac{5N}{9N}\right\} \left\{\frac{3}{4}, ?, ?, ?, ?\right\}$$

They had found other members of the set by multiplying or dividing the members of the set by a form of the identity element, such as $\frac{3}{3}$ or $\frac{4}{4}$. Then the teacher said, "Let's study a few equivalent number pairs and see if we can find any relationship between them. Look at $\frac{1}{2} = \frac{2}{4}$, $\frac{3}{4} = \frac{6}{8}$, $\frac{2}{3} = \frac{4}{6}$. Do you notice any similarities? Work with these number pairs during your spare time and see what you can discover. Test your findings on other equivalent number pairs. We'll discuss your findings tomorrow."

The next day the members of the class discussed their findings. The majority of the pupils had found that the products of numerator (first pair) times denominator (second pair) and denominator (first pair) times numerator (second pair) were equal. They had verified their findings by testing a large number of instances. The teacher said, "You've discovered a valuable tool for working with number pairs. The equality that you've just mentioned is usually stated, 'The cross-products of two equivalent number pairs are equal.' What do we mean by *cross-products*?" The pupils discussed the meaning of cross-products; then they were given several verbal problems with instructions to see if they could use the cross-product development as recorded below.

1. The pull of gravity on the moon is $\frac{1}{6}$ the pull of gravity on the earth. A track champion can high-jump 7 feet on the earth. What would be the height of a bar he or she could clear on the moon? (all other things being equal)?

$$\text{Proportion: } \tfrac{1}{6} = \tfrac{7}{N} \qquad\qquad \text{Cross-products: } 1 \times N = 6 \times 7$$
$$N = 42$$

2. A large gear turns three times while a small gear turns 15 times. How many times will the large gear turn if the small gear turns 60 times?

Proportion: $\tfrac{3}{15} = \tfrac{N}{60}$

Cross-products:

$3 \times 60 = 15 \times N$

$15N = 180$

$\tfrac{15N}{15} = \tfrac{180}{15}$

$N = 12$

Analysis

Ratio and proportion can be valuable tools for verbal problem solving in the elementary school. The task for today's teachers is to establish a balance in teaching topics, for it is possible to overdo ratio in the manner of the late 1800s. It should be used only as one possible tool in problem solving.

PERCENT

Percent has been taught as another means of viewing decimals. Actually, percents were used long before decimals were developed. The term *percent* is derived from the Latin *per centum*, meaning "by the hundred." Thus, the origin of percent and its major uses are more closely associated with rates and ratio than with decimals.

Many believe that the teaching of percent should cause little if any difficulty because of the close relationship of percents, ratios, and decimals. Those experienced in teaching the upper elementary grades often disagree with this conjecture. There are several reasons why the topic of percent often does confuse children and adults, among which are its languages.

Foundation Work

Computation with percent is not usually developed until the fifth or sixth grade. However, an understanding of the theory of percent is necessary earlier to ensure proper interpretation of social studies, science materials, and situations outside of school. The meaning of "percent" can be introduced effectively at the fourth-grade level by using materials from science and social studies. One teacher introduced percent by saying, "In your social studies book, you read today that 8 out of 10, or 80 percent, of the population of an African country live along the coast or rivers. What is meant by 80 percent?"

In class discussion, pupils judged that 80 percent must be equivalent to 8 per 10. Also, they felt that the term *cent* must have something to do with 100. Because they knew that 80 per 100 and 8 per 10 were equivalent ratios, they reasoned that 80 percent meant 80 per 100.

Several other examples from science and social studies were then used for interpretation: "The United States once produced 40 percent of the world's steel. Now the United States produces 17 percent of the world's steel." "Major auto-leasing firms expected a 15 to 20 percent gain in summer volume over last year's activity. Instead, they posted a 20 to 30 percent advance." "Foreigners now buy almost 40 percent of London's theater tickets."

From the discussion of these and other situations that use percent, the pupils decided that percent means per hundred or by the hundred. Then they checked reference books to verify their thinking, and they read up on the historical development of percent.

Since many percent ideas occur in daily life before decimals are introduced in the school curriculum, it is important to provide children with some way of visualizing the meaning of percent. One of the best devices is squared paper. Individual children can use 10-by-10 pieces of squared paper to indicate various percents. Through this device, the percent can also be interpreted as a fraction. For example,

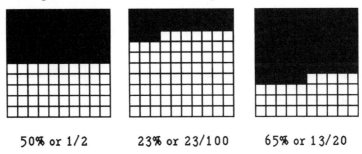

50% or 1/2   23% or 23/100   65% or 13/20

Problems Involving Percent

The majority of problem situations that employ percent involve three problem structures.

1. The pupils may be asked to find the percent of a number; for example, "What is 25 percent of 64?"

2. The pupils may be asked to find what percent one number is of another; for example, "What percent of 64 is 16?"

3. The pupils may be asked to find the total (100 percent) when only a percent is known; for example, "Sixteen is 25 percent of what number?"

Several approaches can be used to solve percent problems that occur in the literature of elementary school mathematics. Among these are (1) the decimal approach, (2) the ratio approach, (3) the unitary-analysis approach, and (4) the equation approach. Pupils' thinking in the solution of each of the three problem structures is presented below for each of the approaches; then a teaching sequence is suggested.

The following problems are solved by using each approach:

1. During a sale, a 5 percent reduction is given on all merchandise. How much would a 40¢ item be reduced?

2. Joe won two games out of the five games he played. What percent of the games did he win?

3. Mr. Brown sold a garden cart for $150. This was 75 percent of the regular price. What was the regular price?

Decimal Approach

In using the decimal approach, the pupil thinks, "Percent means hundredths. I change percent to a decimal and then work the problem."

PROBLEM 1

Pupil: I am to find 5 percent of 40. I change 5 percent to .05 because percent means hundredths. Then I multiply .05 × 40 to obtain the answer of 2.

PROBLEM 2

Pupil: I am trying to find what percent 2 is of 5. This is 2 to 5. I need to change this to hundredths. Percent means hundredths.

$$\begin{array}{r} .40 \\ 5\overline{)2.00} \end{array}$$

Therefore, .40, or 40 percent.

PROBLEM 3

Pupil: Seventy-five percent means .75. To find the whole when I know a part, I must divide the number by the decimal.

$$\begin{array}{r} 200 \\ .75\overline{)150.00} \end{array}$$

Ratio Approach

All problems are solved by developing a pair of equivalent ratios, with a place holder representing the number sought. This approach employs the idea that percent means per hundred, implying a rate.

PROBLEM 1

Pupil: Five percent is absent, which means 5 per 100 are absent. The ratio per 40 will be equivalent to the ratio per 100. Thus I set up equivalent ratios to solve the problem.

$$\frac{5}{100} = \frac{N}{40} \quad 100N = 200 \quad N = 2$$

(For the early work, the student developed equivalent number pairs. Later, he or she may use the equality of the cross-products.)

PROBLEM 2

Pupil: Joe won two games per five played. Now I must find out how many he would win per 100.

$$\frac{2}{5} = \frac{N}{100} \quad 5N = 200 \quad N = 40$$

This means 40 per 100, or 40 percent.

PROBLEM 3

Pupil: I'm to find the number of which $150 is 75 percent. Or, $150 is 75 percent of what number? I think 75 to 100 is equal to $150 to N.

$$\frac{75}{100} = \frac{150}{N} \quad 75N = 15,000 \quad N = 200$$

To use the ratio approach, the pupils must understand ratio and proportion and be able to solve simple equations. Actually, these are not difficult to understand. Pupils should be solving simple equations and working with some ratios by the fourth-grade level. If they have not studied ratio by the time percent begins, it is quite possible to teach ratio and percent simultaneously. The use of ratio eliminates the need for previous study of decimal computation.

Unitary-Analysis Approach
The unitary-analysis approach, sometimes called the 1 percent method, was once very popular in schools in the United States. It has some advantages, particularly for the slower student, because it is easily understood and requires similar thinking for all three types of problems.

PROBLEM 1

Pupil: I want to find 5 percent of 40.

First I'll find what 1 percent would be, then I'll multiply that by 5.

One percent is one-one hundredth, so I can find 1 percent by dividing 40 by 100.

$$100\overline{)40.0}^{\,.4}$$

One percent of 40 is .4.

Five percent of 40 is $5 \times .4 = 2$.

PROBLEM 2

Pupil: I'm finding what percent 2 is of 5.

5 games = 100% of the total

1 game is one-fifth of that; I can find that by dividing by five. $\frac{100\%}{5} =$ 20% of the total

2 games = $2 \times 20\% = 40\%$

PROBLEM 3

Pupil: I'm to find what number 150 is 75 percent of.

75 percent of the number is 150.

I can find 1 percent of the number by dividing by 75: $\left(75\overline{)150}^{\,2}\right)$ 1 percent of the number is 2.

100 percent of the number is 100×2. The number is 200.

The solution of these problems by unitary analysis reveals several weaknesses of the method. Solution of type-1 problems often requires rather difficult division of decimals. (The teacher may decide that the use of a calculator is an appropriate way to overcome this.) Also, note the cumbersome development in problems 1 and 2. Probably the chief use of unitary analysis is in type-3 problems, because unitary analysis does add understanding to this problem structure. In spite of these difficulties, many children prefer this method to any of the others.

Equation Approach

The equation approach makes use of the logical thinking required for unitary analysis. It also has some of the features of the formula. The writing of the mathematical sentence required in the equation approach ties it closely to the type of mathematical thinking wanted in problem solving.

PROBLEM 1

Pupil: The essential mathematical statement is, "Find 5 percent of 40," or, "What number is equal to 5 percent of 40?" Now I translate the statement into a mathematical sentence.

$$N = 5\% \times 40 \left(5\% \text{ is equivalent to .05, or } \frac{5}{100}\right)$$
$$N = .05 \times 40$$
$$N = 2$$

PROBLEM 2

Pupil: The essential mathematical question is: Two is what percent of 5? I write this as a mathematical sentence.

$$2 = N \times 5$$
$$2 = 5N \text{ (I divide both sides of the equation by 5.)}$$
$$\frac{2}{5} = N$$
$$\frac{2}{5} = .40 = 40\% = N$$

PROBLEM 3

Pupil: I have to find the regular price when I know 75 percent of the regular price. A mathematical statement might be: 75 percent of the number equals 150. Now I write a mathematical sentence.

$$75\% \times N = 150 \text{ (75\% is equivalent to .75)}$$
$$.75N = 150 \text{ (I divide both sides of the equation by .75)}$$
$$N = \frac{150}{.75}$$
$$N = 200$$

The format of the equation approach becomes similar to that of the decimal approach, but the equation approach places greater emphasis on the structure of the problem and an understanding of the rationale.

Analysis

The teaching of a variety of approaches for solving percent problems is a way of accommodating for individual differences. One child may find the unitary-analysis approach to be "friendly," and may prefer to use only that approach. Another child may prefer to emphasize the equation approach. One of the authors has observed children seeking help knowing when to use one approach over another. These children should be reassured that whichever approach makes sense to them is appropriate to try using for that problem.

It may be that future research will suggest that for most children one of these approaches is more intuitive and should be emphasized. Or, research may suggest a preferred sequence in terms of teaching the three types of percent problems. Given our present level of understanding about how children construct the necessary cognitive structures for understanding percent problems, however, it seems prudent to offer instruction in each of these approaches to solving each of the three types of percent problems sometime before high school.

GOALS IN TEACHING PROBABILITY AND STATISTICS

What are the major topics in probability and statistics that should be taught in the elementary school? As yet, a body of subject matter in these areas has not emerged as dominant to the school mathematics program.

The National Council of Teachers of Mathematics *Standards* (1989) suggest the following topics for probability and statistics in the elementary program.

For kindergarten through grade 4:

1. Collect, organize, and describe data.

2. Construct, read, and interpret displays of data.

3. Formulate and solve problems that involve collecting and analyzing data.

4. Explore concepts of chance.

For grades 5 through 8:

1. Systematically collect, organize, and describe data.

2. Construct, read, and interpret tables, charts, and graphs.

3. Make inferences and convincing arguments based on data analysis.

4. Develop an appreciation for statistical methods as powerful means for decision making.

5. Model situations by divising and carrying out experiments or simulations to determine probabilities.

6. Model situations by constructing a sample space to determine probabilities.

7. Appreciate the power of using a probability mode through comparison of experimental results with mathematical expectations.

8. Make predictions based on experimental or mathematical probabilities.

9. Develop an appreciation for the pervasive use of probability in the real world.

TEACHING PROBABILITY AND STATISTICS

Descriptive Statistics

Charts and Graphs

The development of graphs can begin as early as the kindergarten level, with the children surveying their favorite TV programs and using colored blocks to record their findings. As the children progress up the ladder of mathematical understanding, the line-segment graph, pictograph, and circle graph can be introduced. Thus, various types of graphs should be developed, and the relationship between them should be understood.

In all cases, it is important that the first thing children learn is to develop the graph, not to read it. Current instructions often reverse this process, but it is more natural and effective if a situation is first used in which children must develop a graph. Current cognitive theory suggests that graphic representations of data are seen very differently by children than they are by adults. "Teaching" children to read graphs before they have learned to produce graphs is likely to lead to confusion and unanticipated misconceptions about graphs.

Technology

With the computer technology available today, it is not usually a wise use of school time to teach children the laborious details of constructing graphs and charts by hand. After an initial experience in which children make a prototype by hand, they should be introduced whenever possible to one or two of the more basic graphing software packages that can put tabular data into a variety of graphic forms. (Many of the better spreadsheet programs as well as integrated software packages have this capability.) Instruction can then focus on the higher-level skills of synthesis and evaluation as children decide what data are best presented graphically and which format most effectively communicates the desired information.

During the course of teaching graphs, the following generalizations should apply:

1. Pictographs, although they are the simplest type to read, give only an approximation of the data. Care must be taken to ensure that the pictographs actually are representative. For instance, one picture can represent 10,000 cars, and two pictures of the same size can accurately represent twice as many. However, the use of a picture of one car to represent 10,000 cars and another that is twice as high to represent 20,000 cars is misleading, because the area of the second drawing is about four times that of the first.

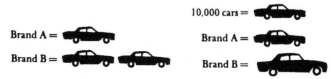

Sales: Brand A = 10,000; Brand B = 20,000

2. The bar graph, while not quite as easy to read as the pictograph, is easier to construct accurately. The bars in a graph normally should be of a constant width. Thus, the area of the bar is proportional to its frequency. Bar graphs can be misleading if units are compressed or extended and if zero is not the starting point.

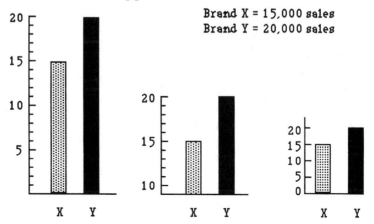

Brand X = 15,000 sales
Brand Y = 20,000 sales

3. Line-segment graphs should be used only when there is a continued trend from one point to the next one. For example, the yearly per capita income in a country in 1960 was $2,000 and in 1980 was $2,500. If there had been a constant increase each year between 1960 and 1980, the line segment connecting the points for 1960 and 1980 would be helpful. If, however, the income had been $1,800 in 1975, the line segment connecting 1960 and 1980 would be misleading. Also, as is the case with bar graphs, line-segment graphs may be misleading if the scale is mixed or if the starting point is not zero. Line-segment graphs are often called *frequency polygons*.

4. A circle graph is particularly helpful if percentages totaling 100 are being graphed or when the graph deals with parts of a whole. A knowledge of angle measurement and decimal division is necessary for the construction of circle graphs without a computer.

5. On occasion it is desirable to use a combination of the formats described previously in constructing a graph. The general impression is conveyed by the pictograph. An accurate assessment can be made by the bar graph.

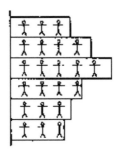

Measures of Central Tendency
Mode

The mode is probably the easiest of the measures of central tendency to introduce. It is simply the value of the category that occurs the greatest number of times. It should be noted that some sets of data have no mode, and other sets of data have more than a single mode. An easy way for children to observe the mode is to have them produce a histogram of their data. The "highest bar" on their graph is the mode. After children become familiar with the mode, they can easily record the value for the mode on their histogram. One example follows. The mode is 24.

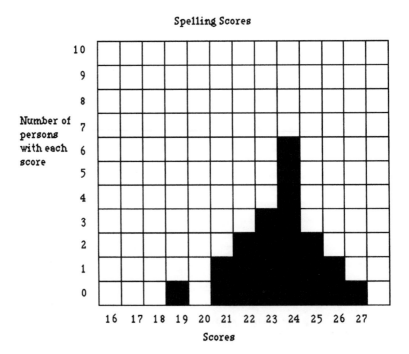

Spelling Scores

Median

The median is the middle value when the data are presented in ascending or descending order. For example, Bill went fishing each day for a week. His catches were 0, 2, 3, 4, 8, 5, and 1. What was a typical day's catch? If children have experience with the mode, they can see that there is not a modal catch. Often children will suggest counting "halfway up" (after arranging the numbers in order: 0, 1, 2, 3, 4, 5, 8) to find a typical catch. In this case, the median would be 3. After many experiences finding the median, children can record both median and mode on their graphs. They soon discover that if there are an even number of observations, it is necessary to "split the difference." For example, with 1, 3, 5, 6, the median is 4.

Mean

The arithmetic mean, often called the *average*, is used to calculate batting averages, test averages, and the majority of measures of central tendencies reported in newspapers. Too often, the mean is thought of as simply adding up the scores and dividing by the number of scores. Although this does produce the average, children need experience at the manipulative level before arriving at the algorithm. One teacher used this lab sheet:

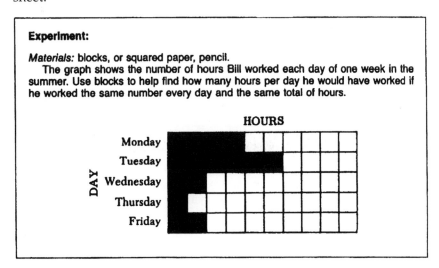

Experiment:

Materials: blocks, or squared paper, pencil.
   The graph shows the number of hours Bill worked each day of one week in the summer. Use blocks to help find how many hours per day he would have worked if he worked the same number every day and the same total of hours.

There were several similar averaging problems on the lab sheet. The typical approach taken by the children follows:

Claudia: I set out blocks to stand for 1 hour of work. Then I moved the blocks for the days when he worked more time to the days that he worked less time to make them all the same. At that rate, he would have worked 3 hours a day.

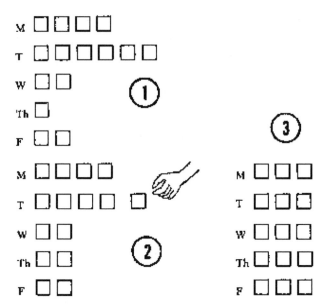

After many manipulative experiences such as this, the children should experiment to find a more rapid, mathematical method of finding the mean.

Since variations in the value of the measures can affect the mean, children should have some opportunities to analyze differing situations that produce the same mean. For example, one teacher said, "Two star running backs each have a 5-yard rushing average. I'll show you the data on the runs they have made. Which one would you choose to run if you needed three yards on a third-down play late in the game? Why?"

Jones	5	4	6	7	7	4	6	5	5	5	avg: 5 yds.
Smith	10	2	3	0	15	0	0	5	10	5	avg: 5 yds.

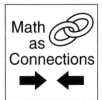

Math as Connections

The children agreed that they would use Jones, since he could be depended on to pick up short yardage consistently. Smith would be used in a situation where they needed longer yardage and could afford more risk. (The notion of risk is a foundational concept for teaching about probability, and will be returned to in later probability lessons. The teacher need not make a formal introduction here, but can refer back to the football problem when probability is more formally introduced.)

During the work on measures of central tendencies, the following generalizations should be developed and emphasized:

1. An incorrect selection of the measure of average used can often distort facts. For example, the mean yearly family income of a certain community is $60,000. But there is one very wealthy person in the community who earns several thousand dollars a day on investments. The median

Increasing

Abstraction

yearly family income of this community is $18,000. The modal yearly family income is $16,000. If the mean income were used in reporting, the type of community could be completely misgauged.

2. The mean provides some features that the median and the mode do not. The mean of a number of means can be taken by the add-and-divide method and be accurate. The mode of a group of modes or the median of a group of medians is not necessarily the actual mode or median of the entire group.

3. The mean is affected by extreme measures on either side of the scale, as the average income of the community described in generalization 1 illustrates. (Economists usually avoid using mean income, preferring instead to use median income, for this reason.)

4. The mode, median, and mean are each appropriate in different circumstances. Circumstances that involve a vote of some sort are suited to the mode. Circumstances where extremes would distort the mean are suited to the median. Circumstances that tend to be fairly stable are suited to the mean.

Critical Analysis

Present-day reporting of statistics is often sketchy, and in some cases the devices used to obtain the statistics are questionable. Analysis of newspaper reports, advertising, and magazine articles can be helpful in developing a spirit of "proceed with caution" among elementary school pupils. When a report states that three out of four doctors interviewed favored a certain medicinal product, pupils should think, "I wonder how many doctors they asked, and how they decided which doctors to ask." It might by possible that they surveyed only the staff doctors working for the company. Also, did they survey medical doctors or people with Ph.D.s? A historian may not be a good authority on the quality of medicinal products.

Analysis of statistical reports is a fascinating project for elementary school pupils. They enjoy looking at reports and raising questions. This is good; however, the teacher should take care that pupils do not become so critical that they no longer consider any information at all accurate. A good start for looking at statistical misinformation is the classic paperback book by Darrell Huff, *How to Lie with Statistics.* The teacher can find a number of examples of common statistical errors. Common errors that can be detected by elementary school pupils include:

1. A shift in definitions. For example, at one point, the writers may use the *mean* as the average, and, at another point, the *median.*

2. Inappropriate comparisons. For example, a small manufacturer may report, "We have the fastest growing sales record in the industry." This might be based on the fact that in one year, the company sold 250

machines, and during the next year, it sold 500 machines. In the meantime, a large producer of the machine may have increased its sales from 250,000 to 450,000. The first company has increased sales by a greater percentage than the second company, but its claim does not mean much.

3. Inaccurate measurement. In any statistical treatment, an inaccurate measurement may cause enough difference to affect the results greatly.

4. An inappropriate method of selecting a sample. [See section on sampling.]

5. Technical errors.

6. Misleading charts. [See section on charts and graphs.]

Probability

With Odds and Without Odds

The teacher gave each group of four children an opaque paper bag in which were 10 yellow marbles and 20 red marbles (different-colored counters of any type could be used). The teacher said, "We're going to play a guessing game for a while. Each of you get out a sheet of paper to keep track of your right and wrong guesses. In the bag there are some marbles. Some are yellow and some are red. Guess a color and, without looking, take out a marble. Mark your guess right or wrong on the paper. Put the marble back in the bag and have another child in your group follow the same procedure. You can use a chart like this [drawn on the chalkboard or overhead]."

R=RED Y=YELLOW	JILL
GUESS	COLOR DRAWN
1. Y	R
2. R	R
3. R	Y

After the children had played the guessing game for about 10 minutes, the teacher asked, "How did your guessing come out? What color did you guess right most often?" The children said that after a short time, they had always guessed red, since they seemed to draw a red marble much more often than a yellow marble. The teacher suggested drawing a graph of their group experiences to get an idea of the mix of yellow and red marbles.

Each of the graphs formed a similar pattern. The teacher then said, "Before we played this game, I put 30 marbles in each of the paper bags. We're going to count them to see how many are yellow and how many are red. But first I'd like to have you guess the number of each color that are in the bags."

Several different guesses were made, but the majority of the children guessed 10 yellow and 20 red.

The next day the small groups used the same set of marbles in the bags. The teacher presented these rules for the guessing game: "There are twice as many red marbles as there are yellow ones. So let's score points somewhat differently. If you score two points for every correct guess of yellow, how many points do you think you should score for every correct guess of red?"

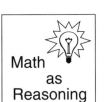

Math as Reasoning

After some discussion and argument, the children arrived at the notion that since there were twice as many red marbles, they should probably only score one point. The game was played in a way similar to that of the first day.

There are many activities and laboratories that can be developed as readiness for probability ideas. Thus, the children should have many experiences similar to the one just discussed.

Later the teacher gave the children a bag with 100 lima beans: 25 with a red dot, 50 without any marking, and 25 with a blue dot. The children worked in groups of three, with instructions to take turns drawing 10 lima beans, record their draw on a graph, return the beans to the sack, and repeat the procedure. In addition to the individual graphs of the draws, each group was to make a continuous graph (a long-run relative-frequency distribution).

Basic Probability Ideas

Difference between Odds and Probability

After the children had conducted a wide variety of experiments involving guessing the outcome of events, the teacher used the following discussion to pinpoint some of the ideas involved in the experiments and games. (Note: More than one day should be used to present the material that follows; also, there should be some experimentation at various points in the development.)

The teacher stated, "Today we're going to be drawing a name out of the hat to see who will be the leader of the lunch line. How many do we have here today?—Thirty-three. Each person's name will appear once. What is the probability of Hank's getting to be first in line?"

The pupils responded that they felt that he had one chance out of 33, or $\frac{1}{33}$. The class members admitted that they were somewhat hazy as to the meaning of the question, "What is the probability of?" To clarify this concept to a certain extent but to avoid treating the definition formally, the teacher asked several questions. Often a debate as to the answer followed. The questions were the following.

1. You said that the probability of Hank's getting to go first was $\frac{1}{33}$. Does this mean that were I to draw a name from the hat 33 times (we put the name back in after every draw), Hank would be sure to win at least once?—No.

2. Would he probably win at least once?—Yes.

3. Were we to draw 66 names (replacing the name after each draw), would Hank win 2 times?—Not necessarily. He might, but he might not.

4. Were we to draw 660 names out of the hat, would Hank ever have to win?—No, but he probably would.

5. From 1, 3, 5, 7, 9, 11, 15, picking a number at random, what is the probability of choosing a number less than 8? Of 5 or more? $\frac{4}{7}$, $\frac{5}{7}$.

From this discussion the class may move to a topic such as coin tossing or opinion sampling. Introductory remarks and possible questions and answers are given in the material that follows.

The teacher said, "We can get a better idea of probability if we try to answer a few more questions and then do some experiments."

1. One of you registers six times for a drawing on a bicycle. There are 2,567 tickets in the drawing. What is the *probability* that you will win? Answer: $\frac{6}{2,567}$. What are the *odds* that you will win? Answer: $\frac{6}{2,561}$.

2. There are 16 girls and 17 boys in our class. What would be the *probability* of drawing a girl's name from a hat containing the names of all class members? Answer: $\frac{16}{33}$. What would be the *odds* of drawing a girl's name from a hat containing the names of all class members? Answer: $\frac{16}{17}$.

3. Bill knew that the answer to a social studies question was either Washington or Lincoln. He decided to pick one of the names at random. He said, "The odds are 50 to 50 that I will be right." What was the probability he would be right? Answer: $\frac{1}{2}$. Discussion should bring out the idea that the *odds* of success are the ratio of chances of success to chances of failure—in Bill's case, 1 to 1. However, the *probability* of success is

$$\frac{\text{chances of success}}{\text{chances of failure} + \text{chances of success}}.$$

After similar questions, the teacher concluded the lesson. The next day, each pupil was given a penny and asked to state the number of heads they would expect in 100 tosses. The children responded that they would expect about 50. Several groups then tossed the coin 100 times and recorded their findings. The outcome was close to 50 in many cases, but not 50 in any of the cases. The teacher used questions to emphasize that although the probability of heads was $\frac{1}{2}$, heads would not necessarily come up half the time. Children then used ten coins to record the result of 1,000 throws. They found that as the number of throws increased, the number of heads thrown more closely approximated the predicted proportion.

Teacher Note: For most children (and many adults), formal notions of probability are in conflict with intuitive notions that they hold. For example, many people mistakenly believe that after a series of coin tosses that have all come up heads there is a greater than 1 in 2 probability of tossing tails on the next toss. These intuitive notions are not simply replaced when the teacher provides experiences and discussions about the more formal "correct" understandings about probability. A wise teacher will elicit predictions from children about how they expect events to occur. The children's predictions will be based on their intuitive notions. When events follow that do not conform to the predictions, the teacher can use this as an opportunity to challenge the intuitive notions that led to the prediction. When a child comes face-to-face with the conflict between his ideas and observed events, there is a greater likelihood that he will be willing to modify his ideas to fit the observed events.

Sampling with a Paddle

One day the teacher brought in a fishbowl filled with red and blue marbles and presented this situation: "At election time, a prediction of the election results is often desired. Let's assume that the blue marbles represent people who are for one candidate and the red ones represent those who are for the other. How could we get an idea of the election outcome without counting all the marbles?"

Pupils suggested that a sample of the marbles could be taken, and they discussed an appropriate method for doing this. The discussion emphasized the term *random sample*. (A random sample is one drawn in such a way that every possible combination of the given size has an equal chance of being selected.)

A paddle constructed of plywood (see illustration) was used to dip into the bowl to select a sample.

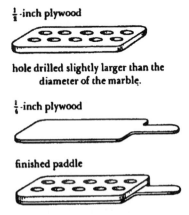

$\frac{1}{2}$-inch plywood

hole drilled slightly larger than the diameter of the marble.

$\frac{1}{4}$-inch plywood

finished paddle

Five samples were drawn, and the following results were obtained. (Each sample was returned to the bowl before drawing the next. If this is not done, the result is inaccurate.)

RED	BLUE
8	2
7	3
6	4
6	4
7	3
34	16

The pupils estimated that the candidate represented by the red marbles would probably win by something like a 2-to-1 margin. (There were actually 800 red marbles and 400 blue marbles in the fish bowl.)

At this point the teacher directed questions to the class concerning the basis of obtaining a good sample. The sampling of people in political and other surveys was emphasized, and the need for a *representative sample* was stressed. (A representative sample matches the population from which the sample is drawn. For example, it would be poor sampling procedure to take an entire national survey from among only people living in small towns.) Some of the generalizations reached were these:

1. Each individual (or object, etc.) should have some known probability of being selected; for example, $1/23,000$ in a sample of voters in a community. The choice of one is not dependent on the choice of another.

2. The sample should be taken by some automatic or prescribed means. It should avoid bias toward or against any portion of the population.

3. There should be some kind of randomness in the selection.

From this discussion, the class may move to a topic such as coin tossing or examining the population of children in the school. When each group had surveyed its sample, the findings were graphed. Then the graphs were compared.

Sampling Using the Tracer Technique

An interesting laboratory can be developed by using the tracer technique. The idea is often used in checking wildlife populations, insect life, and so on. The technique is to introduce a number of "labeled" animals into a population of animals that cannot easily be counted. For example, 30 banded cardinals were released in an area in which the approximate population of cardinals was of interest to scientists. The observers kept track of the proportion of cardinals banded. Thus, if after many observations the ratio of banded to nonbanded cardinals was 1 to 10, the scientists would approximate the cardinal population to be about 330 (300 nonbanded and 30 banded).

In the classroom, the teacher used a larger bag with 200 blue marbles, and the children took turns drawing a marble and replacing it. After a number of draws and the making of a graph of the draws, the children felt reasonably sure that all the marbles were blue. The teacher then asked, "How could we find out about how many blue marbles there are without counting them all?" After several suggestions that did not prove productive, the teacher related the technique used with the cardinals. Then several of the children suggested putting 20 red marbles in the bag, shaking it up, and then drawing samples of 10 marbles 10 times. Other children noted that it would be very important to replace the marbles after each draw and to be very sure that the marbles were completely mixed up.

The children made the table shown from the results of drawings. Then they found the average number of red to blue marbles and predicted that there were about 200 blue marbles in the bag, after which they counted the marbles to check their result.

	MARBLE COLOR	
DRAW	RED	BLUE
1	0	10
2	1	9
3	0	10
4	2	8
5	1	9
6	0	10
7	2	8
8	1	9
9	0	10
10	2	8
Totals:	9	91

At the end of this activity, groups of four children were each given 200 marbles (any different-colored counters could be used) and allowed to place any multiple of 25 marbles in the bag. Each group then traded bags with another group and used the tracer technique to estimate the number of marbles in the bag. Later, similar activities were conducted.

Other Explorations

The following ideas are given for the development of activities dealing with probability and statistics. What teaching strategies could be used with each? What ideas does each develop?

1. Make a survey of vehicles (cars, trucks, or buses, for example). Possible information for graphing the data: make, year, color, time of day for

survey, location of street for survey, day of week for survey, length of time for count, weather at time of count, direction of traffic flow, streets two-way or one-way, etc.

2. Find the frequency of letters in use in the English language. Questions to be considered: What books should be surveyed? How many letters would make a good sample? What type of table would best describe the information? How could this information be used to develop simple codes? How could it be used to break a code? (*Note:* See *The Gold Bug* by Edgar Allan Poe for an interesting detective story using this technique.)

3. Conduct the same type of survey on the length of English words.

4. How many different phone numbers can be generated from the typical seven-digit sequence? Why are there more area codes in highly populated areas?

5. Study the newspapers for a week. What surveys are reported? How much information is given on each? What are the strengths and weaknesses of each survey?

6. Develop the idea that there may be physical properties of objects that cause bias. Use variously biased spinners and compare the actual outcome with predicted outcomes.

Technology

Computers

There are a number of computer-assisted instruction programs that simulate probability situations, generate random happenings, or present problem situations related to probability. See the references in "Selected References" at the end of the chapter. You can also see some fascinating work on the world wide web at The Math Forum: http://forum.swarthmore.edu.

Analysis

Once pupils have mastered the basic ideas of sampling, graphing, averages, and so on, a variety of statistical projects may be undertaken. A survey of the TV interests of an elementary school is one such project. The following steps were used in one such survey:

1. The class agreed upon the nature of the problem: "What are the television viewing interests of the pupils in our school?"

2. The class discussed the selection of a "representative sample" of the school. (It was agreed that surveying every student would be too time-consuming. Also, the pupils wanted to test sampling techniques.) A sample was selected.

3. An appropriate method of gathering data was decided upon.

4. The data were gathered.

5. Interpretations were made from the data.

With activities such as those described in this chapter, extreme care should be taken to make the pupils aware of the difficulties that arise in statistical work and the inaccuracies that may occur. For example, in one fifth grade, the pupils thought they could report the reading interests of fifth graders in general (throughout the United States) from a sample taken in one community of 1,200 people. Such errors in thinking should be addressed. In fact, it is sometimes wise to let pupils jump to false conclusions and then, by discussion, have them discover the fallacies in their own thinking.

Many worthwhile learning experiences can be developed by exploring the ideas of probability and statistics. The teacher should be alert to situations in the sciences and social studies that can be interpreted more effectively with probability statements and simple statistics.

Since graphs, statistics, and probability are a part of the daily life of all children and adults, care must be taken to include a balanced amount of them in all basic-skill and essential evaluation measures.

JIMINY CRICKETS

One hot summer night in Florida, a guy named Walt was sitting on his front porch and listening to the crickets chirping. Later that year during a cold snap in December, he noticed the crickets again one evening, and something peculiar caught his attention. Over the next year he listened to the crickets every time he had a chance to sit out on his front porch. He drew up this chart:

TEMP(°C)	CHIRPS/MIN	TEMP(°C)	CHIRPS/MIN	TEMP(°C)	CHIRPS/MIN
8°	40	15°	90	19°	115
9°	46	16°	90	20°	120
10°	52	16°	96	20°	126
11°	64	17°	98	21°	120
12°	66	17°	100	22°	130
13°	70	18°	101	22°	137
13°	77	18°	103	23°	143
14°	80	18°	108		
15°	86	19°	110		

Ask the students if they think that there is a relationship between the temperature and the number of cricket chirps per minute.

To check, have them make a scatter graph on their own paper. Ask them if they notice a pattern. Have them draw a trend line.

Based on the trend line, ask them questions about the data and the trend it indicates. For example:

(a) If a cricket chirps 56 times a minute, what would you estimate the approximate temperature to be?

(b) On a really hot night the temperature is 28°C. How many chirps per minute would you estimate the crickets to be making?

(c) How cold will it get before the crickets stop chirping?

MEAN M&M'S

Materials: One 40-g package of M&M's for each student or group of students.

Form into groups. Each group counts the number of M&M's in its own package. Then as a class find the mean number of M&M's per package to the nearest whole M&M.

The groups repeat this exercise for the individual M&M colors. Again, round off the means to the nearest whole M&M.

Is there a mode among the five colors? A bimode?

Calculate the sum of the five color means. Is it the same as the mean determined for the whole package?

Each group finds the mode for its individual package of M&M's. If there was a color mode for the class, is it the same?

Line up all your M&M's by color in alphabetical order (brown, green, orange, red, yellow) to find the median.

To close, eat the M&M's (*or share them with your teacher*).

SELF-TEST—HOW WOULD YOU RESPOND TO EACH OF THESE STATEMENTS?

- _____ There are many applications of statistical inference outside the classroom.

- _____ The study of probability and statistics during the elementary years should be concerned with exploring problems and experimenting with the predictability of simple events (coin toss, for example) rather than formal work on probability and statistics.

- ____ Data collecting and sorting can lead to graphing and modeling activities even in the primary grades.

- ____ Prediction is an important use of statistics.

- ____ Children must know how to read a graph before they are taught to construct their own graphs.

- ____ In comparing bar graphs representing the number of immigrants by country of origin for each of several years, the relative size of the units and the starting point become unimportant.

- ____ Early experiences in finding the mean can be developed by using manipulatives before computation is used.

- ____ Children should be sufficiently familiar with the mean, median, and mode to recognize and explain their advantages and limitations.

- ____ Analysis of advertising in newspapers and magazines is best left to the secondary school, because it can serve little purpose in elementary mathematics.

- ____ Critical-thinking techniques should be developed from the earliest experiences with statistics.

- ____ Very young children can understand probability when they are encouraged to experiment with concrete materials and make predictions.

- ____ Good teaching strategy includes numerous laboratory experiences using the social situations in which ratios are used.

- ____ Using the cross-products approach is helpful in problem solving.

- ____ The use of squared paper is not a recommended strategy for helping pupils visualize percents.

- ____ Elementary school mathematics texts commonly suggest using decimal, ratio, formula, and equation approaches as well as unitary analysis in solving percent problems.

- ____ From time to time, pupils should be encouraged to solve the same problem in different ways.

- ____ Percent is the application of a particular notation system to quantity rather than a mathematical topic per se.

SELECTED REFERENCES

Behr, M. J., Harel, G., Post, T., & Lesh, R. (1992). Rational number, ratio, and proportion. In D. A. Grouws (Ed.), *Handbook of research on mathematics teaching and learning* (pp. 296–333). New York: Macmillan.

Campbell, S. K. (1974). *Flaws and fallacies in statistical thinking.* Englewood Cliffs, NJ: Prentice Hall.

Clements, D. (1989). *Computers in elementary mathematics education.* Englewood Cliffs, NJ: Prentice Hall.

Cobb, P. (1988). The tension between theories of learning and theories of instruction in mathematics education. *Educational Psychologist, 23*(2), 87–104.

Gay, S., & Aichele, D. B. (1997). Middle School Student's Understanding of Number Sense Related to Percent, *School Science and Mathematics, 97* (1), 27–29.

Johnson, J. (1997). Mathematics Detective. *Mathematics Teaching in the Middle School, 2*(3), 162–163.

National Council of Teachers of Mathematics (1981). *Teaching probability and statistics, 1981 yearbook.* Reston, VA: National Council of Teachers of Mathematics.

Schwartz, J. E., & Beichner, R. (1999). *Essentials of educational technology.* Boston: Allyn & Bacon.

10 Measurement and Geometry

LOOKING AHEAD

Current Condition of Geometry Instruction

An examination of current textbooks for teaching mathematics in the elementary school will reveal that a moderate quantity of geometry is included in most books. There is a wide range of quality in terms of the types of activities that are recommended. Some elementary mathematics textbooks treat geometry as a subject consisting of definitions, rules, and procedures. Others lead children to explore concepts, to articulate intuitions, and to become actively involved in meaningful learning. In spite of the fact that it is possible to find textbooks that provide excellent ideas for the teaching of geometry, children's achievement in geometry is often very poor.

One of the unfortunate facts about the teaching of mathematics in elementary school today is that teachers often omit the lessons on geometry. Even when geometry is taught, the focus of the lessons tends to be on lower-level thinking skills. By the time that children reach high school and the emphasis shifts to deductive proofs, the necessary prerequisite learning has not taken place. As a result, high school geometry students often "learn" the material of their geometry classes without developing a deep, conceptual understanding of the topic. There is a great need today for elementary teachers to conceptualize a broad-based, integrated, developmental model of geometry teaching in the elementary school.

Reasons for This Condition

A number of factors have operated concurrently to produce this state of affairs in today's elementary geometry classroom. Perhaps the most notable of these factors is the current emphasis on accountability in schools. Teachers are under a great deal of pressure to enable their students to perform well on achievement tests. These tests tend to emphasize computation far more than they emphasize geometry. As a result, teachers come to think of geometry as a "softer" component of elementary mathematics instruction. They begin to feel that time spent on geometry is time that could be more productively spent on drill and practice of the material that will help the children perform well on the achievement tests. This is unfortunate because meaningful learning of geometry can often help children with other areas of the elementary mathematics curriculum.

Closely related to the first factor is the spatial nature of the topic of geometry. This spatial nature of geometry is so different from the analytic, procedural, rule-oriented nature of most of the curriculum that teachers are not sure how to approach it. Much, but not all, learning of geometry begins with intuitive knowledge. Children develop more sophisticated knowledge of geometry by performing actions on objects, and by reflecting on those actions. If a teacher's view of mathematics teaching is rule-bound and procedural, it is easy for that teacher to conclude that there is not much geometry to be taught in the elementary school.

A final factor that contributes to less-than-adequate geometry instruction in today's elementary schools is the geometry knowledge of the teacher. Many teachers have not had the depth and type of experiences with geometry that would enable them to teach geometry from a conceptual standpoint. This is not a factor for which we can blame the teachers. On the contrary, it is an indication that the schools have not provided the type of instruction that we are now beginning to realize is necessary: an education that focuses on sense-making, relationships between ideas, and meaningful mathematics.

Fortunately, learning of mathematics is beginning to be better understood. Learning theorists and researchers are providing educators with models of learning and teaching that have the potential to transform the way geometry is taught in schools.

CAN YOU?

- Describe the six levels of geometric thinking defined by the van Hiele Theory?

- Explain van Hiele's view of the roles of instruction and maturation in the development of geometric thinking?

- Give some examples of how geometry instruction may help children in other areas of mathematics?

- Suggest ways in which teaching of geometry and measurement might be connected to each other?

- Suggest ways in which teaching of geometry and measurement might be connected to other areas of mathematics?

- Explain how it is that measurement is always an estimate?

- Suggest a rationale for teaching children measurement in nonstandard units?

- Give reasons why young children find it difficult to learn to tell time?

- Offer a possible explanation of why children often show confusion between area and perimeter?

- Suggest a way to help children avoid confusion between area and perimeter?

THE HEART PROBLEM

On Valentine's Day a teacher captures the children's attention by folding a large, construction paper heart in half so that the two halves match, thereby making it into a card. He asks if anyone knows what it is called when a shape can be folded in this manner. Since no one knows, he introduces the terms *symmetry* and *line of symmetry* to the children. Following this he asks the children if they think all shapes are symmetric, or have symmetry. The children discuss this, using examples of symmetric and non-symmetric shapes that they are familiar with in their environments. They quickly conclude that not all shapes are symmetric. The teacher then provides the children with collections of geometric shapes and asks them to

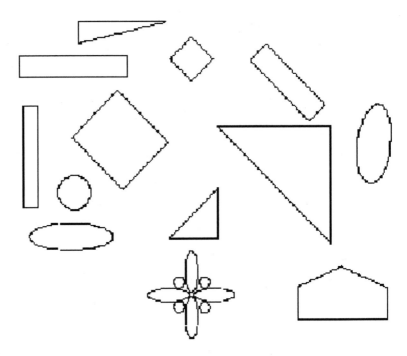

Figure 10-1   Shapes for Exploring Symmetry

work with a partner to sort the shapes into symmetric and non-symmetric shapes. He also provides small plastic mirrors and suggests that the children might find them helpful in finding lines of symmetry.

Following this work with partners, the children are called back to the large group. The teacher asks volunteers to begin displaying shapes that they think are symmetric.

Student 1:   We think this rectangle is symmetric, because you can fold it like this: top to bottom.

Student 7:   We picked the rectangle, too, but our line went the other way . . . like this: side to side.

Teacher: Does a line of symmetry have to go from top to bottom; does it have to be vertical? Can it go from side to side; can it be horizontal?

Student 4:   There can be lots of different lines of symmetry. The circle was really neat! You can draw a line of symmetry anywhere!   Others agree.

Teacher: How about one like this?

Several Students: NO!

Teacher: Why not?

Student 4:   OK. The line has to go through the center of the circle.

Student 2:   We put this square in the symmetric pile. We used the mirror on it and found this line of symmetry.

Student 3:   We found another line of symmetry on the square. Look, you can put the mirror on it from corner to corner and it matches.

Teacher: Can you explain what you mean when you say, "It matches"? What matches?

Student 3:   When you put the mirror from corner to corner the picture matches . . . It's the same picture as the rest.

Student 4:   It makes, like a triangle in the mirror; and there's the same triangle on the paper. They're the same. They match.

Teacher: So, when you say "matching" you mean that the parts are symmetric. There is a diagonal line of symmetry on the square. Did any of the rest of you find that the square had this line of symmetry? If you haven't done so yet, place the mirror the way they've suggested and see for yourself.

Student 1:   Hey, the rectangle probably does that too! I'll try it . . . hey, it doesn't work!

Teacher: The rectangle doesn't have a line of symmetry from corner to corner?

Student 5:   Well, it sort of does. If you cut it along that line you could turn one of the pieces over and it would match the other one.

Teacher: What an interesting idea! What do the rest of you think? Does this qualify as a line of symmetry if you have to flip one of the halves?

The lesson proceeded with a discussion about whether it was symmetry if you have to turn one of the pieces over. Eventually the teacher led the children to consider what sorts of shapes tended to have the diagonal line of symmetry. After the children figured out that they all fit into a general square outline, the teacher challenged them to draw some shapes that were symmetric. He encouraged them to try to draw some that had diagonal lines of symmetry.

An Analysis of the Heart Problem

In this lesson it is important to note the teacher's method of dealing with new vocabulary. Rather than introducing a new geometric term and attempting to give the children a definition for it, the teacher began by illustrating a concept and then naming it. Following this, the teacher continued to use the term correctly, providing a model for the children. When children used informal language to mean "symmetry" ("... it matches...."), the teacher questioned the meaning of the informal language. In this way, the teacher led the children to become comfortable with using geometric terminology. Furthermore, as the children used the new vocabulary correctly, their own conceptual understanding of it was strengthened. There was some interaction between the concept and the term: first the concept gave meaning to the term, then later the use of the term began to enrich the concept.

Another noteworthy item in this lesson was the potential for informal learning that was provided. The teacher's explicit goal was to provide children with an initial understanding of symmetry and lines of symmetry. The teacher knew, however, that a great deal of implicit learning would be taking place as well. An example of this is the child's discovery that one of the parts of the rectangle could be flipped to become congruent with the other part. While the teacher did not plan for this, he capitalized on it and encouraged the child who had made the discovery. At some later time the teacher will provide more formal instruction about flips, slides, and turns—topics related to motion geometry. Much informal and intuitive learning of geometry can be expected as children engage in geometry activities.

A CONCEPTUAL FRAMEWORK

During the last decade, the majority of research on children's learning of geometry has focused on the theory developed by van Hiele-Geldof and van Hiele. This theory proposes that children progress through increasingly sophisticated levels of thought as they learn geometry (see Figure 10–2). Research on the theory has confirmed the basic structure of the van Hiele model and has continued to refine and enhance it.

Instruction, not maturation, leads to higher levels of thinking.

The van Hiele theory suggests that progress through the levels is determined by instruction rather than by biological maturation. This clearly implies that it should be the primary role of teachers to provide activities that will help children to move to progressively higher levels of thinking. Without appropriate experiences, progress through the levels is limited. It is not uncommon to find adults who approach geometry at the lowest van Hiele levels. On the other hand, research using Logo to teach children geometry has succeeded in moving children in the primary grades toward level-2 thinking. Since the levels are believed to be hierarchical, progress toward level-2 thinking in primary school should enable progress toward level 3 in later elementary grades. This progress is necessary if children are to learn meaningfully the material of high school geometry. This is because high school geometry requires level-4 thinking.

The van Hiele theory suggests, and further research has tended to confirm, that children do not bypass levels as they proceed from less so-

Level 0: Pre-recognition	Children perceive geometric shapes, but are unable to identify many of them. They can distinguish between broad categories, such as curvilinear and rectilinear shapes, but they cannot recognize different types within these broad categories. They do not construct mental representations, or visual images, of shapes.
Level 1: Visual	Children recognize basic shapes as wholes. They have mental representations of types of shapes. These mental representations are broadly conceived visual prototypes. For example, any triangular shape would fit the prototype of a triangle, even if the sides were curved. A child at the visual level would call a curved shape a triangle if it had a generally triangular shape.
Level 2: Descriptive/analytic	Children use specific properties of shapes, rather than visual wholes, to distinguish between them. Reasoning is in terms of combinations of properties.
Level 3: Abstract/relational	Children can begin to follow informal logical reasoning about properties of shapes. Concepts such as class inclusion (squares as special cases of rectangles) are understood. Definitions become logical organizers rather than lists of properties.
Level 4: Formal deduction	Students become capable of constructing original meaningful proofs. They can produce a logical argument on the basis of "givens."
Level 5: Rigor/metamathematical	Students extend their reasoning power to the elaboration and comparison of alternate axiomatic systems of geometry. They become capable of reasoning in the absence of reference models.

Figure 10-2   The van Hiele Levels of Geometric Thought (as articulated by Clements and Battista, 1992)

phisticated to more sophisticated thinking. If a teacher presents material that requires level-4 thinking to a student who is functioning on level 1, that student will not learn the material meaningfully. At best, the student will learn to recite the right words or perform the right operations to satisfy the teacher. The teacher will appear to have had success in teaching the material, but the student will have learned the material in a rote fashion.

> **Teaching above a child's level engenders rote learning and negative attitudes toward mathematics.**

This type of learning will not empower the student with the ability to use the geometric knowledge to solve problems. An even greater difficulty with this scenario is that this type of teaching typically engenders negative and destructive attitudes and beliefs about mathematics. Children forced to learn geometry in a rote fashion will believe that mathematics is nothing more than increasingly complex lists of steps to follow or arguments to recite.

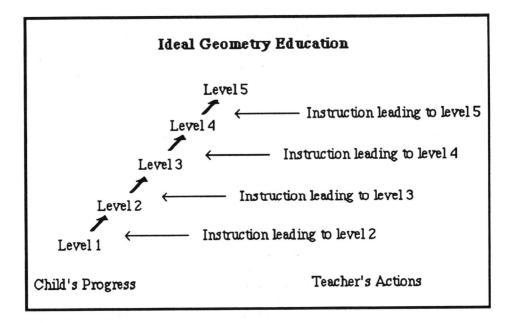

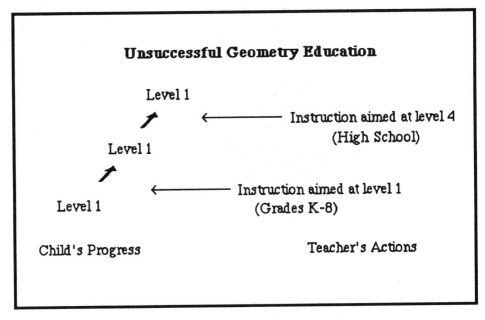

Appropriate instruction must take into account the child's level of thinking. This implies a continuous sensitivity on the part of the teacher. The teacher must realize that the child may not be interpreting the teacher's explanations and representations on the same level on which the teacher is presenting them. For the elementary teacher, the concern is primarily with levels 1, 2, and 3. Most elementary geometry instruction should be designed to help children progress from a visual to a descriptive level. In the middle school, instruction should enable children to progress toward informal deductive reasoning.

TOPICS

Geometry

Some Fundamentals of Geometry

Points, Lines
The abstract, formal, geometric definition of points and lines is difficult for children. Informal discussions about a line continuing infinitely in two directions are appropriate, but forcing children to memorize this definition and use it when talking about lines is not. Some teachers have found it useful to illustrate points by asking children to think about what color to make the *point* at which all the boundaries cross in the following diagram. Can that point be measured? Another useful illustration of a point is the point at which three states meet. Which state owns that point? How big is the point? Again, informal discussion to provoke thinking is appropriate for elementary children.

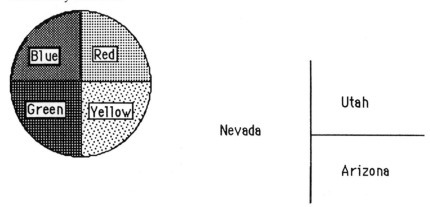

Perpendicular and Parallel Lines; Special Grids
The concepts of perpendicular and parallel lines can be important building blocks for reasoning at levels 3 and 4 in the van Hiele model. Fuys, Geddes, and Tischler (1988) have successfully helped children develop these concepts by using special grids which they refer to as "ladders" and "saws".

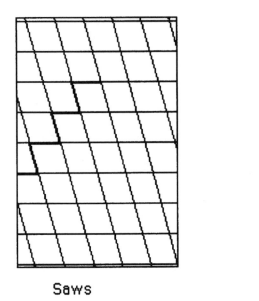

Saws

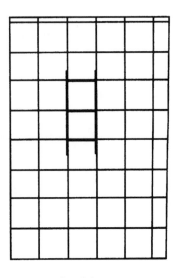

Ladders

Once children have progressed to the point where they are reasoning about the properties of shapes rather than their overall visual appearance, attention can be focused on the right angles that occur in the ladder grids. Children can be questioned about the effect of having two right angles side by side or across from each other. (The ambiguity of this latter question is purposeful: children will need to decide what is meant by "across from each other.") The questions of whether or where the rails of the ladder meet can be discussed further.

In the saws, the questions about whether any of the lines will meet can be pursued. Differences between the saw grid and the ladder grid can be discussed. Children progressing toward level 3 can be asked to identify equal angles in the saw grid and to justify their reasons for deciding that these angles are equal. All angles that are the same can be colored the same color.

The Saws Problem
(*Note:* this vignette is appropriate for children who are already making progress toward level-3 thinking.)

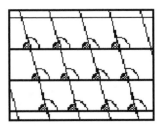

Teacher: Now, we know all the gray angles are equal, and we know all the white angles are equal. Can we mark any more angles?

Sue: I think the other small angles are also equal to the gray ones, but I can't give a reason.

Jose: I know. They look the same as the gray ones, but we need to know for sure.

Bill: We could measure them.

Louise: I can show that all the unmarked small angles are equal to each other. Turn the paper sideways, and you can see that its another case of a line crossing parallel lines. Its just like what we did to mark the gray and the white angles.

Jose: Well, then, all the large, unmarked angles are equal to each other, too!

Dianne: That will take care of all the angles!

Sue: But we still haven't shown if the small, unmarked ones are equal to the gray ones.

Teacher: Notice how the gray and the white angles combine into one large angle? They fit together on a straight line.

Jose: Right; they add up to 180°. So . . . ?

Teacher: Turn the paper sideways again. Now look for . . .

Sue: Look! The white angles and the small unmarked angles add up to 180°!

Dianne: So they have to be the same as the gray ones because white plus gray is 180°!

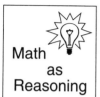

Math
as
Reasoning

Analysis of the Saws Problem

The children in this lesson are making significant progress toward abstract reasoning. They are able to use properties of parallel lines as stable components in a chain of reasoning. They are aware of the need for mathematical reasons rather than visual evidence for supporting their conjectures. At the same time, visual evidence is not ignored. There is a variety of levels of thinking operating within the classroom. The teacher in this case watches and listens carefully. Her job is to allow the children to reason and argue, follow their thinking, and intervene with a potent question at an appropriate moment. The success of this lesson depends very heavily on the teacher's belief in the children as active constructors of their own knowledge and on her understanding of the mathematics involved.

An opportunity for the teacher to show a connection between geometry and one of the fundamentals of algebra is evident in the Saws Problem.

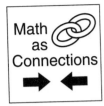

Math as Connections

When Dianne notes that "white plus gray is 180°," she is showing an understanding of variables. Since the children have not measured the gray and the white angles, Dianne must refer to them with names rather than with their measures. Her comment shows that she realizes that the angles could be of various sizes, but must sum to 180°. The teacher can explicitly comment on what Dianne has implied, or she can make a mental note of Dianne's comment and mention it later when the children are beginning to study variables.

Symmetry, Similarity, and Congruence

Symmetry, similarity, and congruence are typically presented as static conditions of shapes. While it is necessary for children to understand these concepts in this way, a good geometry program will go beyond this. One of the goals of geometry instruction is to help children develop the ability to visualize shapes and flexibly manipulate the mental images that they construct. Exercises in changing nonsymmetric or non-congruent shapes so that they become symmetric or congruent can help children develop these visualization abilities. A good exercise will focus on analysis of which elements need to be changed and which elements can remain unchanged. In the following figure, the two shapes are not congruent. However, only the lengths of the sides need to be changed in order to transform one of the shapes to be congruent with the other. This analysis leads directly to a consideration of similarity. In a geometric sense, shapes are similar if all their properties except size are alike.

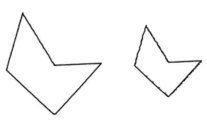

Pairs of children can each create a shape on a geoboard. Then one child, without looking at his partner's shape, must follow directions given by his partner to transform his shape into one congruent to his partner's. The other child can see both shapes and must give specific directions for the partner to follow in making the transformation.

Shapes

A primary grade lesson on shapes may begin with the teacher presenting a collection of colored plastic shapes on the overhead projector. The children can be asked to state how they could sort this collection into groups. As they respond, the teacher asks them to explain the differences and similarities that they are using to sort the shapes.

Since children may invent grouping schemes that the teacher did not have in mind, the teacher again must be sensitive to the children's level of thinking. She should accept their ideas, encourage them to express those ideas clearly, and at the same time keep in mind the goal of bringing about growth in thinking levels. If children's classification schemes are entirely visual, she may, after the children finish, provide a classification on the basis of properties and ask the children if they can figure out the basis on which the shapes are grouped.

A set of triangles to be sorted:

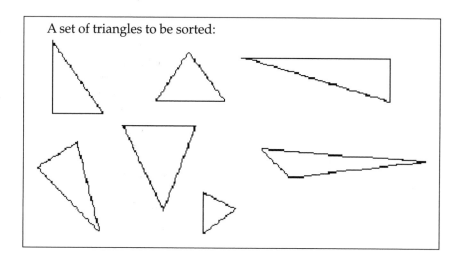

Visual sort produced by children:

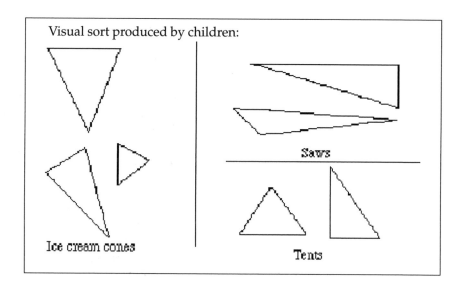

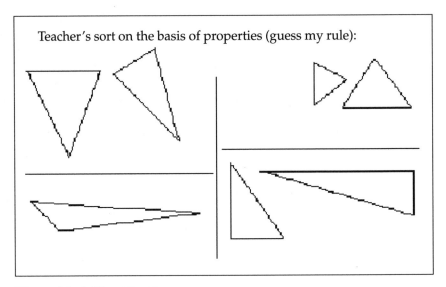

Teacher's sort on the basis of properties (guess my rule):

Hierarchical Classification

Are squares rectangles, or are rectangles squares? It is pointless to teach children this relationship as a definition or rule. The understanding of this relationship is dependent on children gaining the ability to mentally form classes of objects and on their ability to decide on class membership. These abilities are characteristic of van Hiele's level 3. Fortunately there are many places in the geometry curriculum where the question can come up. Are equilateral triangles isosceles? Are rectangles parallelograms? Each time questions such as these occur, children will respond to them on their own levels of thinking. Those children who are progressing toward level 3 will begin to construct the concept of class inclusion. Those children progressing toward level 2 will think the questions are unchallenging: the shapes are different and there is no point in asking if one of them *is* the other. The teacher's role is to pose the questions and let them have their effect on the development of the child.

Motion Geometry

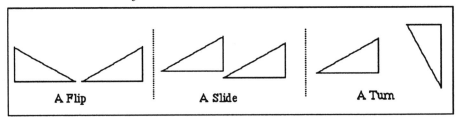

A Flip   A Slide   A Turn

Three different types of motions are studied as components of motion geometry. Informally these three motions are referred to as *flips, slides,* and *turns.* Wheatley and Cobb (1990) have shown that mental imagery involving flips, slides, and turns can be improved through activities such as the following.

A set of plastic pieces as shown in Figure 10-3 are given to a child. The child is shown the arrangement in Figure 10-4 for a few seconds. She then attempts to use the pieces in her collection to imitate the arrangement in Figure 10-4. If she needs to do so, she may have another look at the arrangement, again for a few seconds.

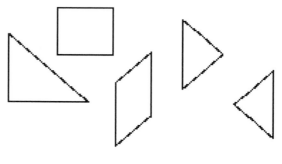

Figure 10-3 A Collection of Shapes

Figure 10-4 An Arrangement to Imitate

This activity seems deceptively simple, but children without much experience with motion geometry find it surprisingly challenging. After engaging in activities at this level of complexity, children will enjoy trying some of the many popular activities with tangrams. Sets of tangrams can be made or purchased. Many commercial sources of tangram challenges are available; children can also make up designs for classmates to try to duplicate.

A Tangram Set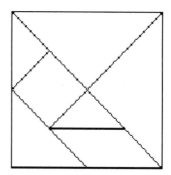

Technology

A computer software package that is helpful in developing children's spatial visualization skills is *The Factory*™ from Sunburst Communications. In this program, children must use mental representations of flips, slides, and turns to reproduce actions performed by the computer.

Coordinate Geometry

Coordinate geometry is an invented system of locating points and lines in space. Based around a grid centered on vertical and horizontal axes, the system allows for explorations of relationships between locations, plotting of functions, and a standard format for communication. The most basic component of coordinate geometry is a grid that uses only positive numbers. In this grid, the horizontal axis, known as the X axis, is located along the bottom of the grid. The vertical axis, or Y axis, is located along the left side. Points on the grid are always referenced by an ordered pair of numbers that represent a specific location. According to convention, the X axis location is always given first. (The location of point M on the simple grid is 3,2.)

A simple coordinate grid (positive numbers only)

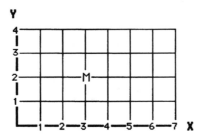

A more complex coordinate grid (negative numbers on X axis)

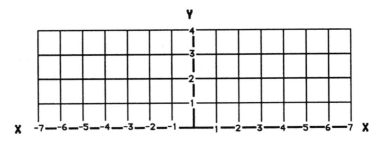

A complete coordinate grid (negative numbers on both axes)

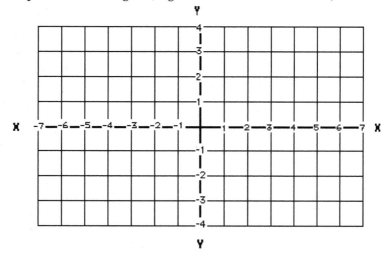

Children Discover the Need for Ordered Pairs

Grid City

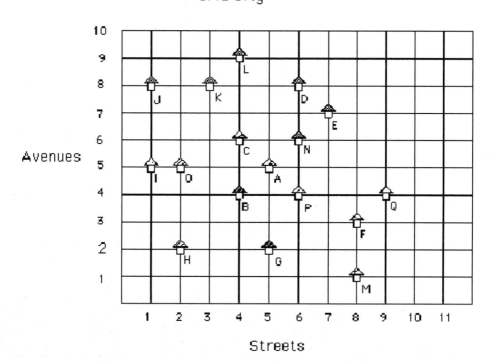

Avenues

Streets

Teacher: "The new mail carrier in Grid City has been receiving too many complaints about mixed up mail. Last week the L family got the Q family's mail and the Q family got the L family's mail. The mail for the K and F families was also switched. Today the mail carrier returned to the post office with the D family's mail. He claimed that there was no house at the address written on the mail: 6th and 8th. That's when the supervisor became involved.

"Based on the three clues you've already been given, I want you to meet together in your cooperative groups to see if you can figure out why this mail carrier is having so much trouble. In about 10 minutes I'll tell you what happened when the supervisor went along with the mail carrier on his route. Perhaps you'll be able to figure it out and tell me what happened."

When the children began to examine the mistakes that had been made, some of them noticed that the addresses of the houses with the mistakes had the same numbers: 6th and 8th was confused with 8th and 6th; 9th and 4th was confused with 4th and 9th; and so on. From this they concluded that the mail carrier needed to know something about the order in which the numbers occurred. They figured out that the supervisor must have forgotten to tell the new mail carrier whether streets or avenues came first in the addresses. As this point came out in the group discussion, the teacher made sure that the children knew that either arrangement would work, but that everyone had to know the system and follow it. She then informed them that the rule for Grid City was that street numbers always had to come first in the addresses.

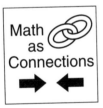

The teacher followed this with several group-presented exercises in which individual children had to show where they would deliver pieces of mail, given specific addresses. Children had to come to a projection of Grid City presented on the overhead projector to show where they would make a delivery. For homework, the teacher asked the children to examine Grid City with symmetry in mind. She would ask them to discuss their findings the next day.

Measurement

The Nature of Measurement

Teachers need to distinguish between two different types of measurement. One sort of measurement involves countable items, such as the number of children in the class or the number of hot lunches being ordered. The other form of measurement involves identifying a location on a continuous scale and letting that location serve as the measurement. When a person reads a thermometer, he is usually aware of the need to estimate in reporting the temperature. Rarely does the top of the mercury appear exactly on a degree mark. What is perhaps not as clear is the fact that measurement on a continuous scale is always an estimate. More precise scales allow us to give better estimates, but they are always still estimates. (Devices that provide a digital readout of a measurement appear not to provide estimates, but the estimate takes place electronically, hidden to the user of the device.)

> **Measurement is always an estimate.**

When teaching children about measurement on a continuous scale, teachers need to keep this estimation aspect of measurement in mind. Normally the context of the measurement task will indicate the degree of precision needed. When attempting to measure the volume of water needed to fill a swimming pool, precision to the nearest milliliter is clearly inappropriate. At times our precision is limited by the measurement tools we have available. School rulers are usually marked in sixteenths-of-an-inch segments. Cabinet makers require thirty-secondths-of-an-inch precision. A cabinet maker would be forced to relax her level of precision if she only had a school ruler with which to measure.

Nonstandard and Standard Units
Children can be led to discover the meaning of and the need for standard units of measurement. Measurement of length is a very tangible activity for making this discovery.

The Desk Problem
The teacher informs the children that there has been a complaint from one of the other grades. The children in that grade feel that they've been treated unfairly because the desks provided for their classroom are smaller than everyone else's desks. She asks for suggestions of how we could find out if this is true.

Amy: We could go and look at them.

Bob: We could have them come and look at ours.

Theresa: We could measure them; then we'd only have to tell them what size ours are.

Teacher: How would that help?

Theresa: Well, then they could measure their desks and we could compare the measurements. The ones with the bigger measurements are bigger desks.

Teacher: Does that seem good to the rest of you? All right, we'll measure our desks. But I want you to use these pencils that I'm passing out as measuring sticks. Count off how many of these pencil lengths it takes to go across your desks. (She passes out pencils of widely varying lengths.)

Steve: But we'll all get different measurements because the pencils aren't the same!

Teacher: Are you sure? Maybe you can predict what measurements some of the people around you will get.

[The students proceed to make predictions. Then they measure their desks using the pencils provided by the teacher.]

Teacher: OK. I want you to tell me one at a time how many pencils wide your desk is and I'll make a chart.

NAME	WIDTH OF DESK
Steve	5 pencils
Amy	7 pencils
Theresa	13 pencils
. . .	. . .

Sally: Steve was right! They're all different! Which one is the right one?

Analysis of the Desk Problem
At this point in the lesson, the teacher then suggested to the children that it would be better if all the pencils were the same length. She then pointed out that for the sake of communication with the other class and with anyone outside the school, measurement with widely accepted standard measures such as the foot or centimeter would be necessary.

An important note about the lesson is the teacher's handling of individual differences. Steve was immediately aware of the difficulty of using different measuring units. For Steve the teacher posed a more difficult question. A common misconception about measurement is that smaller units will result in smaller measures. In fact, smaller units result in a larger number of units per given length. By challenging Steve to predict the measurements obtained by others, the teacher focused the lesson on this common misconception for the student who needed an extra challenge.

Measuring Time
Measurement of time is a difficult concept for young children. Very sophisticated concepts are involved in understanding units of time, passage of time, comparisons between lengths of time, and telling time. These concepts develop gradually as children think about time and as teachers and others discuss time with children.

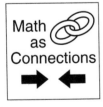
Math as Connections

Telling time involves developing an understanding that hands and numbers or digits on a clock stand for a constantly changing point in time. In order for time-telling to be meaningful to children, they must have constructed a mental structure of time and its passage. Number lines, because they are also used for early work with numbers and arithmetic, can be helpful representations of the numbers on a clock. A number line from 0 to 60 can be used to represent minutes; a number line of equal length, marked from noon to midnight, can be used to represent hours.

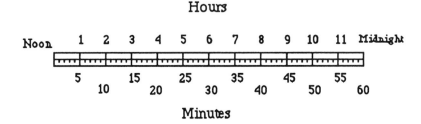

Although reading the time from a digital clock is easier for children, and they will experience relatively early success with it, they also need to learn to tell time from a regular clock. Early questions should deal with only the hour hand; eventually precision can be refined to include telling the number of minutes past the hour.

Area/Perimeter; Volume/Surface Area

One of the perennial difficulties that children have with measurement is a confusion between area and perimeter. Even children who succeed in doing computations for area and perimeter problems often show confusion about units. Typically teachers try to correct the "labeling" problem without understanding the underlying confusion. This confusion that the students experience may be the result of lessons on perimeter having been presented before lessons on area were presented. Presumably, it has been felt that children can more easily learn to measure in linear units than in square units. Unfortunately, when area is introduced after perimeter, children assimilate the activities into their existing understanding of perimeter. The qualitative difference between linear units and square units is not understood.

Rather than proceed in this manner, teachers should first present a problem requiring computation of area. In order to solve the problem, which calls for square units, measurement of linear units must take place. Linear measurement is embedded in the context of an area problem. After area problems have been successfully solved, the concept of perimeter can be presented as a different type of problem. This same sequence is suggested for problems involving volume and surface area. Hopkins and Brahier (1997) suggest several volume activities using ships and and tonnage that can be effectively used.

Scale Drawings and Maps

Work with maps can lead to extremely rich geometric and measurement explorations. Many crucial and complex abilities are required in order for children to be able to make sense of maps. Ideas such as perspective and scale take time to develop. A suitable long-term project that will involve children in constructing these important ideas is mapping the classroom. Mapping the school, the schoolgrounds, and a field-trip site are additional possibilities. Children enjoy the game aspect of being given a treasure map that requires them to follow mathematical directions to locate a hidden object.

Angles and Angle Measure

Technology

Young children have many misconceptions about what an angle is and how one is measured. Work with Logo can help children develop the notion of an angle as a turn. The idea of measurement of an angle on the basis of the amount of the turn rather than the length of the sides is also facilitated by working with Logo.

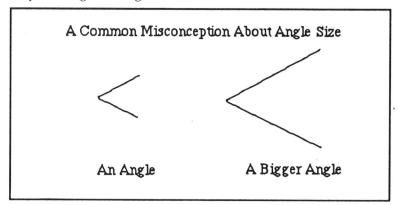

A Common Misconception About Angle Size

An Angle   A Bigger Angle

ACTIVE LEARNING

Manipulatives

A wide assortment of geometry manipulatives are available commercially. Many, such as tangrams, miras, geoboards, and measurement tools, have been referred to in this chapter. The important thing for the teacher of geometry to keep in mind in selecting and using manipulatives is that there is no inherent value in manipulatives. The value in using manipulatives derives from the teacher's skill in helping children make connections between those manipulatives and the concepts that they are supposed to represent. For this reason, some manipulatives are more helpful than others. In addition, some concepts are represented well with manipulatives while other concepts are not. The teacher who uses manipulatives must constantly assess the children's understanding to determine whether the important connections are being made.

> ...there is
> no inherent
> value in using
> manipulatives ...

Measurement Activities

Figures 10-5 and 10-6 represent paths taken by two sailboats as they sailed from the starting line of a race to the first buoy.

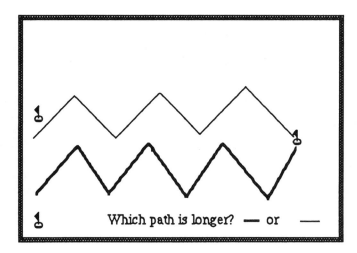

Figure 10-5

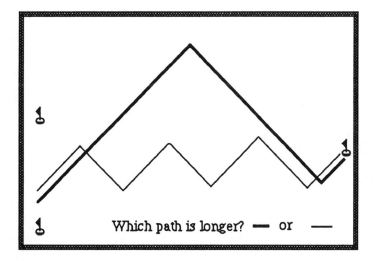

Figure 10-6

Measurement activities must involve the children in actually doing the measurements. In Figures 10-5 and 10-6, the children must actually measure the paths to determine which is shorter. When children are at young ages, the measurements can first be done by estimation, then later by nonstandard units, then finally by standard units. Following the measurement, a discussion of why the shorter path is shorter can be fruitful. Since the answer will necessarily focus on the angles, children who are not yet reasoning about the properties of shapes may find this to be a pointless question. They might say that "it just is" shorter. As these children listen to other children talk about the angles, they will begin to be aware of properties of shapes. This is an important part of their development.

Games

Many mathematical games have geometric concepts embedded in them. The fact that much learning of geometry occurs as children act on and reflect on their intuitions about shapes makes game-playing a very worthwhile activity in geometry learning. Marina Krause, in *Multicultural Mathematics Activities*, (National Council of Teachers of Mathematics, 1983) has collected a number of excellent games and activities that combine geometry, art, logic, and probability. *Arithmetic Teacher* is another good source of games. Recent issues have contained articles dealing with quilting, tesselations, American Folk Art design, and symmetry in art.

A very powerful learning activity that can be provided in relationship to games is to have the children systematically vary some of the rules for the game. This activity is appropriate only after children have played a game enough to have developed some insight into the game. At this point, children can work as small groups to analyze the game's rules and select one that can be modified to create a new version of the game. They should predict the effect that changing the rule will have on the play of the game; then they should play the game with the new rules to see if their prediction was correct. This trial playing of the new game will also show them if there are any unexpected results of the rule change that will make the game unplayable or uninteresting. Following a successful play of the modified game, the small group can share their new rules with the rest of the class.

WHY TEACH GEOMETRY AND MEASUREMENT?

Geometry and measurement provide an interesting and enjoyable application of the concepts and skills taught in other strands of the elementary mathematics curriculum. In addition to this, there is reason to believe that increased ability to visualize spatial objects enhances a child's ability to work mentally with numbers. Furthermore, since progress through the van Hiele levels depends on instruction rather than on maturation, instruction in the elementary school can be seen as a prerequisite to study of geometry in high school. This early preparation for meaningful learning in high school can perhaps help to prevent the development of negative attitudes and beliefs toward mathematics in children.

CAN YOU FIND IT?
Which of these can you find in the design? Shade in the shape, and mark in the matching letter.

A. Triangle—Isosceles
B. Triangle—Scalene
C. Quadrilateral—Not Symmetric
D. Quadrilateral—Two Lines of Symmetry
E. Pentagon—Concave
F. Pentagon—Convex
G. Hexagon—One Pair of Parallel Sides
H. Hexagon—Symmetric
I. Heptagon—Seven Sides
J. Heptagon—Not Symmetrical
K. Octagon
L. Trapezoid

WHO AM I?
Sit in a semicircle and play "Who Am I?" with the kids. Divide the semicircle into two teams. Think of ways (as below) to describe different objects for the students. When they think they know what it is, they raise hands. Call on the first child to raise a hand. If the student is correct, that team gets a point; if not, the other team gets to try.

I am a shape with three sides. Who am I?
I am a shape with two equal angles and one other angle. Who am I?
I am a shape with four corners all the same shape and four sides
    all the same length. Who am I?
I am a shape with five sides. Who am I?
I am a shape with four sides and four different angles. Who am I?
I am a shape with one side and no corners. Who am I?

SELF-TEST—HOW WOULD YOU RESPOND TO EACH OF THESE STATEMENTS?

- ____ Teachers who are concerned about their students' performance on standardized tests should omit the teaching of geometry.

- ____ Progress through the van Hiele levels will occur most rapidly if teachers allow children to mature before they expect sophisticated thinking from children.

- ____ The main concern, for elementary teachers, in the framework of the van Hiele model, is to help children move from Level 1 to Level 2.

- ____ The teacher who presents material at a higher van Hiele level than the level on which her students are functioning can do harm to their development.

- ____ A major goal in teaching measurement is to enable children to make exact measurements.

- ____ Teachers should avoid the use of nonstandard measures because they can easily confuse children.

- ____ Since digital clocks are now so prevalent, children should not be pressured to learn to tell time on clocks with hands.

- ____ Area problems should precede perimeter problems.

- ____ Children can learn from systematically changing the rules of games they have learned to play.

SELECTED REFERENCES

Claus, J. E. (1991). Pentagonal tessellations. *Arithmetic Teacher, 38* (5), 52–56.

Clements, D. H., & Battista, M. T. (1990). The effects of Logo on children's conceptualizations of angle and polygons. *Journal for Research in Mathematics Education, 21,* 356–371.

Clements, D., & Battista, M. (1992). Geometry and spatial reasoning. In Douglas A. Grouws (Ed.), *Handbook of research on mathematics teaching and learning.* New York: Macmillan.

Edwards, L. D. (1991). Children's learning in a computer microworld for transformation geometry. *Journal for Research in Mathematics Education, 22*(2), 122–137.

Fan, C. K. (1997). Areas. *Mathematics Teaching in the Middle Grades,* 2(30), 148–153; 160.

Fuys, D., Geddes, D., & Tischler, R. (1988). *Journal for Research in Mathematics Education Monograph 3: The van Hiele model of thinking in geometry among adolescents.* Reston, VA: National Council of Teachers of Mathematics.

Harrell, M. (1997). Allium to Zircon: Mathematics. *Mathematics Teaching in the Middle Grades,* 2(6), 380–388.

Hopkins, M. & Brahier, D. (1997). That's Gross (Tonnage). *Teaching Children Mathematics.* April.

Krause, M. (1983). *Multicultural mathematics activities.* National Council of Teachers of Mathematics.

Kriegler, S. (1991). The tangram—It's more than an ancient puzzle. *Arithmetic Teacher, 38* (9), 38–43.

Tracy, D. M., & Hague, M. S. (1997). Toys 'R' Math. *Mathematics Teaching in the Middle School,* 2(3).

Wheatley, G. (1991). Enhancing mathematics learning through imagery. *Arithmetic Teacher, 39* (1), 34–36.

Wheatley, G., & Cobb, P. (1990). Analysis of young children's spatial constructions. In L. Steffe & T. Wood (Eds.), *Transforming children's mathematics education* (pp. 161–173). Hillsdale, NJ: Erlbaum.

Wood, E. F. (1989). *Staff development for mathematics teachers: Assumptions to Consider,* ERIC Document No. 308 084.

Zaslavsky, C. (1991). Symmetry in American folk art. *Arithmetic Teacher, 38* (1), 6–12.

Index